ADVANCES IN ACCOUNTING EDUCATION: TEACHING AND CURRICULUM INNOVATIONS

ADVANCES IN ACCOUNTING EDUCATION: TEACHING AND CURRICULUM INNOVATIONS

Series Editor: Bill N. Schwartz

Recent Volumes:

ADVANCES IN ACCOUNTING EDUCATION: TEACHING AND CURRICULUM INNOVATIONS

EDITED BY

BILL N. SCHWARTZ

*Howe School of Technology Management,
Stevens Institute of Technology, Hoboken, NJ, USA*

ANTHONY H. CATANACH Jr.

*School of Business, Villanova University,
Villanova, PA, USA*

United Kingdom – North America – Japan
India – Malaysia – China

Emerald Group Publishing Limited
Howard House, Wagon Lane, Bingley BD16 1WA, UK

First edition 2009

British Library Cataloguing in Publication Data
A catalogue record for this book is available from the British Library

ISBN: 978-1-84855-882-3
ISSN: 1085-4622 (Series)

Awarded in recognition of
Emerald's production
department's adherence to
quality systems and processes
when preparing scholarly
journals for print

INVESTOR IN PEOPLE

CONTENTS

LIST OF CONTRIBUTORS

T. S. Amer	The W. A. Franke College of Business, Northern Arizona University, Flagstaff, AZ, USA
Robert L. Braun	Department of Accounting, Southeastern Louisiana University, Hammond, LA, USA
B. Douglas Clinton	Department of Accountancy, Northern Illinois University, DeKalb, IL, USA
Jeanette A. Davy	Department of Management, Wright State University, Dayton, OH, USA
Catherine A. Finger	W. P. Carey School of Business, Arizona State University, Glendale, AZ, USA
Carol M. Fischer	Department of Accounting, St. Bonaventure University, St. Bonaventure, NY, USA
Michael J. Fischer	Provost and VP for Academic Affairs, St. Bonaventure University, St. Bonaventure, NY, USA
Brian Patrick Green	College of Business, University of Michigan-Dearborn, Dearborn, MI, USA
Daryl M. Guffey	School of Accountancy and Legal Studies, Clemson University, Clemson, SC, USA
Ronald P. Guidry	Department of Accounting, Illinois State University, Normal, IL, USA
Bob G. Kilpatrick	The W. A. Franke College of Business, Northern Arizona University, Flagstaff, AZ, USA
Claire Kamm Latham	College of Business, Washington State University, Vancouver, WA

D. Jordan Lowe	W. P. Carey School of Business, Arizona State University, Glendale, AZ, USA
Roland Madison	Department of Accountancy, Boler School of Business, John Carroll University, Cleveland, OH, USA
D. David McIntyre	Stetson School of Business, and Economics Mercer University, Macon, GA, USA
Jeffrey J. McMillan	School of Accountancy and Legal Studies, Clemson University, Clemson, SC, USA
Donald L. Rosenberg	Department of Accounting, Towson University, Towson, MD, USA
Janet A. Samuels	W. P. Carey School of Business, Arizona State University, Tempe, AZ, USA
Jacqueline J. Schmidt	College of Arts and Sciences, John Carroll University, Cleveland, OH, USA
Deborah L. Seifert	Department of Accounting, Illinois State University, Normal, IL, USA
Kenneth J. Smith	Department of Accounting and Legal Studies, Salisbury University, Salisbury, MD, USA
Pamela A. Smith	Department of Accountancy, Northern Illinois University, DeKalb, IL, USA
William W. Stammerjohan	School of Accountancy, Louisiana Tech University, Ruston, LA, USA
Pierre L. Titard	Department of Accounting, Southeastern Louisiana University, Hammond, LA, USA
Nancy L. Wilburn	The W. A. Franke College of Business, Northern Arizona University, Flagstaff, AZ, USA
Angela M. Woodland	College of Business, Montana State University, Bozeman, MT, USA

CALL FOR PAPERS

Advances in Accounting Education is a refereed, research annual whose purpose is to meet the needs of individuals interested in the educational process. Articles may be non-empirical or empirical. Our emphasis is on pedagogy, and articles *must* explain how teaching methods or curricula/programs can be improved. We publish more articles than the other accounting education journals; we average around 13–14 per issue.

Non-empirical papers should be academically rigorous. They can be thought pieces (e.g., anecdotal experiences with various pedagogical tools, position papers on particular issues, or historical discussions with implications for current and future efforts). Reasonable assumptions and logical development are essential. The papers must place the topic within the context of the course or program and discuss any relevant tradeoffs or policy issues.

For empirical reports, sound research design and execution are critical. Articles must develop a thorough motivation and literature review (possibly including references from outside the accounting field) to provide the basis for the efforts and place the study in a solid context.

SUBMISSION INFORMATION

Send one hard copy by regular mail (including any research instruments) to the editor. By email send two files; one with a copy but without a cover page and one solely with a cover page. Manuscripts should include a cover page, listing all authors' names and address (with telephone numbers, fax numbers, and e-mail addresses). The authors' names and addresses should not appear on the abstract. To assure an anonymous review, authors should not identify themselves directly or indirectly. References to unpublished working papers or dissertations should be avoided.

Submit manuscripts to:

Anthony H. Catanach Jr.
Villanova School of Business
Villanova University
800 Lancaster Avenue
Villanova, PA 19085-1678, USA
Tel.: +1-610-519-4825
E-mail: anthony.catanach@villanova.edu

WRITING GUIDELINES

1. Each paper should include a cover sheet with names, addresses, telephone numbers, fax numbers, and e-mail address for all authors. The title page also should include an abbreviated title you should use as a running head (see item no. 6 below). The running head should be no more than 70 characters, which includes all letters, punctuation, and spaces between words.
2. The second page should consist of an Abstract of approximately 150–200 words.
3. You should begin the first page of the manuscript with the manuscript's title. DO NOT use the term "Introduction" or any other term at the beginning of the manuscript. Simply begin your discussion.
4. Use uniform margins of 1 1/2 inches at the top, bottom, right, and left of every page. Do not justify lines, leave the right margins uneven. *Do not* hyphenate words at the end of a line; let a line run short or long rather than break a word. Type no more than 25 lines of text per page.
5. Double space *among all* lines of text, which includes title, headings, quotations, figure captions, and all parts of tables.
6. After you have arranged the manuscript pages in correct order, number them consecutively, beginning with the title page. *Number all pages.* Place the number in the upper right-hand corner using Arabic numerals. Identify each manuscript page by typing an abbreviated title (header) above the page number.
7. We prefer *active* voice. Therefore, you can use the pronouns "we" and "I." Also, please avoid using a series of prepositional phrases. We *strongly encourage* you to use a grammar and *spell-checker* on manuscripts before you submit to our journal.
8. All citations within your text should include page numbers. An appropriate citation is Schwartz (1994, p. 152) or Ketz (1995, pp. 113–115). You do not need to cite six or seven references at once, particularly when the most recent references refer to earlier works. Please try to limit yourself to two or three citations at a time, preferably the most recent ones.

9. You should place page numbers for quotations along with the date of the material being cited. For example, According to Beaver (1987, p. 4), "Our knowledge of education research ... and its potential limitations for accounting ..."

10. *Headings*: Use headings and subheadings liberally to break up your text and ease the reader's ability to follow your arguments and train of thought. First-level headings should be upper-case italics, bold face, and flush to the left margin. Second-level headings should be in bold face italics, flush to the left margin with only the first letter of each primary word capitalized. Third-level headings *should* be flush to the left margin, in italics (but not bold face), with only the first letter of each primary word capitalized.

11. You should list any acknowledgments on a separate page immediately after your last page of text (before the *Notes* and *References* Sections). Type the word "Acknowledgment," centered, at the top of a new page; type the acknowledgment itself as a double-spaced, single paragraph.

12. You should try to incorporate endnote/footnote material into the body of the manuscript. When you have notes, place them on a separate section before your references. Begin notes on a separate page, with the word "Notes" centered at the top of the page. All notes should be double-spaced; indent the first line of each note five spaces.

13. Your reference pages should appear immediately after your "Notes" section (if any) and should include only works cited in the manuscript. The first page of this section should begin with the word "References" centered on the page. References to working papers are normally not appropriate. All references must be available to the reader; however, reference to unpublished dissertations is acceptable.

14. You should label TABLES and FIGURES as such and number them consecutively (using Arabic numerals) in the order in which you mention them first in the text. Indicate the approximate placement of each table/figure by a clear break in the text, inserting:

TABLE (or FIGURE) 1 ABOUT HERE

Set off double-spaced above and below. Tables should be placed after your References section: Figures should follow tables. Double-space each table/figure and begin each on a separate page.

15. Parsimony is a highly desirable trait for *manuscripts* we publish. Be *concise* in making your points and arguments.

16. *Sample Book References*

Runkel, P. J., & McGrath, J. E. (1972). *Research on human behavior. A systematic guide to method.* New York: Holt, Rinehart and Winston.

Smith, P. L. (1982). Measures of variance accounted for: Theory and practice. In: G. Keren (Ed.), *Statistical and methodological issues in psychology and social science research* (pp. 101–129). Hillsdale, NJ: Erlbaum.

17. *Sample Journal References*

Abdolmohammadi, M. J., Menon, K., Oliver, T. W., & Umpathy, S. (1985). The role of the doctoral dissertation in accounting research careers. *Issues in Accounting Education,* 59–76.

Thompson, B. (1993). The use of statistical significance tests in research: Bootstrap and other methods. *Journal of Experimental Education, 61,* 361–377.

Simon, H. A. (1980). The behavioral and social sciences. *Sciences* (July), 72–78.

Stout, D. E., & Wygal, D. E. (1994). An empirical evidence of test item sequencing effects in the managerial accounting classroom: Further evidence and extensions. In: B. N. Schwartz (Ed.), *Advances in Accounting* (Vol. 12, pp. 105–122). Greenwich, CT: JAI Press.

EDITORIAL REVIEW BOARD

xv

STATEMENT OF PURPOSE

Advances in Accounting Education is a refereed academic journal whose purpose is to meet the needs of individuals interested in the educational process. We publish thoughtful, well-developed articles that are readable, relevant, and reliable.

Articles may be non-empirical or empirical. Our emphasis is pedagogy, and articles MUST explain how instructors can improve teaching methods or accounting units can improve curricula/programs.

Non-empirical manuscripts should be academically rigorous. They can be theoretical syntheses, conceptual models, position papers, discussions of methodology, comprehensive literature reviews grounded in theory, or historical discussions with implications for current and future efforts. Reasonable assumptions and logical development are essential. Most manuscripts should discuss implications for research.

For empirical reports, sound research design and execution are critical. Articles should have well-articulated and strong theoretical foundations. In this regard, establishing a link to the non-accounting literature is desirable.

REVIEW PROCEDURES

Advances in Accounting Education will provide authors with timely reviews clearly indicating the review status of the manuscript. Authors will receive the results of initial reviews normally within eight weeks. We expect authors to work with a co-editor who will act as a liaison between the authors and the reviewers to resolve areas of concern.

EARNINGS MANAGEMENT AND CORPORATE SOCIAL RESPONSIBILITY: AN IN-CLASS EXERCISE TO ILLUSTRATE THE SHORT-TERM AND LONG-TERM CONSEQUENCES

Carol M. Fischer and Michael J. Fischer

ABSTRACT

This chapter describes an in-class exercise to illustrate the implications associated with earnings management and corporate social responsibility (CSR). Student teams act as senior managers, evaluating scenarios in which they must decide whether to engage in earnings management and socially responsible actions. All decisions have the potential to change the firm's net operating income. The "auditor" reviews earnings management decisions based on accounting choices, imposing a penalty if the auditor disallows a decision. Earnings management decisions also affect the firm's earnings quality, operationalized through adjustments to the price–earnings (P/E) ratio. Several decisions affect the firm's social responsibility rating, which ultimately affects the P/E ratio (reflecting the long-term effects of CSR). The class discusses the implications of engaging in earnings management and practicing social responsibility, as

Advances in Accounting Education: Teaching and Curriculum Innovations, Volume 10, 1–25
Copyright © 2009 by Emerald Group Publishing Limited
ISSN: 1085-4622/doi:10.1108/S1085-4622(2009)0000010003

well as the ethical issues associated with these decisions. Survey results indicate that this is an effective pedagogical tool, as students are highly engaged in the exercise. Data analysis also suggests that propensity to engage in accounting manipulations decreases over the course of the exercise.

In a speech in September 1998, Arthur Levitt, then Chairman of the Securities and Exchange Commission (SEC), expressed grave concerns about earnings management practices that effectively misrepresented the performance of American companies (Levitt, 1998, pp. 14–19). Since that time, earnings management has received a great deal of attention from regulators and the public. Several high-profile frauds of the early 2000s, including Enron, Global Crossing, WorldCom, Adelphia, and Tyco, shared one central theme: all these companies engaged in aggressive earnings management, in which firms misstated earnings and presented misleading accounting information (Giroux, 2004, p. 1). Earnings management, a practice that senior managers may have once viewed as part of their normal responsibilities, is now typically unacceptable to a public that is demanding increased transparency in financial reporting.

The public's demand for increased transparency extends beyond traditional financial measures. Many shareholders, consumers, and other constituents believe that companies must exhibit social responsibility and consider this factor in their decision making (Papmehl, 2002, p. 22). Voluntary social responsibility reporting and the ready availability of independent assessments of a company's social responsibility facilitate this process. For example, *Fortune* started publishing annual rankings of socially responsible companies (characterized as the most "accountable" companies) in 2005 (Fortune, 2007).

Business professionals involved in financial reporting should explicitly consider the ethical implications of their decisions. Thus, it is important for accounting educators to explicitly discuss ethical issues. Although accounting educators have long realized the value of integrating ethics in the accounting curriculum (see, for example, Rankin, 1991, p. 42; Sprouse, 1989, pp. 108–109; Kelly, 1987, p. 9), the highly publicized accounting frauds in recent years have further highlighted the importance of this issue (Gaa & Thorne, 2004, p. 1; Mills, 2003, pp. 153–156, 213–217).

We have incorporated the exercise described in this chapter into several accounting courses to encourage students to think about the consequences of earnings management and to consider the implications of corporate social responsibility (CSR). More importantly, the exercise engages students in hypothetical situations similar to those they may encounter once they begin working. The students consider and discuss the implications of various earnings management scenarios with the members of their management team. The exercise addresses both the short-term impact and the long-term effect on financial performance, as well as ethical issues, prompted by a discussion of the quality of reported earnings and the CSR scenarios. We have organized the discussion as follows: Section 1 provides a brief literature review; Section 2 describes the earnings management exercise; Section 3 discusses student reaction to the exercise and provides an analysis of team behavior; and Section 4 concludes with recommendations for implementing this exercise.

LITERATURE REVIEW

Although ethics has a 2000-year old intellectual history in Western culture, it has not enjoyed status as a traditional business subject in the curricula of institutions accredited by the Association to Advance Collegiate Schools of Business (AACSB) (Swanson, 2005, p. 248). In her attempt to mobilize accounting educators to assume more responsibility for ethics education, Swanson (2005, pp. 250–251) suggests three essential steps: 1) require a stand-alone course in ethics; 2) integrate ethics across the curriculum; and 3) provide supplemental initiatives such as hosting guest speakers, service learning, and establishing endowed chairs in ethics. Educators have debated these issues in the accounting literature for many years, but we continue to see renewed calls for an increased focus on ethics in accounting education (Haas, 2005; Bernardi & Bean, 2006; Fisher, Swanson, & Schmidt, 2007).

There is some evidence that ethics education can make a difference in student attitudes and behaviors. In a longitudinal study examining the socialization of accounting majors, Clikeman and Henning (2000, p. 12) found that senior-level accounting students oppose earnings management more strongly than they did as sophomores and to a greater degree than their peers who major in other business disciplines. Dellaportas (2006, pp. 397–98) reported that students who completed a discrete course in ethical issues in accountancy experienced a significant positive increase in their moral reasoning skills. Earley and Kelly implemented a number of educational interventions in an undergraduate auditing class in an effort to enhance students' ethical reasoning and found that students' moral reasoning scores improved for scenarios grounded in an accounting context. This finding was robust across a semester that pre-dated the Enron scandal as well as one that occurred after the Enron scandal (Earley & Kelly, 2004, p. 54). Rau and Weber employed a prisoner's dilemma game in a financial accounting course in an effort to increase students' moral reasoning by encouraging trust and reciprocal altruism. Although their students' moral reasoning scores did not increase one week after the intervention, there was a moderately significant increase in moral reasoning scores three months later for one dilemma (Rau & Weber, 2003, pp. 407–408).

There is strong support for an increased emphasis on ethics in accounting education. Haas argues that accounting educators must begin to give the same priority to ethics education as to other areas of accounting. In a survey of New York State colleges, she reported that two-thirds of the colleges make time to discuss ethics in the introductory accounting course. She characterized this finding as disappointing because the introductory course is taken by all business majors and represents the only opportunity to reach this broad audience with a discussion of ethical issues in accounting. Thus, one-third of respondents are not taking advantage of this opportunity. Furthermore, Haas (2005, p. 68) found that only 24% of respondents require accounting students to take a course in ethics. In a survey of accounting administrators of the largest accounting programs in North America, Madison and Schmidt (2006, p. 104) found that department chairs consistently opined that professors should devote substantially more time to ethics in the accounting curriculum. The International Accounting Education Standards Board, a committee of the International Federation of Accountants, recently proposed guidelines for educating future accounting professionals to achieve high standards of ethical behavior (Verschoor, 2006, p. 19). Importantly, a recent survey suggests that many accounting students are sensitive to the importance of ethical issues and support an increased emphasis on ethical issues in the curriculum (Bernardi & Bean, 2006, pp. 56–57).

Earnings Management, CSR, and Ethics

Levitt's (1998) warnings of aggressive earnings management techniques brought more attention to an issue that was raised by Bruns and Merchant almost a decade earlier. In their survey of 649 managers (40% of whom were finance, control, and audit managers), the majority of respondents did not consider earnings management to be unethical (Bruns & Merchant, 1990, p. 22). In evaluating responses to different scenarios involving operating decisions, they found a lack of consensus among respondents, suggesting that there is not a well-accepted ethical code related to earnings management behavior. Although managers generally viewed accounting manipulations more harshly than operating decision manipulations, the researchers were troubled by the implications of these responses for the integrity of financial reports (p. 24). They pointed out that even if the financial reporting is accurate and in compliance with Generally Accepted Accounting Principles (GAAP), "the truth has not necessarily been disclosed completely," as the company is unlikely to disclose "the borrowed nature of some of the profits" (p. 24). Since most operating manipulations sacrifice long-term profitability for short-term profits, Bruns and Merchant characterize this behavior as unethical.

Fischer and Rosenzweig (1995, p. 434) also suggest earnings management is an issue that is especially well suited to ethical discussions, as sensitizing students to the ethical implications of earnings management may even reduce the likelihood that they will engage in such behaviors as accounting professionals. White (2003, pp. 280–281) expands on this idea by encouraging students to reflect on their responses to an earnings management survey by leading them through a process of value self-confrontation.

CSR is addressed in the accounting literature primarily from the perspective of social responsibility reporting. KPMG's (2005, p. 4) most recent international survey of corporate responsibility reporting found that 64% of the top 250 companies of the Fortune 500 discuss CSR in their annual reports or in a separate report. Beyond the reporting issues, Owen (2005, pp. 400–401) suggests that there is a role for accounting educators to strengthen the ethics component of the curriculum by addressing CSR.

A recent international study examines the relationship between CSR and earnings management, producing different results depending on the type of earnings management examined (earnings smoothing, loss avoidance, and earnings aggressiveness). The researchers find that a greater commitment to CSR is associated with a reduced tendency to smooth earnings and engage in loss avoidance, but increased earnings aggressiveness (Chih, Shen, & Kang, 2008, pp. 192–195). They suggest the reduced tendency to smooth earnings and engage in loss avoidance is a result of CSR-minded companies' focus on nurturing future relationships with stakeholders. Thus, such companies avoid short-term earnings management. However, they also found that CSR-minded companies engage in more aggressive financial reporting (through accruals management), perhaps because in trying to satisfy CSR objectives, agency problems are aggravated and the managers have an incentive to hide the firm's true economic performance. These findings suggest that CSR and earnings management behaviors may be related and both are relevant to ethical issues in business.

This chapter describes an in-class exercise that places students in a position of actually making decisions about whether to engage in hypothetical earnings management behaviors. Additionally, the exercise includes CSR scenarios to highlight the impact of such decisions on performance. We believe this is an effective way to engage students in a discussion of the ethical issues associated with both earnings management and CSR.

EARNINGS MANAGEMENT AND CSR EXERCISE

We administer the exercise during a single class session and have found that it is ideal to set aside a 75-minute period for the exercise to give students sufficient time to process what has occurred and to share their reactions during a class discussion following the exercise. We have conducted the exercise with classes ranging from 12 to 40 students. We do not grade this exercise because we cover the topics of earnings management and CSR in the courses in which we use the exercise. We have administered the exercise at different points in the semester, but we prefer to use it in one of the last class meetings to stimulate discussion about earnings management, CSR, and ethics one last time before the final exam. The exercise serves as a review and helps students to understand better the distinction between accounting and operating manipulations, as well as the implications of earnings management and the impact of socially responsible actions. Although we do not include test questions explicitly based on the exercise, the final exam typically includes both objective and essay questions related to earnings management and social responsibility accounting.

We use a PowerPoint presentation for this exercise; however, we could also administer the exercise without the technology. Students work in groups, with each group representing the senior managers of a firm who must make decisions throughout the year that can change actual net operating income (NOI) relative to the forecasted amount. We display the rules of the exercise, presented in Table 1, on the screen and review them with the students.

The exercise endows each team with a forecasted income amount and then gives teams a series of eleven decision scenarios, all of which have the potential to change NOI. The scenarios we created were influenced by the Bruns and Merchant (1990) survey and include both accounting and operating choices that managers can use to manipulate earnings, thus affecting earnings quality. Earnings quality, or the ability of reported

Table 1. Instructions to the Exercise.

- Senior management teams make decisions for several items (turns)
- Decision at the end of each turn determines the change in your net operating income (NOI) (yes/no decisions)
- If you decide to engage in an action, roll the die to see how much your revenue or expense will increase (e.g., rolling a "3" gives you 3 times the base amount) *unless the impact is a fixed amount*
- Certain decisions involve accounting choices that may "push the envelope" with respect to GAAP; the "auditor" will roll a die for each team that makes this choice
  - Risk levels (hidden) of 1–6 are assigned to each of these scenarios
  - The higher the risk, the more likely the auditor will disallow the decision (e.g., if risk level = "4" and the auditor rolls 1, 2, 3, or 4, the decision is disallowed and a penalty imposed; if the auditor rolls 5 or 6, you are safe).
- NOI, social responsibility, and earnings quality measures will be updated at the end of each turn

---

earnings to reflect true economic performance, is decreased through the artificial or temporary enhancement of earnings that is sometimes achieved through earnings management. Although there are various models to measure earnings quality (Bellovary, Giacomino, & Akers, 2005), there is not a single accepted approach to produce an accurate measure. We choose to use the price–earnings (P/E) ratio to proxy for earnings quality in this exercise, since it reflects the value that the market places on a firm's earnings and is influenced by the market's perception of the quality of the firm's earnings (Revsine, Collins, & Johnson, 2002, pp. 238–244,).

We intended the five accounting manipulations included in our exercise to be questionable under GAAP. For each of these decision scenarios, there is a risk that the auditor will disallow the team's decision. We explain that the risk that the auditor will disallow the decision is higher for more aggressive accounting practices. If the auditor (represented by the instructor) disallows an accounting decision, the firm incurs a penalty, representing the cost of additional audit time. If the auditor does not disallow the decision, however, the earnings quality declines through a reduction in the P/E ratio.

The exercise also includes three operating decision scenarios, all of which affect the P/E ratio. Thus, although there is no audit penalty (and no direct reduction of current NOI) associated with earnings management achieved through operating manipulations, there is an impact on the value of the firm. This notion is based on the assumption that operating manipulations to manage earnings are often made to achieve short-term earnings at the expense of long-term performance (Bruns & Merchant, 1990, p. 23).

Finally, the remaining three decision scenarios affect the company's social responsibility rating. Although the social responsibility rating is highly subjective, the public has become increasingly concerned with CSR. The social responsibility rating in this exercise is neutral at the beginning and then increases or decreases with certain decisions. When we present the initial instructions to the students, we describe the social responsibility rating so that they are aware of the type of rating we use in the exercise. As we complete the CSR scenarios, we indicate the changes in the rating by a simple +/− tally that is posted on the blackboard.

We use the social responsibility rating at the end of the exercise to adjust the P/E ratio of the firm because most people view CSR as contributing to the long-term success of a company by influencing its reputation (Mirvis, 2008, p. 45). Thus, a firm's decision to engage in socially responsible behaviors will enhance the market's perception of the firm in the long run. However, unlike decisions that directly affect reported income, the impact of social responsibility is more difficult to measure, and its impact is uncertain. For this reason, we do not advise the students of the social responsibility adjustment to the P/E ratio until the end of the exercise.

We do not explicitly instruct the students to achieve any specific goal. On the basis of student comments during and after the exercise, they often focus on improving NOI. As discussed later, however, the team with the highest NOI is not necessarily the team with the highest market capitalization or the best long-term prospects. Teams that balance high earnings with high-quality earnings and CSR are most likely to have the highest P/E ratios and market capitalization, which are associated with greater long-term success for the firm.

Each group uses a die to determine the impact of earnings management decisions on reported income. The die introduces an element of chance into the earnings management decisions. The risk serves two purposes: first, it incorporates risk into the exercise to reflect the risk associated with most business decisions. Second, it serves to more fully engage students in the exercise, as they try to improve their performance through "lucky" rolls. We also have a die, which we use in our role as the "auditor." In addition to the basic rules, we present the students with base information to help them respond to the scenarios within a context (Table 2). The base information is admittedly sparse, leaving the students to speculate about and discuss many issues throughout the exercise.

Students usually have a few questions before the exercise gets underway. Most of the questions simply require clarification of the rules, but often a student asks how many turns there will be. We do not reveal this

Table 2. Base Information.

- Publicly held manufacturer with 12/31/year-end
- Three different locations in small towns in the United States
- Projected annual net sales of $10,000,000 (all on credit)
- Gross profit margin of 40%
- Net operating profit margin of 8%
- Thus, forecasted operating profit before adjustments = $800,000; each team is "endowed" with this amount
- Base P/E ratio = 16; ending P/E ratio will be multiplied by net operating profit to determine market capitalization

---

information in advance. (We explain to them at the end of the exercise that keeping the number of turns unknown helps to prevent "gaming" behavior.) Students sometimes ask the magnitude of the penalties. We reveal that they lose their income boost and an additional amount, but we do not indicate the magnitude of the penalties. Any confusion about the rules is alleviated by the time we complete the first "round" of the exercise.

In addition to the PowerPoint screen, we use a section of the blackboard, where we keep a running total of each team's NOI. Since all teams begin with forecasted NOI of $800,000, we write the names of each team on the board and start them all off with $800,000. We also show the P/E ratio (initially 16) and the social responsibility rating (initially neutral) of each team. We update these values with each round of the exercise, as described in the following paragraphs.

We present the accounting scenarios in three steps. The student teams must make their decisions after seeing the basic scenario. Next, we provide additional information about the audit risk. Finally, we reveal the impact on the P/E ratio and/or social responsibility rating. The structure appears in Table 3, which illustrates the first earnings management decision in the exercise. When the first screen appears, the teams must decide whether to engage in the action. We rotate the order in which teams make their decisions, asking each team to announce their decision to the class. It is important to rotate the order because the students view the exercise as a competition and may be influenced by the decisions announced by teams earlier in the rotation. If a team chooses to engage in the action, the students roll their die and announce the result. We immediately update their NOI figure on the board.

After every team has made a decision, we reveal the second screen. For the scenario in Table 3, which involves an accounting manipulation, the second screen shows the risk level associated with the decision. (If the

Table 3.   Presentation of Earnings Management Decision Involving an
Accounting Manipulation.

Screen 1

The estimated bad debt expense is currently 5% of net credit sales. A range of 4%–5.5% is considered reasonable. The company could reduce its allowance, which would reduce bad debt expense. *Do you reduce the allowance?*

NOI boost: die roll × $40,000

Screen 2

The estimated bad debt expense is currently 5% of net credit sales. A range of 4%–5.5% is considered reasonable. The company could reduce its allowance, which would reduce bad debt expense. *Do you reduce the allowance?*

NOI boost: die roll × $40,000
Risk level: 3

Screen 3

The estimated bad debt expense is currently 5% of net credit sales. A range of 4%–5.5% is considered reasonable. The company could reduce its allowance, which would reduce bad debt expense. *Do you reduce the allowance?*

NOI boost: die roll × $40,000
Risk level: 3
Penalty: lose NOI boost+$120,000
Earnings quality drops if change is made – P/E ratio drops 1 point

decision is an operating manipulation, there is no risk of disallowance by the auditor, so this screen does not appear. This type of scenario is illustrated in the second earnings management decision shown in Table 4.) We then roll a die separately for each group that has decided to engage in the action, tracking the results so that we can update the blackboard by adjusting for any disallowed NOI and penalties. Rolling the die on the desks or tables of the students affected by the outcome increases the tension and results in an immediate broadcasting of the outcome to the rest of the class, as the students typically groan – or cheer – when they see the result. Since the auditor will allow some teams to make a change that is disallowed for others, we explain that different auditors will sometimes reach different conclusions about the acceptability of an earnings management practice. Also, different circumstances at the firms may influence auditor judgments. This explanation alleviates any concerns about the inconsistency of auditor

Table 4. Presentation of Earnings Management Decision Involving an Operating Manipulation.

Screen 1
The company could reduce spending on research and development. *Do you reduce spending on R&D?*
NOI boost: die roll × $100,000

Screen 2
The company could reduce spending on research and development. *Do you reduce spending on R&D?*
NOI boost: die roll × $100,000 Earnings quality drops if R&D spending is reduced – P/E ratio drops 3 points

decisions. After we determine which groups, if any, had their decisions disallowed by the auditor, we reveal the third screen, which describes the penalty and the impact on the P/E ratio and social responsibility rating, if any. Those teams whose decisions were allowed by the auditor discover that there are still consequences to their decision, as earnings quality drops (as reflected by a decrease in the P/E ratio) because of the accounting change. At the end of the turn, we update the NOI, P/E ratio, and social responsibility rating displayed on the blackboard for all teams.

The second scenario, presented in Table 5, involves an operating manipulation. The only difference in the presentation of this type of scenario is that there is no risk of auditor disallowance. Thus, there are only two screens to be revealed. The first describes the earnings management decision, and the second screen reveals the implications for earnings quality and, if applicable, social responsibility. We show these consequences by indicating that the P/E ratio has dropped if earnings quality decreased and/ or showing additional plusses (+) or minuses (−) in the firm's social responsibility rating. The scenario presented in Table 4 reduces earnings quality, resulting in a drop in the P/E ratio, but does not affect the firm's social responsibility rating.

This process continues through all of the exercise. The different earnings management scenarios that we use have evolved over time based on feedback from students and colleagues. In addition to the scenarios shown in Tables 3 and 4, we currently use the scenarios shown in Table 5; an individual instructor could expand or change the scenarios to meet his or her needs. We show the order in which the scenarios appear in Table 6.

Table 5. Earnings Management Scenarios.

Panel A: Accounting Manipulations

Industry practice, which we have followed, is to use accelerated depreciation; however, a change from accelerated to straight-line depreciation would reduce depreciation expense. *Do you change to SL?*

NOI boost: die roll × $30,000
- Risk level: 2
- Penalty: lose NOI boost+$90,000
- Earnings quality drops if change is made – P/E ratio drops 1 point

Warranty expense has consistently been 9%–10% of net sales. A range of 7.5%–10% is common in the industry. The company could reduce its allowance for warranty claims to 8%, reducing the warranty expense for the current year. *Do you reduce warranty expense?*

NOI boost: die roll × $50,000
- Risk level: 5
- Penalty: lose NOI boost+$150,000
- Earnings quality drops if change is made – P/E ratio drops 3 points

An annual review of the company's property, plant, and equipment determined that the company has equipment that is overvalued and should be written down. However, the controller believes that he can make a case for deferring the write-down by arguing that there is uncertainty about the permanence of the decline in the equipment's value. *Do you defer the write-down?*

NOI boost: die roll × $50,000
- Risk level: 4
- Penalty: lose NOI boost+$150,000
- Earnings quality drops if write-down is deferred – P/E ratio drops 2 points

The company has to clean up a hazardous waste site. The total cost, given the current methods available for such clean-up, is estimated to be $1–$2 million over a 10-year period. The company argues the cost is not reasonably estimable due to uncertainty about the costs and the possibility that new and cheaper methods of clean-up could be on the horizon...therefore, the company argues that it does not have to book a liability this year. If the liability is booked, it will reduce NOI. *Do you book the liability?*

NOI decrease this year: $100,000
- Risk level: 4
- Penalty: record expense of $100,000+$200,000
- Earnings quality reduced if liability is not booked – P/E ratio drops 1 point

Panel B: Operating Manipulations (Including CSR)

Your company has been approached by a member of the local community who is coordinating a fundraiser to benefit United Way. They are requesting corporate sponsorship, which would require a contribution of $25,000. You have not budgeted for such a contribution. *Do you make the contribution?*

NOI decrease: $25,000
- Donate: social responsibility rating increases (+)
- Don't donate: social responsibility rating decreases (−)

Table 5. (*Continued*)

The company can offer a deferred payment plan, allowing customers to delay payment for goods ordered and shipped in November and December until the following February. This would allow the company to accelerate sales, increasing income for the current year. *Do you offer the plan?*
NOI boost: die roll × $25,000
- Earnings quality drops – P/E ratio drops 2 points

The company could reduce spending on advertising. *Do you reduce spending?*
NOI boost: die roll × $75,000
- Earnings quality drops – P/E ratio drops 3 points

The company has been asked to voluntarily perform a clean-up operation at their plant that would positively affect the long-term health of the community residents. The total cost of this clean-up, given the current methods available for such clean-up, is estimated to be between $1 and $2 million over a 10-year period. *Do you conduct the clean-up?*
NOI decrease: die roll × $50,000
- If clean-up is conducted: social responsibility rating increases (+++)
- Decision not to conduct clean-up: social responsibility rating decreases (− − −)

The company manufactures junior-sized sporting equipment. Quality control personnel have advised that one product just barely meets government safety standards, and has recommended a production change that will increase costs. Since the product currently meets standards, however, the company is not compelled to make this change. *Do you make the change?*
- NOI decrease this year: die roll x $ 50,000
- Offset by NOI increase: die roll x $20,000
- Social responsibility rating increases (++)
- *Decision not to make change*: Social responsibility rating decreases (− −) and NOI decreases $200,000 due to bad publicity if die roll is 4 or higher

---

In total, there are 11 earnings management decisions. Eight of the decisions affect earnings quality, reinforcing the idea that even if a decision is legal and within the boundaries of GAAP, it still affects financial reporting and the value of the firm's financial reports to the market. Three of the scenarios affect the firm's social responsibility rating, which is a simple +/− rating. We explain to the students that social responsibility is not easily measured in a single summary figure, but that we are using a neutral/positive/negative rating scheme to proxy for the market's assessment of the firm's level of CSR.

Since we update NOI, the P/E ratio, and the social responsibility rating at the end of each round, students are consistently aware of the cumulative impact of their decisions and their position on all of these dimensions relative to the other teams. The availability of key data about all the teams

Table 6.   Timeline: Order of Scenarios.

Decision #	Summary of Decision	Type of Decision
1	Reduce allowance for bad debts	Accounting
2	Reduce spending on R&D	Operating
3	Contribute to United Way	Operating/CSR
4	Change depreciation method	Accounting
5	Reduce warranty expense	Accounting
6	Offer a deferred payment plan	Operating
7	Conduct voluntary clean-up	Operating/CSR
8	Reduce spending on advertising	Operating
9	Defer write-down of equipment	Accounting
10	Improve product quality	Operating/CSR
11	Record liability for hazardous waste clean-up	Accounting

parallels the situation that senior managers face when their competitors announce earnings and other financial details to the market, making all aware of their position relative to their competitors.

At the end of the exercise, the students learn that the social responsibility rating affects the company's market capitalization through an adjustment to the P/E ratio. Specifically, the students add (subtract) one for each plus (minus) in their firm's social responsibility rating. Thus, there is a long-term reward for socially responsible behavior and a penalty for behavior that is not socially responsible, as reflected in a higher (or lower) P/E ratio. We intend for this adjustment to convey the trade-offs associated with these decisions. In the short run, NOI will be decreased (increased) by socially responsible (irresponsible) decisions, but in the long run, the impact of these decisions is just the opposite.

After the last scenario, the screen indicates that there are no more decisions. We summarize the NOI, P/E ratio, and social responsibility rating, calculate market capitalization of each team, and display this information on the blackboard. The summary leads into a discussion of which team performed the best. Since there is no single measure of what is "best," some of the class discussion focuses on identifying the best performer.

Debriefing: The Class Discussion

The class exercise concludes with a debriefing session, in which we acknowledge the obvious differences between the exercise and real life, but point out that the students can still learn important lessons from the exercise. We begin the discussion with three questions: (1) What factors influenced your decisions? (2) Did all teammates agree? and (3) Which team did the "best"? During the debriefing, we also discuss how the students felt during the exercise. They always talk about how important it was for them to "win" (although we never define winning and actually do not use the term "win" in an effort to avoid characterizing the exercise as a game). Students also talk about the pressure that they experienced when other teams were ahead of them. We discuss how this pressure mimics the situation that financial executives face when their competitors report results that are better than their own company. And, while we are engaged in just a class exercise, the students develop an appreciation for the pressure that financial executives feel to beat the competition and meet earnings forecasts.

We also talk about the element of risk present in the exercise, which often seems unfair to students. Some teams that engage in earnings management get a large boost in NOI, whereas others have their decision disallowed by the auditor and face a penalty on top of that. Over the course of the exercise, students learn that teams with the NOI boost also experience deteriorating P/E ratios, as their earnings quality declines when they engage in earnings management. Thus, they begin to weigh the risk of accounting manipulations, which requires them to consider the extent to which a decision violates the spirit of GAAP and compromises the quality of reported earnings.

We typically have at least a few student teams that have differences of opinion about the team decisions. (We are aware of their disagreements because we can overhear the discussions that take place as we present each scenario.) Some students insist that they would have made different decisions if they had made the decision on an individual basis, whereas others acknowledge that they were influenced by peer pressure during the exercise and may well be influenced similarly in a real world environment.

Often there is no clear-cut best performer, as the team with the highest NOI may not have the highest market capitalization or the best P/E ratio and social responsibility rating. There is typically a lively discussion of what constitutes the best performance and the ability to enhance short-term performance at the expense of long-term viability.

The debriefing also includes a discussion of the consequences of earnings management. We address the general consequences borne by society: financial statements that are less reliable, a financial reporting system with less integrity, and capital markets that are not as efficient at allocating capital. We also discuss the individual consequences borne by the managers involved in these situations: personal stress, loss of employment, financial penalties, and potential jail time. These consequences are particularly salient to our students because of the location of our university, close to Coudersport, Pennsylvania, the former headquarters of Adelphia Communications. Other instructors can make a similar point by referring to a number of highly publicized financial reporting frauds.

During the debriefing, we also discuss the internal satisfaction that comes from making ethical decisions, particularly in the face of pressure to manage earnings. We refer back to earlier discussions about ethics during the course, relating their decisions during the exercise to judgments that they made during class discussions about Adelphia, Enron, and other accounting frauds. We finish by highlighting a point made earlier in the course: the role of financial reporting is to provide useful, reliable information to the public. Thus, it is never right to intentionally mislead the public about the firm's financial performance.

Finally, the discussion concludes with a brainstorming session concerning how the profession might address earnings management. We discuss several approaches to reduce earnings management, including the use of outside directors, better audit programs for detection, and harsher penalties for those who are caught engaging in aggressive earnings management. Since earnings management is often legal, improving the ethical climate in which managers prepare financial statements may be the best approach for reducing earnings management designed to mislead financial statement readers. We can improve the ethical climate through executive education, senior executives who model ethical behavior, and enforceable professional codes of conduct. Removing the incentives to engage in earnings management, perhaps through restructured executive compensation plans, can also serve to reduce earnings management behavior.

STUDENT REACTION AND DECISION MAKING

Student Reaction to the Exercise

We have used a version of this exercise in class for several years, with four undergraduate sections of first-semester intermediate accounting and nine sections of contemporary accounting theory (a required course in our MBA program), one section of graduate level auditing, and three sections of graduate level accounting theory and research. The exercise has generated a very positive response each time. Students often want to discuss the exercise further after class, and tell us that it makes them think about these issues much more than the assigned readings and general class discussion on the topic. The informal feedback we have received on this exercise has encouraged us to continue to use the exercise each semester.

When we initially developed the exercise, we administered it in class without any formal measurement of student decisions or feedback. Early in the process, in an attempt to obtain feedback regarding student perceptions of the experience, we conducted a survey of participants shortly after the class exercise. We sent the survey to a total of 47 undergraduate students and 17 graduate students. We asked students to complete the survey anonymously and to return it to the instructor. We received 27 surveys from the undergraduates and 16 surveys from the graduate students, for response rates of 57% and 94%, respectively. The results of the survey appear in Table 7.

In addition to asking the questions shown in Table 7, the survey had space for open-ended comments or suggestions. Just over half of the students who completed the surveys included comments, some of which appear in Table 8.

The survey responses clearly indicate that students were engaged in this exercise and saw the connection to course material. Three students made helpful suggestions for improving the exercise. Specifically, one student suggested adding more rounds to reduce the impact of luck on the outcome

Table 7. Student Feedback: Mean Responses to Survey Questions.

Question	Undergraduate Students ($n = 27$)	Graduate Students ($n = 16$)
How much did you pay attention during the exercise?	4.93	4.93
Did the class exercise help you to better understand managers' motivations for engaging in earnings management?	4.44	4.40
Were you motivated to win[a] the exercise?	4.63	4.40
Did you understand the rules of the exercise?	4.85	4.53
Did the game cause you to think about earnings management issues?	4.37	4.47
Do you feel the exercise fit in with the course material?	4.78	4.73
How much did you enjoy the class exercise?	4.89	4.93

Note: Scale of 1 to 5, with 1 = "not at all" to 5 = "very much."
[a]In the initial version of the exercise, we indicated that the winner would be the team with the highest NOI. The current version of the exercise does not define "winning" or explicitly instruct students to maximize income.

Table 8.   Selected Student Comments.

Panel A: Under Graduate

The exercise helped to realize different risks with different situations and made my moral and
  ethical side help me make the decision

I thought the exercise was very educational – it was practical and informative. I liked how it was
  synchronous with what class lectures had been about. I also thought it was fun to "pretend,"
  yet have a real goal in mind

I think it's a GREAT EXERCISE!!! One suggestion: I think if there were a couple of extra
  rounds more groups, might have eventually learned a lesson about the drawback of earnings
  management (as their luck would have run out)

It showed me how a person might feel when making a decision that they know might not be the
  most ethical choice. It is easy to say that I would never make an unethical decision while
  reading about companies that have made them, but when we were all put in the situation, we
  all wanted to do whatever it took to get the most money. I think it is a great demonstration of
  the pressure we will face in the workforce

Panel B: Graduate

I think the exercise was very enjoyable. It really helped us to think about decisions managers
  must make with regard to earnings management

I was confused before the exercise started, but quickly caught on. I don't think I was as
  motivated as I could have been because it wasn't actually "my" money. Also, I would have
  made different decisions had I been working on my own and not in a group

Awesome in-class exercise. It kept my attention while helping me to understand the underlying
  motivation of managers when engaging in earnings management

I thought this exercise was a great learning tool. It illustrated various situations and the
  penalties that come along with getting caught. Excellent!

---

of the exercise. Another student recommended clarification of some of the
instructions. A third student suggested modifying the match between risk
and reward on some of the scenarios. Subsequent modifications of the
exercise incorporated all of these suggestions. Most of the comments
included sentiments to the effect that the students really enjoyed it, either
because the exercise itself was fun or because it was nice to have a break
from the usual class routine. Some of the student comments reflect the tone
of the class discussion that followed the exercise, suggesting that students
continue to think about these issues after the class period. Although the
survey does not prove that the class exercise is superior to a lecture on
the same material, the level of student engagement and positive reaction to
the exercise convince us that students are likely to better understand
earnings management and CSR issues after the class exercise. In addition,
this approach complements the traditional lecture by providing an active
learning experience.

Student Decision Making

Since incorporating modifications to the earnings management and CSR exercise, we have administered it each semester with continued good student response. We collected data about student decision making during the last three administrations of the exercise. We asked the students to record their decisions in a log, which we collected at the end of the exercise. We used the logs to determine how many groups engaged in each action and to summarize the results of the exercise across sections. These data provide additional insights into the students' decision making in the exercise.

We collected these data for a total of 18 groups, averaging five students per group. Two of these recent administrations were to graduate level contemporary accounting theory classes (with four and five groups, respectively), whereas the third administration included in these data was to a joint meeting of two graduate level classes in auditing and accounting theory and research, which included a total of nine groups.

The earnings management and CSR exercise includes eight opportunities for earnings management (five accounting decisions and three operational decisions) and three opportunities to engage in socially responsible behaviors. Every student team engaged in at least two earnings management actions and at least one socially responsible decision. Only one of the 18 student teams did not choose to engage in any accounting manipulations; one other team chose not to manage earnings through operating decisions. Table 9 shows the percentage of teams choosing to take each action throughout the exercise. For the scenarios involving earnings management through accounting choices, the table also shows the percentage of teams that were overruled by the auditor after making the decision to manage earnings.

Overall, this table indicates that at least some of the student teams chose to take each possible action throughout the exercise. The pattern of decisions is interesting with respect to the accounting decisions. We present these scenarios in turns 1, 4, 5, 9, and 11. As shown in Table 9, the percentage of teams choosing to manage earnings through accounting choices decreases as the exercise proceeds. Although 89% of the teams engaged in the first accounting scenario in the exercise, the percentage of teams choosing to engage in earnings management through accounting decisions dropped off to 33%, 28%, 11%, and 6%, respectively, for the next four accounting scenarios. Thus, the likelihood of choosing to manage earnings through accounting decisions decreased dramatically throughout the exercise. After the first two scenarios, students seem better able to

Table 9.   Percentage of Groups Engaging in Each Decision
($N = 18$ Groups).

Turn	Type of Decision	Percentage of Groups Taking Action (%)	Audit Override Frequency[a] (%)
1	Accounting	89	50
2	Operating	33	N/A
3	Social responsibility	89	N/A
4	Accounting	33	17
5	Accounting	28	20
6	Operating	33	N/A
7	Social responsibility	44	N/A
8	Operating	67	N/A
9	Accounting	11	50
10	Social responsibility	100	N/A
11	Accounting	6	100

[a]Only accounting decisions were subject to audit; the audit override frequency represents the percentage of groups engaging in earnings management on this turn that had the decision disallowed by the auditor.

distinguish between operating and accounting manipulations, and avoid the accounting manipulations. This is most likely due to the "audits," which disallow team decisions (and impose monetary penalties). The audit results for the five accounting scenarios appear in Table 9. The audit override frequency indicates the number of groups that had their decisions disallowed by the auditor for each scenario. For example, 16 of the groups decided to engage in earnings management on the first turn, but eight (50%) had their decisions disallowed by the auditor. (The audit override frequency of the last scenario is 100% because only one group chose to engage in this action and the decision was disallowed by the auditor in that one instance.)

Table 10 presents information about the ending position of the groups across the variables that we tracked (NOI, P/E ratio, market capitalization, and social responsibility). For discussion purposes, it is interesting to compare the ending results to the ending values for a hypothetical firm that did not engage in any of the earnings management actions and took all the socially responsible actions throughout the exercise. Such a firm would finish the exercise with an expected value of NOI of $495,000, a P/E ratio of 22, and market capitalization of $10,890,000. Although both the NOI and market capitalization of such a firm are below the averages achieved by the student teams, the P/E ratio is significantly higher than both the average and the highest achieved by any of the student teams, suggesting that the

Table 10. Ending Position on Key Variables: Lows, Highs & Averages ($N = 18$ Groups).

	Net Operating Income[a]	P/E Ratio[b]	Market Capitalization[c]	Social Responsibility[d]
Minimum	$215,000	10	$3,440,000	−2
Maximum	$1,225,000	17	$18,445,000	+6
Mean	$874,444	13	$11,484,444	+2
Median	$897,500	13	$11,270,000	0

[a]Started at $800,000; adjusted for decisions throughout the exercise.
[b]Started at 16; adjusted for decisions throughout the exercise, and at the end by adding (subtracting) the social responsibility rating.
[c]NOI times P/E ratio.
[d]Started at 0; adjusted with additions for positive actions and subtractions for negative actions throughout the exercise; ending value used to adjust ending P/E ratio.

long-term viability of such a firm might be better than that of the student teams. This is an issue that we discuss with the students during the debriefing.

The lowest NOI reported by a group ($215,000) is well below average. Of the 18 groups, only five (28%) reported ending NOI below the original forecasted NOI of $800,000, and only two (11%) reported NOI below $600,000. The group that reported the lowest NOI was also the group with the lowest market capitalization. However, the team that achieved the highest NOI did not report the highest market capitalization. In fact, there were five student groups that reported higher market capitalization than this group. Thus, it appears that this group sacrificed long-term success (as proxied by the P/E ratio) for short-term gains in NOI.

There was considerable variation in the ending market capitalization amounts. The top three groups in terms of ending market capitalization all had high P/E ratios (16 or 17) and the highest possible social responsibility ratings (+6). In contrast, five of the six firms in the bottom third had P/E ratios of 13 or lower and social responsibility ratings of zero (neutral).

The social responsibility ratings were generally at least neutral (zero). We calculated the ratings by starting with a neutral rating and adding (subtracting) one for each plus (minus) acquired during the exercise. The rating could range from negative six to positive six; however, since every team engaged in at least one socially responsible action, the lowest social responsibility rating among the 18 groups was −2; this group was the only one with a negative rating. Nine of the student groups ended up with a neutral (zero) rating, whereas one group had a positive rating of 4, and the other seven groups had a positive rating of 6.

In general, the results across the three administrations were similar. We do not provide detailed analysis, as there are only three administrations reflected in our data, and the number of groups varies considerably across these administrations.

RECOMMENDATIONS FOR IMPLEMENTATION

On the basis of our experience, we believe that the earnings management and CSR exercise are most effective when students have been exposed to these issues before the exercise. Students will get more out of the in-class exercise when they understand how GAAP offers opportunities for earnings management, and they are familiar with the concerns of the SEC and accounting profession concerning earnings quality. We also discuss ethics in all of our accounting courses, including those in which we have administered this exercise. Previous discussion of the role of ethics in accounting enables students to thoughtfully consider and discuss the ethical implications of earnings management. Prior exposure to CSR also contributes to a richer discussion of the scenarios in the exercise.

We have administered the exercise with as few as four and as many as eight groups. Although students could make each decision individually, we believe that completing the exercise as part of a group is preferable. First, it is far more practical for most classes. More importantly, a single individual typically does not make the types of decisions involved in the different scenarios without consulting with others. Furthermore, the peer pressure that students experience as part of a group (and from competing groups) helps to keep the students engaged. However, it is likely that group decisions differ from individual decisions. One of the students in our survey made this point (Table 8); we now discuss this issue in the debriefing session. Informal feedback from our students has suggested that there are typically several individuals who do not agree with at least some of their team decisions. An interesting extension to this exercise might involve surveying the students early in the semester concerning their views on the earnings management behaviors included in the exercise and comparing their individual responses to the actual group behavior. Instructors could also survey participants about their level of agreement with group decisions during and after the exercise.

An anonymous reviewer suggested another possible change to the exercise, in which the auditor always detects earnings management, but may decide that the action is not material or does not really constitute earnings management given the situation at hand. To implement this change, the instructor could assign some scenarios a risk level of 1 (no loss of NOI boost and no penalty – thus getting a pass from the auditor) or 2 (loss of NOI boost, but no penalty). This requires the students to differentiate between unimportant earnings management decisions and blatant earnings management activities. If the risk level assigned is high, that is, greater than or equal to 3, the level of the penalty is based strictly on the excess time spent by the auditor (determined by roll of die) as a result of this action – all rolls of the die would affect the penalty, not just the rolls that are less than or equal to 4, when the risk level is 4, as it presently is in the exercise. For example, if the risk level is greater than or equal to 3 and the auditor rolls a 5, then the penalty is 5/6 of the base amount given when the original decision to manage earnings is made – plus the boost they made by making the decision would also go away. If the auditor rolls a 1, then the penalty would be 1/6 of the base amount (plus the boost would go away). This change to the structure of the exercise would maintain the roll of the die as a way to engage the students, but omit the possibility that a team engages in overt earnings management without suffering the consequences of a penalty.

In summary, the earnings management exercise has been one of the best class activities that we have used in more than 20 years of teaching. Student reaction is consistently positive, the exercise complements course material very well, and the experience is thought-provoking. Thus, we believe this exercise is a very effective pedagogical technique. Perhaps just as importantly, it is a lot of fun. We always look forward to the class in which we conduct the earnings management exercise, as we come away reenergized from enjoying the time with our students.

ACKNOWLEDGMENTS

We acknowledge the contributions of Mike Dambra, Dave DuBrava, and Rob Westin, who developed the initial idea for this exercise and presented it to a graduate level class as part of a class assignment. We are also grateful for the helpful comments and suggestions of Connie Esmond-Kiger on an earlier version of the earnings management exercise. Finally, we greatly appreciate the recommendations of the editor and two anonymous reviewers.

REFERENCES

Bellovary, J. L., Giacomino, D. E., & Akers, M. D. (2005). Earnings quality: It's time to measure and report. *The CPA Journal, 75*(November), 32–37.

Bernardi, R. A., & Bean, D. F. (2006). Ethics in accounting education: The forgotten stakeholders. *The CPA Journal, 76*(July), 56–57.

Bruns, W. J., & Merchant, K. A. (1990). The dangerous morality of managing earnings. *Management Accounting, 72*(August), 22–25.

Chih, H., Shen, C., & Kang, F. (2008). Corporate social responsibility, investor protection and earnings management: Some international evidence. *Journal of Business Ethics, 79*(April), 179–198.

Clikeman, P. M., & Henning, S. L. (2000). The socialization of undergraduate accounting students. *Issues in Accounting Education, 15*(February), 1–17.

Dellaportas, S. (2006). Making a difference with a discrete course on accounting ethics. *Journal of Business Ethics, 65*(Spring), 391–404.

Earley, C. E., & Kelly, P. T. (2004). A note on educational interventions in an undergraduate auditing course: Is there an "Enron effect"? *Issues in Accounting Education, 19*(February), 53–71.

Fischer, M., & Rosenzweig, K. (1995). Attitudes of students and accounting practitioners concerning the ethical acceptability of earnings management. *Journal of Business Ethics, 14*(June), 433–444.

Fisher, D. G., Swanson, D. L., & Schmidt, J. J. (2007). Accounting education lags CPE ethics requirements: Implications for the profession and a call to action. *Accounting Education, 16*(December), 345–363.

Fortune (2007). Most 'Accountable' Companies: Our Annual Ranking of Business Responsibility. Available at http://money.cnn.com/magazines/fortune/global500/2007/accountability/full_list.html

Gaa, J. C., & Thorne, L. (2004). An introduction to the special issue on professionalism and ethics in accounting education. *Issues in Accounting Education, 19*(February), 1–6.

Giroux, G. (2004). *Detecting earnings management*. Hoboken, NY: Wiley.

Haas, A. (2005). Now is the time for ethics in education. *The CPA Journal, 75*(June), 66–68.

Kelly, T. F. (1987). Educating future accountants. *The CPA Journal, 57*(August), 8–12.

KPMG. (2005). *KPMG international survey of corporate responsibility reporting 2005.* Amsterdam, The Netherlands: KPMG International.

Levitt, A. (1998). The numbers game. *The CPA Journal, 68*(December), 14–19.

Madison, R. L., & Schmidt, J. J. (2006). Survey of time devoted to ethics in accountancy programs in North American colleges and universities. *Issues in Accounting Education, 21*(May), 99–109.

Mills, D. Q. (2003). *Wheel, deal and steal: Deceptive accounting, deceitful CEOs, and ineffective reforms*. Upper Saddle River, NJ: Prentice Hall.

Mirvis, P. H. (2008). What do surveys say about corporate citizenship? *The Corporate Citizen, 2*, 43–47.

Owen, D. (2005). CSR after Enron: A role for the academic accounting profession? *European Accounting Review, 14*(July), 395–404.

Papmehl, A. (2002). Beyond the GAAP. *CMA Management, 76*(July/August), 20–25.

Rankin, L. J. (1991). Student capabilities and instructional methods: A framework for curriculum development, assessment, and research. In: G. L. Sundem & C. T. Norgaard (Eds), *Models of accounting education* (pp. 38–48). Torrence, CA: Accounting Education Change Commission.

Rau, S. E., & Weber, J. (2003). Can the repeated prisoner's dilemma game be used as a tool to enhance moral reasoning? *Teaching Business Ethics, 7*(November), 395–416.

Revsine, L., Collins, D. W., & Johnson, W. B. (2002). *Financial reporting and analysis.* Upper Saddle River, NJ: Prentice Hall.

Sprouse, R. T. (1989). The synergism of accountancy and accounting education. *Accounting Horizons, 3*(March), 102–110.

Swanson, D. L. (2005). Business ethics education at bay: Addressing a crisis of legitimacy. *Issues in Accounting Education, 3*(August), 247–253.

Verschoor, C. C. (2006). IFAC committee proposes guidance for achieving ethical behavior. *Strategic Finance, 88*(December), 19–2055.

White, L. F. (2003). Cooking the books or managing earnings: Students draw the line. *Advances in Accounting Education, 5*, 263–287.

ESTABLISHING AN eMENTOR PROGRAM: INCREASING THE INTERACTION BETWEEN ACCOUNTING MAJORS AND PROFESSIONALS

Nancy L. Wilburn, T. S. Amer and Bob G. Kilpatrick

ABSTRACT

This chapter describes an eMentor program used as a cocurricular professional development activity for accounting majors at a university that is located in a relatively small city, geographically distant from the primary location of its major recruiters. The key element of the program is the use of e-mail as a communication channel to link students in our accounting program with accounting and business professionals. We provide information regarding our eMentor program's mission and objectives, recruiting professionals and students to participate, and an examination of data collected to evaluate the program. In addition, we identify the topics discussed during the interactions between professional mentors and students. Finally, we provide insights based on our experiences on running a successful eMentor program.

Results indicate that the program is an overall success since a high proportion of students and professionals agree/strongly agree that the program meets its mission and objectives, and virtually all of the

Advances in Accounting Education: Teaching and Curriculum Innovations, Volume 10, 27–59
ISSN: 1085-4622/doi:10.1108/S1085-4622(2009)0000010004

professionals agree/strongly agree that the program is a worthwhile use of their time. Most student–mentor pairs have had several e-mail contacts and at least one phone contact, with a majority of students initiating some contact. The topics discussed most frequently centered on college curriculum choices and professional career path options, including the benefits of internships and externships.

In *Issues Statement No. 4, Improving the Early Employment Experience of Accountants,* the Accounting Education Change Commission (AECC) recommended that students should

- Seek opportunities to obtain first-hand knowledge of the business world and practice environment.
- Obtain information about career opportunities and the job search (AECC, 1993, p. 2).

Accounting departments can help students undertake these objectives by facilitating their interaction with accounting professionals. A mentoring relationship between accounting students and professionals can be an excellent way of accomplishing these objectives. However, for many universities located in traditional "college towns" (i.e., relatively small cities that are geographically distant from major metropolitan areas where most recruiters are located), frequent student–professional interaction presents a challenge. Utilizing e-mail can overcome not only this geographic challenge but also the challenges posed by the busy schedules of both professionals and students as well as traffic problems in large cities, both of which may reduce the frequency for face-to-face meetings, even when geographical distance is not an issue.

The primary objective of this chapter is to describe the development of an eMentoring program that brings students and professionals together in a mutually beneficial mentoring relationship. Linking students with professionals can enhance students' abilities to network and increase their knowledge of the profession, thus facilitating their transitions from college to the "real world." Indeed, increasing this interaction is even more important than ever, given the recent changes in the accounting environment that have resulted in a more complex professional workplace. For example, corporate accounting scandals such as those of Enron, Worldcom, and Tyco have placed accountants to a greater degree in the public eye and have prompted questions about their professional responsibilities.

The resulting Sarbanes-Oxley legislation has increased the role accountants play in establishing controls in the reporting environment and has changed the scope of their work in both public and corporate accounting. Professionals who serve as mentors also can benefit from such a program by experiencing satisfaction through helping students and by maintaining a connection with the accounting program and university. Indeed, this program also benefits our Accounting department by addressing two key elements of our college mission – preparing students for their professional careers and fostering a sense of community among our students, faculty, and alumni.

Additionally, we present the results of data from questionnaires we used to assess the effectiveness of the program and to understand the nature of the communications between the mentors and the students. Finally, we describe some challenges that we encountered during the evolving implementation of the program and recommendations in establishing such a program at other universities.

MENTORING IN THE ACCOUNTING LITERATURE

Mentoring is generally defined as an interpersonal relationship between a less experienced individual (the mentee, or protégé) and a more experienced individual (the mentor), where the goal is to advance the personal and professional development of the mentee (Kram, 1985). Previous accounting literature on mentoring describes a continuum of mentor–mentee relationships. At one end is (1) the "within the professional organization" setting, at the other end is (2) the "within the university" setting, and in the middle is (3) the "between the professional organization and university" setting. Fig. 1 graphically portrays these various relationships.

Accounting studies have largely focused on the types of mentoring relationships within public accounting firms (relationship (1) in Fig. 1).

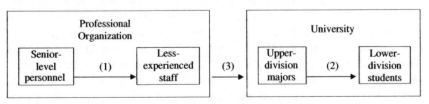

Fig. 1. Continuum of Mentor/Mentee Relationships.

Dirsmith and Covaleski (1985) were among the first to document the different nature of mentor–mentee relationships between various levels of staff, managers, and partners within large public accounting firms. While their findings suggest that informal mentoring relationships are more effective in enhancing career development, Viator (1999) found that more formal structures (e.g., meeting regularly and setting goals and objectives) and methods for matching mentors and mentees are associated with greater employee mentorship satisfaction. As a possible explanation of these seemingly inconsistent findings, Siegel, Rigsby, Agrawal, and Leavins (1995) found that the more successful mentoring relationships begin as a formal structure and evolve to an informal structure as the mentees gain experience. Regardless of the type of structure, mentor relationships at most public accounting firms are successful in not only developing mentees' careers but have a positive influence on their intentions to stay with their firm (Viator & Scandura, 1991).

Prior accounting studies also examine mentor relationships between students within the university setting (relationship (2) in Fig. 1). For example, Etter, Burmeister, and Elder's (2001) study of the effects of student supplemental instruction for introductory accounting courses can be described as a formal, discipline-based approach to the relationship, in which upper division students essentially provided academic tutoring for lower division students. On the contrary, Fox and Stevenson's (2006) study describes a less formal, student-based relationship, in which pairs of upper division accounting majors shared their experiences and various approaches to coursework with groups of underperforming first-year students (rather than providing specific course tutoring). Results of these studies indicate that both approaches had positive impacts on improving the academic performance of the mentees.

Accounting studies on mentor relationships between professionals and students (relationship (3) in Fig. 1) are more descriptive in nature. Weinstein & Schuele (2003) describe a university accounting department's mentoring program that was established during a period in which enrollment in accounting programs was declining and whose purpose was to encourage introductory accounting students to decide to major in accounting. Falgiani, Coe, and Thompson (2004) describe a mentoring program established by a local chapter of the Institute of Management Accountants (IMA), whose goal was to help accounting majors develop their managerial accounting knowledge by promoting IMA memberships and providing certification information. Both of these mentoring programs were relatively successful in accomplishing their objectives.

PROGRAM IMPLEMENTATION

Developing the Program's Mission, Objectives, and Design

Our accounting program has admitted 70 upper division accounting majors on average and has graduated about 40–45 each year for the past 3 years, (we have experienced significant growth in our program the past 2 years, and most of those students have not yet graduated). Historically, about two-thirds of our students meet the 150-hour requirement by graduation. We have an active Beta Alpha Psi chapter through which members can interact with professionals through firm office tours, on-campus presentations by professionals, and special social events. Students can also interact with professionals through annual "meet the firms" types of events and may have the opportunity to listen to professionals who serve as guest speakers in various classes. However, most students do not regularly interact with business or accounting professionals, especially in a one-on-one mentoring relationship. The idea to develop a mentoring program was proposed by one of the authors (who has been the program champion and was the accounting department chair at that time) to our Accounting Advisory Council (AAC). The AAC enthusiastically endorsed the idea as a way for AAC members to become more involved and enhance our students' educational experience. Due to the geographic distance of our university from the primary location of the large public accounting firms and businesses that recruit our majors, we decided to have our program emphasize e-mail communications, hence the name, "Accounting eMentor Program."

The first step in the design of the eMentor program was to develop a mission and key objectives. A five-member committee comprised of faculty and professionals from our AAC formulated the operating principles of the program. As a starting point, the committee used suggestions from "Practitioners as Mentors" (Weinstein & Schuele, 2003), which describes a mentoring program to recruit accounting majors to a university in a major metropolitan area. Following the AECC's recommendations, we focused our mentoring efforts on the professional development of already-declared accounting majors.

The committee surveyed first-semester, junior-level accounting majors to gather ideas on the benefits and design of such a program and to determine what characteristics of professionals are important to them in assigning mentors (refer to Appendix A for the survey). Based on the responses, we drafted our program's mission and objectives and presented them to the

Table 1. Program Objectives.

A. Students
 1. To provide students with insight, advice, and answers to questions from professionals
    regarding matters such as curriculum choices, goal-setting, careers, and interviewing.
 2. To enhance the students' understanding of the industry they are preparing to enter.
 3. To enhance and complement faculty advising.
 4. To help students make more informed decisions.
 5. To help students become more polished and improve their business etiquette.
 6. To enhance student motivation and improve retention.

B. Professionals
 1. To provide professionals with a feeling of satisfaction through helping students.
 2. To provide professionals a continuing connection with the Accounting Department, the
    College of Business, and the University.

---

accounting faculty and AAC for feedback and refinement. The resulting mission of our Accounting eMentor Program is "to bring accounting majors and professionals together in a mutually beneficial mentoring relationship." The program's objectives for students and professionals are presented in Table 1.

The accounting faculty and AAC established the program guidelines, process, and responsibilities of program participants, which appear in Table 2. We also developed guidance for the professionals in making the initial contact, improving their communications with students, as well as identifying potential topics for discussion (refer to Appendix B). In addition, we provide the professionals with a PowerPoint primer on our accounting program to ensure they are familiar with our state's current regulations regarding professional certification education requirements, as well as our curriculum structure and recommendations for meeting the education requirements. The primer helps ensure the professionals understand our program so that they can reinforce the advice provided to the students by our faculty.

We established two important program design parameters: (1) the program should be flexible for both the students and the professionals and (2) the program should be relatively easy to administer and assess. The first design parameter allows for the students and mentors not to feel constrained in the nature and direction of their relationship by encouraging other forms of interaction such as phone communications and person-to-person contact and by allowing the student and the professional to mutually agree on the frequency of contacts. The second design parameter minimizes the time

Table 2.   Program Guidelines, Process, and Responsibilities.

A. General
   1. The program is not intended to be a job placement service or recruiting tool.

B. Process
   1. Professionals and students must complete a profile information form submitted through e-mail to the Program Coordinator to participate in the program.
   2. Professionals will receive information through e-mail ("A Primer on Northern Arizona University Accounting Program") regarding the Accounting Program and the 150-hour law.
   3. Each student will be assigned a professional as a mentor, and both will be notified through e-mail of the other's contact information.
   4. The frequency and type of contacts should be mutually agreed upon by the professional and student and will primarily be through e-mail, although other types of contact such as phone calls, short meetings, and shadowing visits may be part of the mentoring relationship and are encouraged.
   5. The normal duration of the mentoring relationship is until the student graduates.
      a. If the professional or student chooses to withdraw from the program, the mentor partner and Program Coordinator should be notified.
   6. Professionals or students who do not adhere to the program guidelines and responsibilities may be removed from the program.
   7. Contact the Program Coordinator if you have any questions, issues, concerns, and so on.

C. Responsibilities of program participants
   1. The professional should review the document, "A Primer on Northern Arizona University Accounting Program," to be an informed mentor.
   2. The professional is responsible for making the initial contact through telephone – an appointment for the telephone call should be set up through e-mail (refer to Appendix B for additional guidance).
      a. The initial contact should be made within a few weeks of the mentoring assignment notification.
      b. Once the initial contact is made, the professional should notify the Program Coordinator through e-mail of the contact.
   3. Students and professionals should follow up on a contact made by the other *within a week* and should follow appropriate e-mail etiquette (refer to Appendix E).
   4. The professional is expected to initiate contact with the student at least once each semester.
   5. Changes in contact information and/or job should be communicated to the mentor partner and to the Program Coordinator.

commitment required to coordinate the program since an individual accounting faculty member performs this responsibility as a voluntary service assignment. As noted later in this chapter, this time commitment remains significant. An important aspect of the program is identifying a program coordinator. Due to the significant time commitment required to administer the program, we believe it is important for the coordinator to also be a champion of the program who cares about the program's success. At our university, the initial program champion continues to serve as coordinator; this faculty member is a tenured full professor who has well-established relationships with AAC members and alumni.

Recruiting Professionals and Students to the Program

The program has been in place for 3 years and has evolved somewhat over this period. We believe it is important for the professionals to be personally familiar with our accounting program and to have sufficient work experience (at least 6 months) to be an effective and supportive mentor. To simplify the recruiting process for professionals at the outset of the program, we focused primarily on alumni, AAC members, and recruiters who were located in our state. However, last year we expanded the geographical locations of the professionals to meet the increase in student demand for the program. Indeed, the use of e-mail as the primary mode of interaction makes geographical boundaries somewhat irrelevant to the implementation of the program.

When the program was initiated, we attempted to recruit professionals through solicitation in our annual newsletter. This general approach resulted in very few responses. Consequently, we changed our approach to a personal invitation, primarily through e-mail from the program coordinator. Additionally, current participants and AAC members have recruited mentors for the program. Almost everyone invited in this manner agrees to participate. As student participants graduate and become "young professionals," we intend to solicit them as mentors. To date, we have had only a few such graduates for whom we have contact information and who have been in the workplace sufficient time. We invited these graduates to participate for last year's mentoring start group and most responded favorably (three of four); indeed, one professional noted, "I participated in this program while I was at [the University] and I feel that I benefited from it, so I'd like to participate in it."

We invite accounting majors with at least two semesters remaining until graduation to participate through e-mail and announcements in junior-level accounting classes. While participation in the program is voluntary, faculty strongly encourage students to participate; as an incentive, the authors (who teach junior-level classes) allow students who participate to earn a nominal amount of extra credit points in their respective courses. We decided to make student participation voluntary rather than mandatory to have better student motivation in the program. However, we believe that providing a nominal incentive for voluntary participation can encourage more students to participate. In an attempt to address the motivation issue and discourage students from signing up simply to earn extra credit points, we made alternative extra credit assignments available to students who do not truly wish to participate in the program. As a result, approximately half of our accounting majors have participated in the program. In last year's start group, the majority (82 percent) were juniors, 14 percent were freshmen or sophomores, and 4 percent were seniors.

Program Processes and Participant Responsibilities

To participate, professionals and students complete a brief profile information form that they submit to the program coordinator through e-mail. The student and professional profile forms appear in Appendices C and D respectively. These forms collect contact information from the participants, as well as the student's requests regarding the mentor's type of firm (public accounting, industry, or government/nonprofit), scope of firm (local, regional, or international/national), and any special requests for characteristics of the professional (e.g., gender, ethnicity). The profile form also requires participants to provide electronic initials to acknowledge that they have read the program description and agree to follow the program guidelines and responsibilities (see Table 2).

Deciding which characteristics students may request in matching a professional to them is a balancing act; indeed, including too many preference choices imposes considerable difficulties in identifying a professional who meets all of a student's specifications. In our initial survey of students, very few indicated that ethnicity and/or gender would be a factor in their eMentor preference for the professional. Although level of experience was identified as relatively important and was used as a specified preference through the first 2 years, we decided to eliminate this as a routine request because we found it increasingly difficult to identify additional experienced graduates as mentors versus recruiting recent graduates (these are the graduates with whom we have the most contact). We decided to accommodate preferences that are important to an individual student by allowing special write-in requests specifying additional characteristics of the prospective mentor. To date, we have been able to accommodate the few special requests that students have made (about 10 percent on average), including Native American, female, recent graduate, or particular firm type (forensic accounting, law, utilities).

Although many students express no preferences for mentor demographics, the most common requests have been for professionals in national/international-level public accounting firms.

Table 3 presents information regarding program participants from the 3 years that our program has been in place. Since the program's inception, 127 pairs of students–mentors have participated. The profile of the professionals in the program indicates 72 percent are "young" versus 28 percent experienced, with 71 percent from public accounting firms, 18 percent from industry, and 11 percent from government/nonprofits. The profile of the professionals' type of firm reflects the typical proportions of job placements of our graduates. To date, turnover of professionals has been minimal; only about 10 percent have dropped out of the program, mostly from attrition as their assigned student/mentee graduates. The most common reasons are nonresponse to a renewal request after the student mentee graduates, withdrawal due to lack of time related to personal/job reasons, or a job change with lack of new contact information. Indeed, our experience is that many professionals (15) have volunteered to be

Table 3. Participant Information.

	N	%
Total Student–Mentor pairs since Program Inception	127	
Profile of professionals ($n = 95^a$):	N	%
Experience level		
Young professional (1–6 years)	68	72
Experienced professional (>6 years)	27	28
Type of firm		
Public accounting		
Big 4	26	27
Mid-tier	24	25
Local	18	19
Industry	17	18
Government/Nonprofit	10	11
Survey response rate (of 127[a])	101	80

[a]Some professionals have had more than one student assigned to them since the program's inception. These professionals complete the survey at the end of each semester in which a new assignment is made and no more than one new assignment is made in a semester; the number of respondents does not agree with the number of professionals profiled because some professionals have completed the survey more than one time, with their responses based on the current mentor assignment. Each student is assigned only one mentor; only twice have students requested reassignment due to lack of responsiveness from the mentor originally assigned.

assigned a second student, and the majority of professionals whose student mentees graduated or changed majors have agreed to be assigned a new student (16).

The program coordinator assigns each student a mentor based on matching the student's requests, if any, for characteristics of the professional, and notifies both the student and the professional through e-mail of the mentor assignment, attaching the profile forms of both participants. Before the initial contact, professionals are responsible for reviewing the primer sent through e-mail regarding the Accounting Program and the 150-hour Certified Public Accountant (CPA) education requirements. The professionals make the initial contact through telephone within a few weeks of the mentoring assignment. Although our mentoring program emphasizes the use of e-mail for communication, we adopted the recommendation of our AAC members to have the initial contact through telephone to establish a more personal relationship and enhance future communications. Several participants noted difficulties in lining up their schedules for the initial phone contact; in response, we revised the student profile form to include a question regarding the best time for the initial phone contact.

Once the participants make initial contact, the professionals notify the program coordinator; the program coordinator follows up in situations where there is no notification. At the outset of the mentoring relationship, the professional and student mutually agree on the frequency and type of contacts, which will be primarily through e-mail; however, we encourage other types of contact such as phone calls, short meetings, and shadowing visits as part of the relationship. The normal duration of the mentoring relationship lasts until the student graduates, and the program coordinator sends both the professional and the student an e-mail each year to encourage them to stay in contact.

Other responsibilities for program participants include the following:

- the professional should initiate contact with the student at least once each semester and to communicate changes in contact information to the student and program coordinator,
- students and professionals should follow up on a contact made by the other within a week and follow appropriate e-mail etiquette, which we provide to students and professionals (refer to Appendix E for this guidance), and
- students and professionals should contact the program coordinator with any questions, issues, concerns, and so on.

EVALUATION OF THE PROGRAM

Survey Results

At the end of the first semester of a new mentoring assignment, we survey both the students and the professional mentors to assess their perceptions of the program's success in meeting its mission and objectives, identify the types and frequency of contacts, and solicit comments or suggestions to help us improve the program. Appendices F and G present the surveys used for the students and professionals respectively. The response rate was 85 percent for the students and 80 percent for the professionals over the 3 years.

Table 4 presents the results of students' perceptions of the program's mission and objectives for students. Table 5 presents the results of professionals' perceptions of the program's mission and objectives for professionals. (A statistical analysis of variance (ANOVA) indicates that there are no significant differences ($p < .05$) in any of the evaluation responses across the 3 years that the program has been in place.) Overall, a high proportion of students and professionals agree/strongly agree (90 percent and 91 percent respectively) that the program brings accounting majors and professionals together in a mutually beneficial mentoring relationship. The proportion of students who agree/strongly agree with statements regarding the program's objectives for students ranges from 93 percent for "the program provides students with insight, advice, and answers to questions from professionals regarding matters such as curriculum choices, goal-setting, careers, and interviewing" to 71 percent for "the program enhances student motivation and improves retention." The proportion of professionals who agree/strongly agree with statements regarding the program's objectives for professionals is 94 percent for providing a feeling of satisfaction through helping students and 98 percent for providing a continuing connection to the accounting program, college, and university. Additionally, 96 percent of professionals agree/strongly agree that the program is a worthwhile use of their time. These relatively high endorsements bode well for the continued success of the eMentor program.

Approximately 40 percent of survey respondents provided additional written comments about the program, the majority of which were positive and constructive. Representative student comments regarding the program include the following:

- The professionals in this mentor program show that they care about you as a student and want to help you.

Table 4. Students' Evaluations of Accounting eMentor Program.

Statement	Percentage of Students ($n = 108$[a])					Mean[b]	Standard Deviation
	Strongly agree (1) (%)	Agree (2) (%)	Neutral (3) (%)	Disagree (4) (%)	Strongly disagree (5) (%)		
Mission: The program brings accounting majors and professionals together in a mutually beneficial mentoring relationship (from the *student's* perspective).	48	42	9	1	0	1.63	0.69
Students' objective 1: The program provides students with insight, advice, and answers to questions from professionals regarding matters such as curriculum choices, goal-setting, careers, and interviewing	53	40	6	1	0	1.54	0.65
Students' objective 2: The program enhances the students' understanding of the industry they are preparing to enter	43	38	19	0	0	1.75	0.75
Students' objective 3: The program enhances and complements faculty advising	27	48	21	4	0	2.02	0.80
Students' objective 4: The program helps students make more informed decisions	45	43	12	0	0	1.68	0.68
Students' objective 5: The program helps students become more polished and improve their business etiquette	32	44	21	2	1	1.94	0.79
Students' objective 6: The program enhances student motivation and improves retention	36	35	26	3	0	1.96	0.86

[a]The student response rate on the survey was 85%.
[b]Mean calculated on a five-point scale.

Table 5. Professionals' Evaluations of Accounting eMentor Program.

Statement	Percentage of Professionals ($n = 101$)					Mean[a]	Standard Deviation
	Strongly agree (1) (%)	Agree (2) (%)	Neutral (3) (%)	Disagree (4) (%)	Strongly disagree (5) (%)		
Mission: The program brings accounting majors and professionals together in a mutually beneficial mentoring relationship (from the *professional's* perspective)	35	56	9	0	0	1.74	0.61
Professionals' objective 1: The program provides professionals with a feeling of satisfaction through helping students	42	52	6	0	0	1.63	0.60
Professionals' objective 2: The program provides professionals a continuing connection with the Accounting Area, the College of Business, and the University	56	42	2	0	0	1.56	0.59
Overall: The program is a worthwhile use of my time	53	43	4	0	0	1.56	0.59

[a]Mean calculated on a five-point scale.

- This is an excellent opportunity to not only become acquainted with a professional in our field but ask questions and seek advice in a manner that is not intimidating.
- The effect depends on the attitude of the mentor and student. I have asked my mentor questions and have got great responses. If students do not put forth anything, they will not get anything out of this program.
- I am glad that I participated in the program because I am gaining insight on the real world and what to expect when I graduate.
- I really liked being able to talk with someone in the field and it totally complemented what I was being told by my advisors.
- My mentor was great! I would recommend this program to anyone who is interested in accounting. It really helped me see what options are out there and which path to take to get there.

Comments from the professionals include the following:

- I think this program is a great idea and my mentee seemed very appreciative of my time and the answers to his questions I was able to provide. He seemed very interested in learning the details of my experiences as a professional versus a student. Our conversation was very worthwhile.
- I think the major benefits to the professionals are the connection as alumni with Northern Arizona University. It is important for me to stay connected with the University and I enjoy helping students.
- I feel that this program is very well structured and has great potential for both students and professionals.

Some of the issues that students and professionals have identified include the difficulty lining up schedules for the initial telephone contact and the desire to actually meet face to face, especially at the beginning of the relationship. Additionally, several professionals expressed the desire for their mentees to be more proactive in the relationship, for example, "Student(s) need to take greater initiative in contacting and assertively questioning the professional(s). This way professionals can be more active and better fulfill the students' expectations."

Type and Frequency of Contacts

As noted above, the design of the eMentor program establishes e-mail as the primary mode of mentor–student contact. Table 6 reports data regarding type and frequency of contacts. During the initial semester of the

Table 6. Type and Frequency of Contacts.

Type of Contact	Frequency of Contacts				
	0 (%)	1 (%)	2–5 (%)	>5 (%)	Average[a]
E-mail	8	17	59	16	2.7
Telephone	16	58	26	0	1.1

[a]Average was estimated, using 7 contacts for the ">5"category.

relationships, 92 percent of both students and professionals report at least one e-mail contact, 75 percent report two or more e-mail contacts, and 16 percent report more than five e-mail contacts (an average of 2.7 contacts). Participants also employ phone contact, with 84 percent of the participants reporting one or more phone conversations in the first semester (an average of 1.1 contacts). In addition, some students and professionals reported having face-to-face meetings, generally on campus when mentors visit during recruiting events and Beta Alpha Psi activities. In the first 2 years of the program, the program coordinator made the mentor assignments in the middle of the semester; consequently, very few meetings in person occurred. To address this issue and the desire for personal meetings, the program coordinator made the mentor assignments earlier in the semester for the most recent group, which significantly increased personal meetings reported to about 25 percent of survey respondents.

The reported use of both e-mail and phone contact modes reveals significant contact between mentors and students during the initial semester of the relationship. After this period, however, contact frequency appears to vary widely across individual relationships. In focus sessions with our AAC members (who have comprised about 20 percent of our mentoring pairs), many reported contacts continuing on a relatively regular basis, but others reported no further contact after the initial semester. A few mentors indicated that they perceived their role as evolving to one of serving as a resource and being available for questions, rather than as one of initiating contact with the student.

We were also interested in how comfortable students felt in making contact with professionals. We report data on this question in Table 7. Before the initial semester of the program, we surveyed students (refer to Appendix A) and asked them to evaluate "how comfortable do you think you would feel in initiating contact with your mentor?" Only 19 percent responded that they would feel very comfortable and 23 percent responded

Table 7. Student Comfort Level in Initiating Contact.

	Very Uncomfortable (%)	Somewhat Uncomfortable (%)	Neutral (%)	Somewhat Comfortable (%)	Very Comfortable (%)
Pre-program survey	12	11	4	54	19
End of initial semester	0	3	11	27	59

that they would feel either somewhat or very uncomfortable. In the survey at the end of the initial semester in the mentor program, we asked students to "[p]lease indicate how comfortable you feel in making contact with your mentor." After the first semester in the program, the students' comfort level increased dramatically, with 59 percent responding that they felt very comfortable and only 3 percent reporting feeling somewhat or very uncomfortable. Although some students may initially feel uncomfortable in making contact, this data gives us confidence that by the time the program ends most students feel comfortable with interactions with their mentor.

Topics Discussed

Beginning in the second year that the program took place, we added questions to the survey. These questions tried to determine what topics the professionals and students discussed, based on the suggested topics listed in Appendix B. These data provide insights into the nature of the communications and can help inform and set expectations of the students and professionals involved in the program. Tables 8 and 9 present the responses from these elicitations from students and professionals respectively. In general, students and professionals reasonably align in their perceptions of the extent to which they discuss various topics.

The three topics most frequently discussed in the first semester of the mentoring relationship, based on the percentage reporting that they spent some or a lot of time on the topic, are (1) "Advice for curriculum path in college (masters degree, double majors, certificates/minors, electives, etc. to meet the 150-hour CPA requirement)," (2) "Career path options; advantages and disadvantages of entry-level positions in public accounting, industry, government, including comparison of small, medium and large firms," and (3) "Benefits of internships, externships, fieldwork experience."

Table 8.   Students' Reporting of Topics Discussed – Perceived Degree of
Discussion.

Topic of Discussion	Extent to Which Topic was Discussed – Percentage ($n = 85$)		
	A lot (%)	Some (%)	None (%)
Advice for curriculum path in college (masters degree, double majors, certificates/minors, electives, etc., to meet the 150-hour CPA requirement)	41	52	7
Importance of grades; skills to develop and extracurricular activities recommended during college	23	57	20
Benefits of internships, externships, fieldwork experience	45	37	18
Resume writing, conducting the job search, preparing for interviews, tips for the interview and follow-up	9	41	50
Professional certifications and preparing for these exams	31	47	22
Current economic outlook for job opportunities and salaries in accounting	27	40	33
Career path options; advantages and disadvantages of entry-level positions in public accounting, industry, government, including comparison of small, medium, and large firms	39	47	14
Description of work performed by an entry-level professional in various types of firms	24	47	29
Ethical situations faced and discussion of how to deal with these situations	8	23	69
Advice for the transition from college to career	23	51	26
Balancing personal life and career	26	52	22

The topic least discussed in the first semester of the mentoring relationship is "Ethical situations faced and discussion of how to deal with these situations." The topics discussed were during the first semester of the mentoring assignment and may evolve over the duration of the relationship as the student progresses through the Accounting Program.

INSIGHTS ON RUNNING A SUCCESSFUL eMENTOR PROGRAM

We believe that an eMentor program similar to the one described in this chapter can be easily adopted by other universities. While overall feedback has been very positive, our program has encountered some inevitable

Table 9. Professionals' Reporting of Topics Discussed – Perceived
Degree of Discussion.

Topic of Discussion	Extent to Which Topic was Discussed – Percentage ($n = 83$)		
	A lot (%)	Some (%)	None (%)
Advice for curriculum path in college (masters degree, double majors, certificates/minors, electives, etc., to meet the 150-hour CPA requirement)	28	58	14
Importance of grades; skills to develop and extracurricular activities recommended during college	20	46	34
Benefits of internships, externships, fieldwork experience	31	52	17
Resume writing, conducting the job search, preparing for interviews, tips for the interview and follow-up	9	25	66
Professional certifications and preparing for these exams	20	47	33
Current economic outlook for job opportunities and salaries in accounting	12	45	43
Career path options; advantages and disadvantages of entry-level positions in public accounting, industry, government, including comparison of small, medium, and large firms	23	62	15
Description of work performed by an entry-level professional in various types of firms	10	58	32
Ethical situations faced and discussion of how to deal with these situations	1	6	93
Advice for the transition from college to career	11	52	37
Balancing personal life and career	5	52	43

challenges. Following is a listing of recommendations based on lessons we
have learned in the 3 years of our program.

Start-Up

Identify a coordinator who will champion the program. A major challenge
is the significant amount of time and effort required to design, implement,
and administer a mentoring program. The coordinator should be a faculty
member who is enthusiastic, cares about the students, and has a strong
relationship with the alumni and/or recruiters.

Provide guidelines for the students and mentors. If the department has
an advisory council, those members should provide input on the design of
the program as they may become the core of professionals who serve as

mentors. Some important items that should be addressed in the guidelines include frequency and types of contacts and who should initiate contact (we recommend providing specific guidelines for the initial contact and minimum number of contacts each semester, with the mentor–student deciding the rest by mutual agreement); minimum response time on contacts; the intended duration of the mentoring relationship; and a list of suggested discussion topics.

Provide a primer on your accounting program for mentors. Do not assume that the professionals are intimately familiar with your current curriculum or your state's CPA licensure requirements. Include this information in your primer, which should be disseminated to your mentors before the start of the mentoring relationship, and communicate to mentors the need to read and be familiar with this information to be informed mentors.

Running the Program

Recruit mentors using a personal invitation. Our experience is that individual contact works best in recruiting professionals. Normally, the program coordinator is the ideal person to make this contact; however, existing mentors and advisory council members can also actively recruit mentors.

Recruit students for voluntary participation. We target first-semester, junior-level accounting majors for the program. Several of our mentors have indicated that freshmen and sophomores are not yet committed to the major or mature enough to participate. Thus, the junior year seems to be the most important year for students to receive benefits from the program in terms of decision-making regarding their career goals and curriculum. Our experience indicates that offering a nominal incentive for voluntary participation can increase student sign-ups.

Minimize "check-off" options for students in indicating desired mentor demographics but do allow students to make special requests. Allowing students to specify many demographic options for their desired mentor may make for better matches; however, it can add significant additional effort for the program coordinator in locating a mentor who meets these specifications, and it makes the matching process much more difficult. However, allowing special requests accommodates preferences that are important to individual students. We have not experienced any concerns from students regarding the mentors assigned to them using our recommended approach.

Make mentor assignments early in the fall semester. Our experience indicates that mentoring assignments work best when made early in the fall semester, as it increases the possibility of face-to-face meetings during recruiting trips and allows more time for students and mentors to communicate in the initial semester when motivation in the program is the highest. We make initial assignments in the fall since this is the semester in which the majority of our recruiting activities occur and new majors begin the junior year; many professionals also prefer to start new relationships in the fall versus the spring to avoid conflict with their "busy season."

Maintain a database of student–mentor pairs. Accurate recordkeeping allows the coordinator to track the assignments of the student–mentor pairs and ensure initial contact is made, maintain up-to-date contact information of the participants, encourage participants to stay in contact with one another, and target only relevant e-mail communications to individual professionals.

Determine the desired level of formality for the mentoring relationships and encourage mentors and students to maintain contact for the duration of the relationship. The level of formality is directly correlated with the effort required for the program coordinator. The approach we describe begins as a formal relationship in the initial semester and becomes less formal in subsequent semesters. We believe this approach strikes an appropriate balance between micro-managing the program and a "hands-off" approach. The program coordinator's effort required is greatest in the initial semester of each relationship, due to soliciting professionals and students, making mentor assignments, communicating with all participants to ensure that initial contact is made, and conducting the end of semester survey. The program coordinator's subsequent effort for previously assigned pairs diminishes considerably, requiring only annual e-mails to professionals to let them know the status of their student (e.g., graduated, changed majors) and remind them to initiate contact with their student at least once each semester, with similar e-mails to students to encourage them to stay in contact with their mentors and be proactive in the relationship.

Assessment

Gather feedback on the program. Collect feedback concerning the program's design and operations as well as suggestions for improvement. This feedback can be gathered through various means, including surveys, focus groups, and ad hoc discussions with participants.

Implement needed changes to the program. Departments must view their mentoring programs as evolutionary, so that feedback can be used to continuously improve the program. Throughout this chapter, we have addressed some of the issues that we have faced in our experience and changes we have made.

SUMMARY AND CONCLUSIONS

This chapter describes the process undertaken to implement an eMentor program used as a cocurricular professional development activity for accounting majors at a university that is located in a geographic area distant from the primary location of its major recruiters. The key element of the program is the use of e-mail as a communication channel to link accounting and business professionals with students in our accounting program.

We report data that we collected to examine the effectiveness of the program and generate insights on the implementation. Responses indicate that the program is an overall success. Most student–mentor pairs have had several e-mail contacts and at least one phone contact in the first semester, with a majority of students initiating some contact. In some cases, professional mentors met personally with students to further their relationships. Professionals and students indicate that the key topics discussed in the first semester of the mentoring relationship are college curriculum choices and professional career path options, including the benefits of internships and externships. A high proportion of both students and professionals agree/strongly agree that the program met its mission and objectives, and virtually all of the professionals agree/strongly agree that the program is a worthwhile use of their time. We believe that an eMentor program similar to the one described in this chapter can be easily adopted by other universities, and we provide recommendations for implementing such a program based on our experience.

Our students benefit from the program by enhancing their abilities to network and increasing their knowledge of the profession and career opportunities, thus facilitating students' transitions from college to the real world. The professionals experience satisfaction through helping students. Our Accounting Department benefits by maintaining a connection with professionals, most of whom are alumni. Overall, we believe these benefits outweigh the significant time and effort required to administer the program. Indeed, the success of our eMentor program has prompted our College's Strategic Planning Committee to recommend expanding the program to other disciplines within the College of Business.

ACKNOWLEDGMENTS

We acknowledge the helpful comments and suggestions on earlier drafts of this chapter by reviewers and session participants of the 2007 American Accounting Association Western Region meeting, Ken Lorek, Bill Schwartz, and two anonymous reviewers.

REFERENCES

AECC – Accounting Education Change Commission. (1993). *Issues Statement No. Four, Improving the early employment experiences of accountants.* Torrrance, CA: AECC.

Amer, B. (2009). *Soft skills at work: Technology for career success* (pp. 44–45). Boston, MA: Course Technology, Cenga. Learning.

Dirsmith, M. W., & Covaleski, A. A. (1985). Informal communications, nonformal communications and mentoring in public accounting firms. *Accounting, Organizations and Society, 10*(2), 149–169.

Etter, E. R., Burmeister, S. L., & Elder, R. J. (2001). Improving student performance and retention via supplemental instruction. *Journal of Accounting Education, 19*(4), 355–368.

Falgiani, A. A., Coe, M. J., & Thompson, J. (2004). How to pursue a grassroots mentoring program. *Management Accounting Quarterly, 5*(2), 61–64.

Fox, A., & Stevenson, L. (2006). Exploring the effectiveness of peer mentoring of accounting and finance students in higher education. *Accounting Education: An International Journal, 15*(2), 189–202.

Kram, K. E. (1985). *Mentoring at work.* Glenview, IL: Scott, Foresman & Co.

Siegel, P., Rigsby, J., Agrawal, S., & Leavins, J. (1995). Auditor professional performance and the mentor relationship within the public accounting firm. *Accounting, Auditing and Accountability Journal, 8*(4), 3–22.

Viator, R. E. (1999). An analysis of formal mentoring programs and perceived barriers to obtaining a mentor at large public accounting firms. *Accounting Horizons, 13*(1), 37–53.

Viator, R. E., & Scandura, T. A. (1991). A study of mentor-protégé relationships in large public accounting firms. *Accounting Horizons, 5*(3), 20–30.

Weinstein, G. P., & Schuele, K. (2003). Practitioners as mentors. *Journal of Accountancy, 195*(6), 39–44.

APPENDIX A. ACCOUNTING AREA COLLEGE OF BUSINESS – NORTHERN ARIZONA UNIVERSITY eMENTOR PROGRAM SURVEY – FOR ACCOUNTING MAJORS

The Accounting Area in conjunction with our Accounting Advisory Council are considering the establishment of an eMentor program, in which students would be mentored by accounting professionals, primarily via e-mail. In order to help us design the program, please answer the following questions:

1. Please evaluate the following statement: *I think this program would be beneficial to students.* (circle one)

   Strongly   Disagree   Neutral   Agree   Strongly
   Disagree   Agree

2. How do you think you could benefit from this program?

3. What would you like or expect in this program?

4. Should the program be (circle one):   mandatory   optional

5. How comfortable do you think you would feel in initiating contact with your mentor? (circle one)

   Very   Somewhat   Neutral   Somewhat   Very
   Uncomfortable   Uncomfortable   Uncomfortable   Uncomfortable

6. Please indicate how important each of the following potential criteria is to you for matching you with a mentor (1 = *very important;* 2 = *somewhat important;* 3 = *not important*) – if you have a preference on the criteria, please circle your preference

   — gender (male or female or no preference)
   — ethnicity (caucasian or minority—specify _____ or no preference)
   — years since graduation (recent graduate or experienced professional or no preference)
   — type of firm (public accounting or industry or government/NFP or no preference)
   — scope of firm (international/national or regional or local or no preference)
   — other (please describe)

APPENDIX B. ACCOUNTING eMENTOR PROGRAM GUIDANCE FOR PROFESSIONALS AND STUDENTS

The Initial Contact and Improving Communications with Students

- Greet the student by name, be relaxed and warm. Introduce yourself and summarize your background for the student. Ask the student about himself/herself.
- Help the student feel at ease; reinforce the objectives of the mentoring program and that it is not a job placement service or recruiting tool and this is not an interview.
- Set a fixed length of time for the initial contact, which should be approximately 15–30 minutes.
- Agree on the frequency and type of future contacts you and the student will have. Encourage the student to e-mail you with their questions and topics for discussion.
- Conversational flow will be cut off if questions are asked so that only a "yes" or "no" reply is required. A good question might be, "What have you thought about taking next semester?" or "What are some things that made you think about accounting as a career?"
- Good mentoring requires effective listening. Listening is more than the absence of talking. Try to understand what the student is saying.
- A student may fear that the mentor won't approve of what he/she says. Mentors need to convey their acceptance of these feelings and attitudes in a non-judgmental way.
- Most people are embarrassed if no conversation is going on. Remember, the student may be groping for words or ideas. If a conversation goes silent, a good rule of thumb is to count to ten. Often a student will continue to explain and you will get a more complete picture of what he or she is trying to express.
- End the meeting at the agreed time. A comfortable concluding phrase might be, "Do you think we have done all we can for today?"

Potential Topics for Discussion

- Advice for curriculum path in college (classes, electives, certificates/ minors, other majors, meeting the 150-hour CPA requirement).
- Importance of grades; skills to develop and extracurricular activities recommended during college.

- Benefits of internships, externships, fieldwork experience.
- Resume writing, preparing for interviews, tips for the interview and follow-up.
- Professional certifications and preparing for these exams.
- Current economic outlook for job opportunities and salaries in accounting.
- Career path options; advantages and disadvantages of entry-level positions in public accounting, industry, government, etc., including comparison of small, medium and large firms.
- Description of work performed by an entry-level professional in various types of firms.
- Ethical situations faced and discussion of how to deal with these situations.
- Advice for the transition from college to career.
- Balancing personal life and career.

APPENDIX C. ACCOUNTING eMENTOR PROGRAM PROFILE-ACCOUNTING STUDENTS

Instructions: Please read the Accounting eMentor Program description for information on the program's mission, objectives, program guidelines and responsibilities, identifying mentors and students, program design parameters, and administration and assessment of program. If you would like to be assigned a professional mentor, please complete the information below and return via e-mail as an attachment to the Program Coordinator, Professor [name] at firstname.lastname@[university].edu. We will notify you as soon as we have assigned a mentor to you. Thank you!

Name	
E-mail address (university e-mail account)	
Phone number	
Best time(s) for the initial phone contact	
Anticipated graduation date	
Type of firm requested: (no preference, public accounting, industry, or government/NFP)	
Scope of firm requested: (no preference, local, regional, or international/national)	
Other special mentor requests	

After you have read the program description, please enter your initials and the date below to indicate your agreement to follow the program guidelines and responsibilities:

Initials	
Date	

(For administrative use only): Name of assigned mentor	

APPENDIX D. ACCOUNTING eMENTOR PROGRAM PROFILE-ACCOUNTING PROFESSIONALS

Instructions: Please read the Accounting eMentor Program description for information on the program's mission, objectives, program guidelines and responsibilities, identifying mentors and students, program design parameters, and administration and assessment of program. If you are willing to serve as a professional mentor, please complete the information below and send as an e-mail attachment to the Program Coordinator, Professor [name] at firstname.lastname@[university].edu. We will notify you as soon as we have assigned a student to you. Thank you!

Name	
Employer name	
Job Title	
E-mail address	
Business address	
Type of firm (public accounting, industry, or government/ NFP)	
Scope of firm (local, regional, or international/national)	
Past experience (briefly describe type of firm and position)	
Educational degree/year/university (list all)	
Professional certifications	
Ethnicity (optional)	

After you have read the program description, please enter your initials and the date below to indicate your agreement to follow the program guidelines and responsibilities:

Initials	
Date	

(*For administrative use only*): Name of assigned student	

APPENDIX E. ACCOUNTING eMENTOR PROGRAM E-MAIL ETIQUETTE

In today's digital world, many people forgo hand-written correspondence (sometimes referred to as "snail mail") in favor of the speed and convenience of a digital form of communication called electronic mail, or e-mail. While e-mail is a quick and easy way to send messages, writers should not assume that *anything goes* with regard to the form, content, and use of electronic communications. In the professional world, what you say, how you say it, and when you respond all carry meaning to the recipient. The informal, abbreviated way you write to friends and family doesn't translate well to the professional realm. In fact, when you send e-mail to people you work with, but may have never met, they instinctively form impressions and opinions of you, based solely upon the quality of your writing. Your friendly, upbeat, and casual attitude when expressed through spelling errors, smiley faces, or inappropriate language can actually backfire to make you look uneducated or worse. At a minimum, you should consider the following items when creating and sending your messages:

1. Who is my recipient? Do I need to "reply all"?
2. How quickly do they need a response (a lag of several days may be unacceptable)?
3. Have I fully answered any questions or provided the information requested?

A checklist of tips that should be part of your professional e-mail etiquette routine is below:

- Don't use all capital letters. This is the equivalent of shouting in written form.

- Refrain from forwarding every joke, cartoon, or touching story you receive. Most people don't have time, especially at work, to deal with them and usually end up deleting them or flagging them as junk mail. This means future legitimate messages from you may be tagged as junk as well. Plus, these messages just take up unnecessary space on the mail server.
- Use proper salutations, such as "Dear Susan," or "Hello Dr. Elrod," or even just the recipient's first name. More informal greetings, such as "Hey, Drama Queen!," are best saved for personal messages.
- Include a meaningful subject line. Something like "Question about Project 2" is more descriptive than "Question."
- Close the message with a simple salutation or your automated signature line. This is especially important when the sender's name is not part of the e-mail address or the system doesn't provide the alias (sender's alternate name) for the recipient.
- Reply promptly, and keep the message short and to the point. Also, avoid the use of excessive punctuation.
- Minimize the use of fancy colors or fonts. Simple, plain text is fine and reduces the possibility of the recipient's mail server not being able to handle the special formatting.
- Avoid the use of text messaging language and abbreviations. Spell out "you" (not "u") and "your" (not "ur"), and use "I" (not "i").
- Only use acronyms if you are sure your recipient knows what they mean.
- Save emoticons for personal communications. Since e-mail can't easily capture the body language or meaning of the sender, they are sometimes used to convey that element. However, they can appear juvenile in the workplace. Instead, focus on making sure that what you write won't be misunderstood based on the language and content you include.
- Don't use profanity. The English language has plenty of rich and meaningful words to help you express yourself without using offensive language.

Source: Adapted from Amer (2009, pp. 44–45).

APPENDIX F. ACCOUNTING eMENTOR PROGRAM SURVEY (STUDENTS)

Please complete this survey if you participated in the Accounting eMentor Program. Thank you for your help so that we can assess the program and make any needed improvements to ensure the program's success!

                                                                                    Estimated time

Please estimate the amount of time spent engaging in contact with your mentor this semester.   _____

Indicate the types and frequency of contacts:	Type of contact	Number of contacts
	Telephone	_____
	e-Mail	_____
	Other (describe):	_____

Have you initiated any contacts? (check one)   Yes _____   No _____

If YES, does your mentor respond on a timely basis? (check one)   Yes _____   No _____

Please indicate how comfortable you feel in making contact with your mentor (place an "x" in the appropriate box below):

Very Comfortable	*Somewhat Comfortable*	*Neutral*	*Somewhat Uncomfortable*	*Very Uncomfortable*

Please indicate the extent to which you have discussed each of the following topics with your mentor (place an "x" in the appropriate box below for each statement):

Topic	A lot	Some	None
Advice for curriculum path in college (masters degree, double majors, certificates/minors, electives, etc. to meet the 150-hour CPA requirement).			
Importance of grades; skills to develop and extracurricular activities recommended during college.			
Benefits of internships, externships, fieldwork experience.			
Resume writing, conducting the job search, preparing for interviews, tips for the interview and follow-up.			
Professional certifications and preparing for these exams.			
Current economic outlook for job opportunities and salaries in accounting.			
Career path options; advantages and disadvantages of entry-level positions in public accounting, industry, government, including comparison of small, medium and large firms.			
Description of work performed by an entry-level professional in various types of firms.			
Ethical situations faced and discussion of how to deal with these situations.			
Advice for the transition from college to career.			
Balancing personal life and career.			

Please evaluate each of the following statements related to the Accounting eMentor Program's mission and student objectives (place an "x" in the appropriate box below for each statement):

Statement	Strongly Agree	Agree	Neutral	Disagree	Strongly Disagree
The program brings accounting majors and professionals together in a mutually beneficial mentoring relationship (from the **student's** perspective).					
The program provides students with insight, advice, and answers to questions from professionals regarding matters such as curriculum choices, goal-setting, careers, and interviewing.					
The program enhances the students' understanding of the industry they are preparing to enter.					
The program enhances and complements faculty advising.					
The program helps students make more informed decisions.					
The program helps students become more polished and improve their business etiquette.					
The program enhances student motivation and improves retention.					

Please provide comments or suggestions to help us improve the program.

Thank you for completing this survey!

APPENDIX G. ACCOUNTING eMENTOR PROGRAM
SURVEY (PROFESSIONALS)

Please complete this survey if you participated in the Accounting eMentor Program. Thank you for your help so that we can assess the program and make any needed improvements to ensure the program's success!

<u>Estimated time</u>

Please estimate the amount of time spent engaging in contact with your student this semester.

Indicate the types and frequency of contacts:	<u>Type of contact</u>	<u>Number of contacts</u>
	Telephone	
	e-Mail	
	Other (describe):	

Has the student responded on a timely basis to your contacts? (check one)   Yes _____   No _____

Has the student initiated any contacts? (check one)   Yes _____   No _____

Please indicate the extent to which you have discussed each of the following topics with your student (place an "x" in the appropriate box below for each statement):

Topic	A lot	Some	None
Advice for curriculum path in college (masters degree, double majors, certificates/minors, electives, etc. to meet the 150-hour CPA requirement).			
Importance of grades; skills to develop and extracurricular activities recommended during college.			
Benefits of internships, externships, fieldwork experience.			
Resume writing, conducting the job search, preparing for interviews, tips for the interview and follow-up.			
Professional certifications and preparing for these exams.			
Current economic outlook for job opportunities and salaries in accounting.			
Career path options; advantages and disadvantages of entry-level positions in public accounting, industry, government, including comparison of small, medium and large firms.			
Description of work performed by an entry-level professional in various types of firms.			
Ethical situations faced and discussion of how to deal with these situations.			
Advice for the transition from college to career.			
Balancing personal life and career.			

Please evaluate each of the following statements related to the Accounting eMentor Program's mission and professionals' objectives (place an "x" in the appropriate box below for each statement):

Statement	Strongly Agree	Agree	Neutral	Disagree	Strongly Disagree
The program brings accounting majors and professionals together in a mutually beneficial mentoring relationship (from the **professional's** perspective).					
The program provides professionals with a feeling of satisfaction through helping students.					
The program provides professionals a continuing connection with the Accounting Area, the College of Business, and Northern Arizona University.					
The program is a worthwhile use of my time.					

Please provide comments or suggestions to help us improve the program.

Thank you for completing this survey!

USING SERVICE-LEARNING IN GRADUATE AUDITING COURSES: A STANDARDS-BASED FRAMEWORK

Angela M. Woodland

ABSTRACT

A mid-semester request for help from a local neighborhood association turned into a graduate auditing class service-learning project. Service-learning projects have the potential to provide accounting students with valuable opportunities to integrate and apply auditing, accounting, and business knowledge, to acquire new knowledge, and to practice exercising professional judgment, due professional care, and communications skills in rich settings and to provide clients with useful information. However, the use of service-learning cases in the classroom poses significant risks. Common concerns are that such cases use too much class time relative to learning achieved using more traditional methods, students might not be able to provide a satisfactory work product for the client, instructors must plan and prepare too extensively, and instructors will assign grades based primarily on subjective grading criteria. I offer a standards-based framework for incorporating service-learning projects into existing graduate auditing courses that allows educators to manage potential risks while exploiting pedagogical benefits.

Advances in Accounting Education: Teaching and Curriculum Innovations, Volume 10, 61–80
Copyright © 2009 by Emerald Group Publishing Limited
All rights of reproduction in any form reserved
ISSN: 1085-4622/doi:10.1108/S1085-4622(2009)0000010005

The accounting education literature is replete with calls for changing accounting course content and teaching methods. (Nelson, Bailey, & Nelson, 1998, p. 303) specifically attribute the demand for change in accounting education in part to outdated pedagogical methods that result in "graduates who are ill-prepared for the changing profession." Albrecht and Sack (2000, p. 43) warn, "[o]ur pedagogy often lacks creativity, involves too much lecture and dependence on textbooks, and does not require enough student contact with business," and specifically advocate responding by moving away from an overreliance on traditional lecture methods.

Educators, educational and professional organizations, and accounting practitioners alike encourage more innovative courses and more active learning opportunities such as those afforded by the use of cases (Milne & McConnell, 2001, p. 62). Albrecht and Sack (2000, p. 53) advocate a shift to more hands-on activities, including real cases. They suggest that cases should include, among others, group work, project management, real companies, and hands-on activities. Throughout his seminal book on experiential learning, Dewey (1938) promoted learning *by doing*. Service-learning in accounting has the potential to allow students to learn by doing in rich case settings through less traditional, hands-on activities, complete with real companies, real documents, and real stakeholders.

This chapter offers a standards-based framework for incorporating service-learning in the graduate auditing classroom illustrated with an actual case. The standards-based approach is designed to exploit the pedagogical benefits while mitigating the associated risks. The chapter is organized as follows. The next section includes a review of the relevant literature. I provide details of the actual case in the second section and lay out a framework for incorporating service-learning into graduate auditing courses in the third section. The final section contains concluding remarks and a call for additional research.

LITERATURE REVIEW

In its survey of auditing and assurance courses in the United States, the 2000–2001 Auditing Section Education Committee (AAA, 2003, p. 242) found that the use of cases in advanced auditing courses increased significantly in the 1990s. Pre-packaged cases based on real experiences are widely available for classroom use in casebooks (Knapp, 2006; Cullinan & Wright, 2003) and in accounting education journals such as *Issues in Accounting Education* and *Journal of Accounting Education*, among others.

Cases based on real experiences are also available to instructors via private and professional sources such as, among others, Deloitte and Touche's Trueblood Case Series and the American Accounting Association's Faculty Development section of its website. Lipe (2006, pp. 419–429) provides an index of cases published through November 2006 in *Issues in Accounting Education*, and Weinstein (2005, pp. 205–206) and Brasel and Hentz (2006, pp. 414–416) provide instructions on accessing databases of accounting cases.

Preparers of pre-packaged cases typically adapt real circumstances to fit neatly in a classroom setting and include instructions for presenting the cases, timetables, and suggested answers. These cases often contain information summarized from client documents and other evidence and do not include extraneous information. Such cases allow students manageable access to relevant, real situations and avoid some of the difficulties of introducing real-time cases or service-learning in the classroom such as organizing information, determining client needs, setting time budgets, and managing documents. In avoiding some of the difficulties of using real-time cases, pre-packaged cases are likely to sacrifice some of the richness of the case environment and the depth of involvement and learning options (Zlotkowski, 1996, p. 7).

Accounting education literature contains repeated calls for providing students with greater access to the complexity and depth of real world environments (PricewaterhouseCoopers, 2003, p. 7; AECC, 1990, p. 309, among others). Colleges and universities across the nation are also recognizing and promoting civic responsibilities and community involvement (Campus Compact, 2006). Service-learning offers the opportunity for rich case environments while also promoting community involvement. Brazelton (2000, p. 69) calls for accounting courses to include more activities that promote middle and upper levels of thinking as described in Bloom's Taxonomy (Bloom, 1956), concluding that "[a]ny idea that makes students think through an entire process is effective." I suggest that service-learning projects require students to think through entire processes.

There is an extensive and developing literature on service-learning in the accounting curriculum. Most notably, Rama (1998), in a serial monograph, offers 4 theoretical essays on service-learning in accounting and 11 papers on implementation approaches. Rama, Ravenscroft, Wolcott, and Zlotkowski (2000) evaluate and summarize service-learning outcomes for all disciplines including accounting. Godfrey (2003, p. 466) and Hoxmeier and Lenk (2003, p. 92) discuss the reciprocal nature of service-learning; clients receive the product or service they need, and students learn relevant course material and acquire skills in the process of providing the service. Hurt (2007, pp. 297–298) and McCoskey and Warren (2003, pp. 407–409) specifically advocate including service-learning in accounting programs as part of addressing calls for change in accounting education.

Implementing service-learning in the classroom is not without risks. In particular, service-learning can consume class time during which students could be learning via more traditional methods. The service-learning cases have not yet been organized or tested. Accordingly, there is the possibility that client records are inadequate, that the services required are too simplistic (or overly complex) such that the desired reciprocal nature of the case is not achieved. There is a chance that the students either will not be able to provide a satisfactory work product for the client or the case itself will not illustrate or develop the skills and understanding initially intended. Additionally, without a clear and complete understanding of the case, establishing a solution may be difficult, along with the consequent grading concerns.

Faculty reward structures are less appreciative of innovations in teaching. Instructors may be reluctant to invest too much time into risky, but innovative teaching methodologies. Heffernan (2001, p. 2) outlines difficulties in incorporating service-learning pedagogies that include time and inflexibility of teaching loads, resistance from faculty and others in the discipline to curricular changes, and lack of institutional support for faculty. Cook, DeBerg, Michenzi, Milano, and Rama (2003, p. 100) suggest that some of these concerns can be addressed by implementing service-learning as part of student organizations, but posit that service-learning in the classroom setting is likely to better promote learning of course materials and application of knowledge in real world settings, whereas service-learning through student organizations is likely to build personal competencies.

Andrews (2007, pp. 21–23) notes, based on reviews of academic publications, that service-learning in accounting education remains relatively infrequent, and, when implemented, occurs most frequently in information-systems courses or as elective credits with tax-based content. For example, Campbell, Reider, & Maloney (2002, p. 13) describe a senior-level service-learning project to provide taxpayer assistance to rural Alaskan native communities, and Anderson and Bauman (2004, p. 118) describe how low income taxpayer clinics can be used as graduate service-learning projects. One study, Still and Clayton (2004, pp. 473–475), describes in detail a service-learning project successfully used in an auditing course. Their project entails working with small businesses or nonprofit organizations to review accounting systems. My study differs in several respects. The type of project I describe is best suited to a graduate auditing course (external, internal, or fraud) and focuses on performing substantive audit/ attestation procedures for a client.

From the AACSB's *Accounting Accreditation Standards Worksheet* as part of Pre-Accreditation Process Documents (AACSB, 2008),

> Learning in a Masters of Accounting program is developed in a more integrative, intensive fashion than undergraduate education … Graduates demonstrate an expanded understanding of the professional responsibilities, the ethical standards of the accounting profession, and the strategic role of accounting in business organizations and society.

If integrative and intensive learning are to be part of a graduate education in accounting, then graduate learning should include experiences that facilitate achievement of these goals.

My study also differs from the previous literature by offering a framework and working example of how a service-learning project in a graduate auditing course can be structured and evaluated using the existing auditing/ attestation standards. I choose to refer to the project described in the chapter as a service-learning project. I also could characterize the project as a client-based problem-based case or real-time case. Regardless of the terminology used, the basic characteristics of service-learning projects discussed in this chapter should still apply.

CASE DESCRIPTION

While reviewing the financial records of a local neighborhood nonprofit association (the association), the new treasurer noticed that the former treasurer had written many checks to herself without authorization or supporting documentation. The new treasurer and board of directors of the association engaged an attorney and discussed the situation with the former treasurer, who, in exchange for not being prosecuted, agreed to fully reimburse the association for unauthorized payments. The immediate problem facing the association was identifying the total unauthorized payments. Neither the treasurer nor the board members had accounting or auditing expertise. The new treasurer asked students in my graduate auditing class to use the situation as an in-class project with the goal of identifying and reporting unsupported payments.

Over a period of five 80-min class periods (and some out-of-class time), the class identified the nature of the engagement, completed the client acceptance process, drafted an engagement letter, planned the engagement, performed agreed-upon procedures, prepared working papers, and issued a report.

Ultimately the students delivered a report to the association that identified $9,212.56 in checks written to the previous treasurer without supporting documentation and $2,350 in checks written to a private school the former treasurer's children attended, also without supporting documentation. These transactions occurred during the period 1999–2005, during which the association's total annual revenue averaged less than $15,000. In addition, the students provided accounting and internal control recommendations to the association's board and treasurer for future use.

This particular case offered a unique, rich setting for learning and reinforcing knowledge about the following subjects: identifying applicable standards, client acceptance, establishing engagement terms, independence, engagement planning, preparing and following time budgets, attestation services and standards, due professional care, working paper preparation, reporting, and management letter recommendations.

Accepting this project was not without risks. First, the costs of the case (mainly class time that could be devoted to other areas or more traditional methods of instruction) could have exceeded the potential pedagogical benefits. Students expressed initial concerns that parallel those discussed in the Bernstein, Tipping, Bercovitz, and Skinner (1995, p. 246) analysis of problem-based learning in medicine. Students worried that the case would be too time-consuming and involve too much work on their part. I worried that the case might be too time-consuming for me and involve too much work on my part. Ultimately, the project was more time-consuming for me than if I had followed the original course plan, but not unreasonably so, and I did take away some ideas for better managing such a project in the future, which I share in the framework sections of this chapter. Students expressed strong satisfaction with the experience in reflective discussions in class, and several students made a point of thanking me for the experience in conversations outside the class.

FRAMEWORK TO INCORPORATE SERVICE-LEARNING INTO GRADUATE AUDITING COURSES

Based on my experiences with this case, I recommend that instructors first screen the project on three basic criteria before applying the standards based-framework: ability of students to perform the service, appropriateness of the service to the course, and adequacy of client records. According to the

Heffernan (2001, p. 3) classification system, this case would fall into the problem-based service-learning category in which students respond much as "consultants" and the association much like a client. A necessary condition for these types of cases is that students possess a knowledge base they can use to meet the client's needs. Graduate auditing students have typically completed a battery of accounting and business courses as well as an introductory course in auditing. Most have had internships and/or relevant job experience. I concluded that my graduate auditing students were well-prepared to handle a real service-learning project in auditing, and I anticipate that many graduate audit classes are similarly prepared.

Instructors can determine if a project is technically and logistically viable by meeting with the client to gather additional information as to what exactly the client expects from the arrangement, deadlines, available records, client organizational structure, and history. The client allowed me to spend some time looking through the organization's financial records, which was useful because she had difficulty describing exactly what documentation was available. As a matter of convenience, I refer to the source of the real case as the "client" throughout this chapter. However, it should be duly noted and clarified to the students in the class and to the case source that a true practitioner–client relationship does not exist.

What remains after assessing the viability and appropriateness of a project is the big question. Are the likely benefits of a particular service-learning project worth the associated costs? The client acceptance decision in public accounting also involves an evaluation of potential costs (risks) and potential benefits (profits), and, even if a particular case does not turn out to be a suitable class project, it certainly poses an opportunity to explore in real time the client acceptance decision, a relevant classroom exercise. Professional standards also provide an ideal framework for organizing and completing the project.

What follows is a standards-based framework for managing service-learning projects in the classroom. I outline the key considerations in following the relevant standards and then discuss related considerations by offering questions to guide the class through the process or to aid in reflection on the work performed. The framework consists of (1) client acceptance procedures, (2) planning, (3) performance, (4) reporting, (5) reflection, and (6) performance evaluation. Throughout the process, I use the real case from my graduate auditing course to illustrate concepts and use my real efforts (successful and not) and the benefit of hindsight to offer ideas and suggestions. Table 1 offers a sample timeline and summary of the framework activities.

Table 1.   Sample Timeline.

Activity	Information	Homework Assigned	Outcome
Before first class devoted to case			
Introduce case	Provide handout with basic information at end of class	Identify nature of engagement and applicable standards, review client acceptance standards	Basic familiarity
Class period 1			
Client acceptance	Provide handout with detailed information on client	Review standards for engagement planning	Client acceptance decision
Class period 2			
Planning	Collect suggested work programs at end of class	Review standards for engagement performance	Suggested work programs
Class period 3			
Performance	Provide client documents, client confidentiality form, final approved work programs, due dates and grading criteria	Continued performance	Working papers
Class period 4			
Performance	Provide client documents	Review reporting standards, draft reports	Working papers
Class period 5			
Reflection	Collect reports, discussion		Assess value of case, emphasize key points
After last class devoted to case			
Performance evaluation			Feedback on work product, reports, and client satisfaction

Client Acceptance Procedures

Heffernan (2001, p. 3) points out that up-front planning is a key element of effective service-learning. Up-front planning is also a key element of case-based learning (and real auditing and attestation engagements) as well. Perhaps even more important is the critical decision of whether to accept clients. Including the class in the client acceptance process is vital to ensuring that the class takes ownership of the project and allows the class to apply the relevant standards in a real setting. Because client acceptance procedures are important, but with consideration of time constraints, I devoted the first of the five 80-min class periods and some initial time outside of class to the client acceptance process as follows.

Identifying Relevant Standards
I began by providing a brief introduction to the case and asked the students to identify the nature of the engagement and which standards apply. If students do not have access to professional materials in class, instructors could use standards research as a homework assignment before the first class. In-class time could be devoted to clearing up any confusion about who issues relevant standards, types of engagements accepted by public accountants, and where to locate guidance. Our particular case fell into the category of an agreed-upon procedures engagement subject to the AICPA's *Statements on Standards for Attestation Engagements* (SSAE).

Client Expectations
Determining the client's specific needs helps the class determine whether the engagement is likely to provide relevant learning experiences as part of the client acceptance process and also is an essential part of establishing an understanding with the client and a necessary element of planning. I gathered as much information as possible up-front as part of the initial screening process, which worked well for determining initial viability and in eliminating confusion. During the first meeting with the potential client, I was careful to emphasize that the work would be used as a learning tool for students who are not seasoned professionals with experience in these types of projects. I also explained that the class would complete a thorough evaluation of whether or not to accept the service-learning project, with the possibility that the class would turn down the project. It also would have been reasonable at this point to suggest possible alternative solutions to the potential client, which would include local accounting firm contacts, names of consultants, professional organizations that may provide referrals, etc.

Conditions for Engagement Performance
Auditing and attestation standards outline the conditions for engagement performance, providing an opportunity to discuss the skills, preparation, and other required characteristics of public accountants. At this point,

I provided students with additional information about the organization, its records, history, and expectations.

In addition to assessing whether the specific conditions for engagement performance are met, there are multiple opportunities for exploring the subject matter. In particular, students could use the client acceptance process as an opportune time to discuss independence, whether the client is capable of being responsible for the subject matter, what constitutes sufficient training and proficiency, and what risks are unacceptable (in this case and in other settings). See Exhibit 1, Panel A for examples of questions an instructor may pose to foster class discussion about client acceptance procedures. My class had a lively discussion of the first three questions but did not show much interest in discussing risks. Because we focused less on the risk-related standards than on other standards relevant to planning and consequently, they had less background from which to draw upon. For future planning purposes, I either will have to increase the background consideration of risks or modify or eliminate the risk reflection questions.

Proper Fit

Public accounting firms do not accept every engagement just because they have the expertise, the risk is low enough, and the client has the ability to pay. Firms often decline certain services because they decide those services are not the best use of their limited resources (primarily staff hours). Likewise, it was important for me to assess whether the subject matter of the service-learning project aligned with the objectives of the graduate auditing course. My course focused primarily on external auditing, so we discussed whether this case, fraud detection in an agreed-upon procedures attestation engagement, would provide learning consistent with the objectives of the course. We noted that attestation services are one type of assurance service often performed by practicing public accountants. Much of the relevant attestation guidance overlaps or is similar in nature to auditing standards. Additionally, we noted that much of the engagement involved matters of clear importance to auditors – client acceptance, planning, working paper documentation, due professional care, and reporting – even if the actual fraud detection procedures were less related to the planned subject matter of the course.

Acceptance Decision

At this point, students evaluated, with limited information, whether they expected to be able to complete the work in a timely manner, whether the

Exhibit 1. Discussion Questions.

Panel A: Client Acceptance

1. Would you be independent if you worked for the client? What if you provided volunteer services or made donations to the nonprofit client? What if a key client employee was related to you or a good friend?
2. Does this potential client have the sophistication necessary to understand the scope of the services you will provide? How can you be sure?
3. Does an accountant have to have experience in performing similar services to accept an engagement? How can you ensure you are skilled enough to accept the engagement? Must all members of the engagement team be CPAs? Must any?
4. What is business risk? What is audit risk? How much risk should public accountants be willing to accept? What risks can insurance mitigate? How does this affect our responsibility to the public interest?

Panel B: Planning

1. How important is it to follow the time budget?
2. What will happen if, when performing the engagement, you encounter unexpected circumstances?
3. Why are engagement letters important? What purposes do they serve? How well do they serve their purposes?
4. Why have working paper documentation standards (auditing standards) changed recently? What behaviors are these changes intended to prevent? How effective are these changes likely to be?

Panel C: Performance

1. Were there any conclusions you drew with less than certainty? How do you suggest dealing with these situations? Do the standards address this?
2. Are the relevant standards adequate? In what areas would you have liked additional guidance? In what areas were the standards too restrictive? How can you respond in these situations?
3. What are the advantages of performing audits in teams? What are the drawbacks?

Panel D: Reporting

1. How can you ensure your report is understandable to the client?
2. Where can you look for reporting examples? Is it okay to borrow language from other reports?
3. How will you best structure the report-writing process? Will everyone submit a report individually or should you prepare the entire report as a team or should one report be divided among team members?
4. What was the most difficult reporting requirement to comply with?
5. What do you think you did well in the report? What do you wish you did better in the report?
6. Do the standards for reporting provide enough guidance? Are the standards for reporting too restrictive?

Panel E: Reflection

1. Overall, are you glad we did this case in class? Would you want to do something like this case again?
2. What did you like most? What did you like least?

Exhibit 1. (*Continued*)

3. What did you learn? What do you wish you had learned?
4. What would you have done differently?
5. How can you use this experience in interviews for jobs?
6. What can you apply from this experience in your career?
7. Do you think the client will be satisfied with the results?

work would be beneficial to them, and whether the work would be beneficial to the client. Initially, my students were reluctant to commit to a decision. A suggestion to overcome such reluctance is to instruct the class to list the three biggest possible benefits to them of accepting the case, and list the three biggest concerns with regard to the case. At the end of this process, the class also could discuss the likely relevant client acceptance factors in public accounting firms' decisions. I allowed students to vote on whether to accept the case. If the instructor and the class together decide at this point not to accept the case, the evaluation will have used only one class period; the time will not have been wasted because it offers valuable insight into the client acceptance process.

Allowing students to ultimately make the client acceptance decision is risky in that they could, because of aforementioned concerns about using real cases in the classroom, vote not to accept an otherwise acceptable client. Alternatively, the instructor, acting as a partner, could make the ultimate decision after considering the results of the client acceptance procedures performed by the students. This method mirrors the decision-making process used in public practice. Also, instructors could specify up-front in their course descriptions that the course has a service-learning component. Universities with established service-learning programs often offer special course designations. University of Missouri, University of Nebraska, and Louisiana State University, among many others, include a special service-learning designation for courses in which such pedagogy will be utilized.

The client in this case approached me, but this is not likely to be a typical opportunity. Many universities have well-established service-learning centers with lists of willing service-learning partners. Service-learning center personnel also are often willing to use their community connections to search for appropriate partners. Additionally, clients might be obtained through faculty connections from participation in local professional organizations and by contacting local volunteer organizations, obtaining lists of local nonprofit agencies, and by advertising in university-alumni newsletters. Service-learning usually focuses on partnering with nonprofit organizations, but instructors might also consider for-profit businesses because client characteristics such as size, willingness, specific needs, available records, etc. may be better determinants of an appropriate fit for the class.

Planning

If the class and instructor spend a good deal of time deciding whether to accept the client, some of the initial planning will already be completed. Consider devoting the second of the five 80-min class periods to planning. Using relevant standards as a guide, I required teams of approximately five students each to prepare an initial work program and time budget under the stipulations that the work program must address the client's expectations and must be able to be completed in two 80-min class periods and outside of class. I required students to develop the work program and the time budget at the same time because joint consideration allows them to more realistically determine what they likely will be able to complete. I exercised final approval of the work program, and issued a final work program for all groups to use that was a combination of the work product of the multiple groups. I found the planning process to be the appropriate time to discuss how practicing accountants typically generate work programs, the requirement to prepare written work programs, working paper requirements, and the function, form, and content of engagement letters.

In our case, the preparation of the work program required us to identify the specific agreed-upon procedures we would perform. Students considered the client's specific requests and also brainstormed ways that fraud could have occurred and offered suggestions for additional procedures.

In our case, I also outlined due dates for completed work (working papers and report to client) and grading criteria. I offer the following standards-based grading criteria: (1) whether working papers support conclusions and are prepared in accordance with applicable standards, (2) the propriety of actual conclusions reached, (3) whether the final report to the client follows applicable standards and effectively conveys the engagement results, and (4) the usefulness and proper reporting format of any management recommendations. I assigned a point value to the project equivalent to 15% of the total points in the course which approximates the time spent on the project relative to the total course time. See Exhibit 1, Panel B for examples of questions the instructor can raise to reflect on the planning process. I did not have the foresight to ask all these questions during the case itself, but did note in later class discussions that the case lent itself to discussions of these matters.

Performance

If the class gives sufficient attention to the engagement acceptance process and if the class performs the planning process in accordance with relevant standards (as applicable), the performance of the case procedures will be less confusing and will allow the students to work most effectively with client records, gather information, and form conclusions. Devoting two 80-min class periods and out-of-class time in performing the procedures in the work programs worked well in my case, but specific case details would dictate time parameters.

Instructor preparation for this stage is more extensive and requires several key decisions. Whether to use original documents or copies, however, is not likely to be a difficult decision. Though original documents provide authenticity to the case, they are difficult to share among teams. More importantly, there is the risk of loss or contamination which might have deleterious effects on subsequent litigation. I chose to have copies of all documents made for each team, which was a time-consuming project for several departmental office workers and for me. To facilitate this process, I first organized the documents into like categories (bank statements, receipts and other supporting documentation for expenses, membership dues records, etc.). I sacrificed some case authenticity by organizing the documents myself, but this sacrifice seemed necessary to reduce time spent on less valuable tasks in class. It also allowed me one last opportunity to assess the viability of case.

Client confidentiality is also a key concern at this stage. Even though our particular client was relatively unconcerned, confidentiality was nonetheless an important area to address. I drafted a confidentiality agreement that students signed before accessing copies of client records. The agreement, while likely not legally binding, was intended to instill in students the importance of client confidentiality in public accounting. Because of time constraints, we did not incorporate a review of client confidentiality rules in the AICPA's *Code of Professional Conduct*, but such a discussion would be appropriate at this point.

After providing students with the financial records, I let them work for the first class period without interruption or intervention (except when clearly necessary) under the theory that there is value in the process of deciding how to approach a task, familiarizing oneself with financial records, deciding how best to divide work among team members, and trying to make sense out of new information. Based on my previous experience in public accounting, this process very much resembles the process practicing accountants encounter on engagements. I did encourage students to e-mail questions after class to resolve any major sources of confusion before the next class period.

Because one of the key concerns in accepting a service-learning project for classroom use is whether the client will receive a valuable product, I decided to encourage information sharing between teams by specifically stating that sharing of information for the good of the client would not be considered cheating and that the case was not intended to be a competition (and would not be graded as such). In hindsight, I should have specified that sharing of research, conclusions, and work product otherwise was not encouraged, as I received surprisingly homogeneous reports.

See Exhibit 1, Panel C for examples of questions the instructor can pose to reflect on the performance process. As a result of our discussion about audit teams, I learned that students perceived a disconnect between audit teams and class teams because audit teams may have more of a hierarchical structure.

Reporting

I found that reporting on the results of the engagement was the most difficult part of the case for students. Students in my classes expressed concern that they did not have much experience in actually drafting reports. For similar projects in the future, I will suggest that students complete the report writing process over a weekend to allow for less in-class time pressure, more experimentation and editing, and for teams to focus on preparing a well-written, accurate report, the only real outcome for the client. This change will likely involve some additional attention to the reporting standards.

In our case, the client requested services that necessitated an agreed-upon procedures report. The standards for characteristics of agreed-upon procedures reports are quite detailed, but the actual wording is not prescribed due to the varying nature of these engagements. This guided flexibility provided a challenging (but rewarding) opportunity to learn about reporting characteristics prescribed by the attestation standards and then actually to apply that understanding by drafting a report. Students additionally offered accounting and internal control suggestions in the form of a management letter, also with its own rules and considerations, and seemed especially enthusiastic about doing so. For both reports, students had to focus on communicating clearly, avoiding ambiguous or judgmental language, sticking to the facts, and choosing professional words and tone while still being understandable to the client.

I struggled with what final report information to present to the client: all team reports, the best team report, or some combination of the best elements of team reports. In our case, only one group differed significantly in its findings from other groups. This discrepancy required that I investigate by reperforming the procedure, a relatively time-consuming process. In the end, I used the reporting format from one group, various wording choices from each of the groups, and common findings from the groups.

I had not considered that findings might vary from group to group, leaving doubt about the truth, causing me to worry that this project might in some way subject me (as a CPA), my students, or the university to legal liability. Since the completion of the project, I have learned that many universities have service-learning centers with personnel who are experienced in handling these types of concerns. Specifically, these centers can provide university-approved service-learning contracts and advice on managing liability. Also, instructors might want to apprise department chairpersons and deans about their plans to perform procedures in a service-learning or case environment for real "clients." Finally, to ensure that rules of practice are not violated, CPAs can contact their respective state boards of accountancy.

See Exhibit 1, Panel D for examples of questions the instructor can pose to promote effective report writing and to reflect upon the reporting process.

Reflection

After the conclusion of audits or attestation engagements, engagement teams often meet for post-engagement reviews. Some firms require this meeting as an attempt to comply with the AICPA's *Quality Control Standards*, as well as a way to reinforce learning and better prepare for next year's engagement. Mintz (2006, p. 100) recommends reflective learning in accounting ethics education to analyze and synthesize experiences. Likewise, reflection is a useful tool to solidify understanding of the key elements of the service-learning project. Reflection may be an effective use of the fifth and final class period devoted to the case. Reflection completes the learning process and also provides valuable information to the instructor about what learning did occur, what learning still needs to occur, and what matters to consider when incorporating real cases in the future.

In our case, I chose questions to be used in reflection, but had difficulty moving the students away from the actual details of the case to the learning process and their actual learning experiences. A reasonable alternative might be to have students develop the reflective questions themselves, then respond.

In our reflection and in other class discussions, students indicated strong satisfaction with the service-learning experience, particularly because of the chance to tie standards to actual practice and because the exercise yielded meaningful results to the client. Students responded to the course positively in evaluations. Using a 4-point evaluation scale, students rated the class 3.92 for stimulating interest in the subject, 3.77 for whether the method of presentation stimulated learning, and 3.85 for whether evaluation methods were impartial. These ratings are somewhat higher than ratings from other semesters taught without the service-learning component. Clearly this is not a statistically valid measurement of the effect of this one service-learning activity, but it does provide some evidence of student satisfaction (or lack of dissatisfaction). One student specifically commented that more such cases should be included in the class because "they also made the material more understandable." Another commented positively that this type of format "made us get involved." Finally, one student offered about the course in general, "I know I will be a better auditor because of what I have learned ..."

In hindsight, I wish I had collected more formal data with respect to student satisfaction with the service-learning experience as a learning tool, and have since found that service-learning centers on campus can provide templates and suggestions for collecting student feedback. See Exhibit 1, Panel E for examples of reflective questions instructors can pose in the final class period.

Performance Reviews

Auditors typically receive performance reviews shortly after completing a significant engagement. I recommend completing grading as soon as possible after the performance of the project. However, it may be useful to obtain the client's comments before issuing the final grades, as meeting the client's expectations may be an appropriate grading criterion. In some cases, it might be possible for clients to later address the class with comments on the service-learning project from their perspective. Alternatively, instructors could consider asking the client to complete a more complete performance evaluation for the class. Service-learning centers on campus also offer templates for this type of evaluation.

CONCLUSION AND CALL FOR RESEARCH

The potential problems associated with implementing service-learning projects in graduate auditing courses may be mitigated by using a standards-based approach. The applicable authoritative standards provide a natural framework for managing service-learning projects and provide a structure for dividing projects into manageable learning opportunities: client acceptance, planning, performance, reporting, reflection, and performance evaluation.

I offer the standards-based framework for implementing a service-learning project in a graduate auditing course based on existing literature and one positive classroom experience. Clearly, empirical evidence of outcomes of service-learning projects in the graduate auditing class setting is needed to validate these ideas. Possible research projects could include comparing measurements of learning in courses with service-learning components to learning in similar courses taught more traditionally, surveys of student perceptions of the value of service-learning projects, surveys of client perceptions of the value of service-learning projects, and surveys of employer perceptions of the value of service-learning in preparing students for work.

REFERENCES

Accounting Education Change Commission (AECC). (1990). Objectives of education for accountants: Position statement number one. *Issues in Accounting Education, 5*(2), 307–312.

Albrecht, W. S., & Sack, R. J. (2000). Accounting education: Charting the course through a perilous future. In: *American Education Series 16*. Sarasota, FL: American Accounting Association.

American Accounting Association (AAA), 2000–2001 Auditing Section Education Committee. (2003). Challenges to audit education for the 21st century: A survey of curricula, course content, and delivery methods. *Issues in Accounting Education, 18*(3), 241–263.

Anderson, S., & Bauman, C. (2004). Low-income taxpayer clinics as a form of service learning. In: B. N. Schwartz (Ed.), *Advances in accounting education* (Vol. 6, pp. 117–132). Greenwich, CT: JAI Press.

Andrews, C. P. (2007). Service learning: Applications and research in business. *Journal of Education for Business, 83*(1), 19–26.

Association to Advance Collegiate Schools of Business (AACSB). (2008). *Accounting accreditation standards worksheet*. Available at http://www.aacsb.edu/accreditation/. Retrieved on September 17.

Bernstein, P., Tipping, J., Bercovitz, K., & Skinner, H. A. (1995). Shifting students and faculty to a PBL curriculum: Attitudes changes and lessons learned. *Academic Medicine, 70*(3), 245–247.

Bloom, B. (Ed.) (1956). *Taxonomy of education objectives.* New York: David McKay.
Brasel, K., & Hentz, B. (2006). Increasing accessibility to academic publications in accounting education: A database for research and teaching. *Issues in Accounting Education, 21*(2), 411–416.
Brazelton, J. (2000). Students may blossom using Bloom's Taxonomy in the Accounting Curriculum. In: B. N. Schwartz (Ed.), *Advances in accounting education* (Vol. 2, pp. 57–85). Greenwich, CT: JAI Press.
Campbell, S., Reider, B., & Maloney, R. (2002). A service-learning approach to achieving taxpayer compliance in Alaskan native communities. In: B. N. Schwartz (Ed.), *Advances in accounting education* (Vol. 4, pp. 1–19). Greenwich, CT: JAI Press.
Campus Compact. (2006). *Welcome to the campus compact website.* Available at http://www.campuscompact.org/. Retrieved on October 25, 2007.
Cook, G., DeBerg, C., Michenzi, A., Milano, B., & Rama, D. (2003). Developing personal competencies through service-learning: A role for student organizations. In: B. N. Schwartz (Ed.), *Advances in accounting education* (Vol. 5, pp. 99–120). Greenwich, CT: JAI Press.
Cullinan, C. P., & Wright, G. B. (2003). *Cases from the SEC files.* Upper Saddle River, NJ: Pearson Education, Inc.
Dewey, J. (1938). *Experience and education.* New York: Collier Books.
Godfrey, M. (2003). Academic service-learning as an information systems curriculum asset. *Issues in Information Systems, IV,* 465–471.
Heffernan, K. (2001). Service-learning in higher education. In: *National campus compact.* Providence, RI: Brown University.
Hoxmeier, J., & Lenk, M. M. (2003). Service-learning in information systems courses: Community projects that make a difference. *Journal of Information Systems Education, 14*(1), 91–100.
Hurt, B. (2007). Teaching what matters: A new conception of accounting education. *Journal of Education for Business, 82*(5), 295–299.
Knapp, M. C. (2006). *Contemporary Auditing, Real Issues & Cases.* USA: Thomson South-Western.
Lipe, M. G. (2006). Using cases published in *Issues in Accounting Education*: Categories and topics at a glance. *Issues in Accounting Education, 21*(4), 417–430.
McCoskey, M., & Warren, D. L. (2003). Service-learning: An innovative approach to teaching accounting: A teaching note. *Accounting Education, 12*(4), 405–413.
Milne, M., & McConnell, P. (2001). Problem-based learning: A pedagogy for using case material in accounting education. *Accounting Education, 10*(1), 61–82.
Mintz, S. M. (2006). Accounting ethics education: Integrating reflective learning and virtue ethics. *Journal of Accounting Education, 24,* 97–117.
Nelson, I. T., Bailey, J. A., & Nelson, A. T. (1998). Changing accounting education with purpose: Market-based strategic planning for departments of accounting. *Issues in Accounting Education, 13*(2), 301–326.
PricewaterhouseCoopers (PWC). (2003). *Educating for the public trust: The Pricewaterhouse-Coopers position on accounting education.* New York: PricewaterhouseCoopers.
Rama, D. V. (Ed.) (1998). *Learning by doing: Concepts and models for service-learning in accounting.* Sterling, VA: Stylus.
Rama, D. V., Ravenscroft, S. P., Wolcott, S. K., & Zlotkowski, E. (2000). Service-learning outcomes: Guidelines for educators and researchers. *Issues in Accounting Education, 15*(4), 657–692.

Still, K., & Clayton, P. R. (2004). Utilizing service-learning in accounting programs. *Issues in Accounting Education, 19*(4), 469–486.

Weinstein, G. P. (2005). A tool for accessing accounting cases. *Journal of Accounting Education, 23*(3), 204–214.

Zlotkowski, E. (1996). Opportunity for all: Linking service-learning and business education. *Journal of Business Ethics, 1*(1), 5–19.

INSTILLING STUDENT RESPONSIBILITY WITH TEAM CONTRACTS AND PEER EVALUATIONS

B. Douglas Clinton and Pamela A. Smith

ABSTRACT

This chapter shares ideas about how to encourage students to take responsibility for their individual learning and their role as a team member through the use of team contracts and peer evaluations. We also share how instructors can more easily determine individual grades for team projects. Team contracts can help instill a sense of responsibility, encourage accountability, and add structure by promoting the clarification of task-specific roles. In conjunction with team contracts, peer evaluations can reinforce the responsibilities assigned through the contract. Peer evaluations provide an opportunity for students to objectively and thoughtfully evaluate team member contributions to the collective result and reward individual participants more equitably related to the outcome obtained.

The chapter provides discussion and examples of student-developed team contracts and a sample peer evaluation form along with a discussion of how these documents have been used in the classroom. Using responses from a convenience survey of undergraduate and graduate students, we conclude by examining student feedback to suggest patterns of the perceptions of students toward the use of these tools.

Advances in Accounting Education: Teaching and Curriculum Innovations, Volume 10, 81–101
Copyright © 2009 by Emerald Group Publishing Limited
All rights of reproduction in any form reserved
ISSN: 1085-4622/doi:10.1108/S1085-4622(2009)0000010006

A great challenge in education is to compel students to take responsibility for their learning and for their role as a team member (AACSB, 2007, p. 15). This chapter presents two tools (i.e., team contracts and peer evaluations) that are useful for instilling student responsibility within a team learning environment. We use relevant literature to support how these tools can help achieve that goal. We provide examples of student-developed team contracts and a sample peer evaluation form, along with a discussion of how these documents have been used in the classroom. Using survey responses from undergraduate and graduate students, we examine student feedback that suggests some patterns of the perceptions of students regarding the use of these tools.

The remainder of the chapter is organized as follows: In the next section, we introduce the concept of team learning – distinguishing it from groups and discussing the benefits and challenges of team learning. In the third section, we provide a two-part example of a team contract and explain its usefulness in overcoming difficulties in a team learning environment. We focus on peer evaluations in Section 4, providing an example and a demonstration of how the form could be completed. Finally, to assist other faculty who may wish to use team contracts and/or peer evaluations, we conclude with a discussion of our experiences – positive and negative – drawing from survey responses of both graduate and undergraduate student participants.

TEAM LEARNING IN THE CONTEXT OF COOPERATIVE LEARNING

Accounting education research refers to teamwork as a component of cooperative learning and provides many examples of ways to implement and integrate cooperative learning into the classroom (Apostolou, Watson, Hassell, & Webber, 2001, pp. 1–61).

The Department of Education defines cooperative learning as follows:

> Cooperative learning is a successful teaching strategy in which small teams, each with students of different levels of ability, use a variety of learning activities to improve their understanding of a subject. Each member of a team is responsible not only for learning what is taught but also for helping teammates learn, thus creating an atmosphere of achievement. (Balkcom, 1992)

A survey of accounting educators found that almost 75% of accounting faculty use team or group work in their classes (Albrecht & Sack, 2000, p. 54).

In addition, Bryant and Albring (2006, pp. 241–265) provide a comprehensive summary and guide on effective team-building techniques for accounting educators. Thus, the use of team work within the context of cooperative learning is something that is widely accepted in accounting education. Our focus is to ensure that the notion of teams is clearly depicted, so that students understand that in a team they are part of something bigger than themselves.

Katzenbach and Smith suggest that a distinction should be made between teams and groups. They state that a team is a "small number of people with complementary skills who are committed to a common purpose, performance goals, and approach for which they hold themselves mutually accountable" (Katzenbach & Smith, 1999, p. 45), whereas a group has been defined as "a collection of two or more interacting individuals with a stable pattern of relationships between them who share common goals and who perceive themselves as being a group" (Greenberg, 1996, p. 178).

The two most significant distinctions here appear to be that teams have complementary skills and hold each other accountable for their performance whereas groups do not. Moreover, Bryant and Albring (2006, p. 243) suggest that, although group members may share common goals, they may be more concerned with individual contributions than the collective outcomes typically sought by teams. Although the significance of the differentiation of groups and teams may be arguable, we believe the distinction is important. Hite (1996, p. 98) has also reinforced the notion that cooperative learning is distinguished from traditional group work in the same sense that teams are distinguished from groups. Traditional *group* work does not necessarily insist on interdependence and individual accountability, which are considered essential characteristics of cooperative learning (Millis & Cottell, 1998, p. 11). Thus, the use of the term *teams* appears more consistent with the cooperative learning approach, which we endeavor to promote.

As we discuss later, interdependence and accountability are important to this discussion in the sense that the use of team contracts and peer evaluations can encourage mutual accountability. Senior- and graduate-level accounting students presumably have complementary interests and, within class levels, their relative accounting skills should be quite similar. Hite (1996, p. 66) suggested establishing teams by intentional methods such as stratifying students by grade point average (GPA), ensuring that each team comprises students at lower, mid, and upper GPA levels. However, research has been mixed on such recommendations. For example, Clinton and Kohlmeyer (2005, p. 109) found absolutely no performance differences between instructor-assigned and student self-selected teams. Thus, further research is needed to substantiate recommendations in this regard.

Common issues of student team learning include "free riders" (also known as "hitchhikers"), social loafers, and the "workhorse" student. The free rider/hitchhiker "makes a conscious decision to let others in the group do most of the work (Beatty, Haas, & Sciglimpaglia, 1996, p. 18)." The free rider/hitchhiker benefits from the other members of the team but provides little in return. This behavior undermines the collaborative objective of teamwork, is counterproductive, and can cause resentment within the team. This is different from social loafers, whose behavior is more complex. Social loafing does not necessarily result from a conscious choice made on the part of the team member. Dependence on other members of the team may be the result of inhibitions or introversion. Alternatively, social loafing can result from cultural or language differences (Beatty et al., 1996, p. 18). However, both the free rider and the social loafer exhibit behavior that is undesirable, and the instructor should seek to reduce or eliminate opportunities for either occurrence.

In the opposite direction, individuals who want to take over the project (i.e., workhorses) inhibit the development of the team members, including themselves since their own behavior denies the opportunity for the cooperative learning they would otherwise receive from the team. We find these students exhibiting dysfunctional behavior in the opposite direction of free riders/hitchhikers and social loafers. The workhorse student inhibits the effectiveness of collaboration, as teammates often regard the student as too controlling. This dominant team member prevents other teammates from providing input that would be meaningful. Consequently, teammates can feel that they have little or no input or control over the team's results. This clearly inhibits participation and the objectives of establishing the team in the first place. All these issues create problems for instructors in assigning individual grades to the students within the teams and in training students to take responsibility for their learning. Accordingly, the instructor would benefit from a mechanism to determine individual contribution, which suggests the potential benefits of the use of additional tools of team contracts and peer evaluations.

TEAM CONTRACTS

According to Bryant and Albring (2006, pp. 251–254), a contract developed by the student team can help members of the team take ownership of their responsibility for the team's outputs and encourage them to function effectively from the onset. The language, "from the onset," is important given that the instructor would like to encourage appropriate team behavior before problems develop. This appears to be a clear advantage of the concept of team contracts. Although peer evaluations are helpful in assigning individual grades, the team contract attempts to establish expectations for individual commitment and necessary skills *prior* to the start of the project.

The focus of building team skills is on the commitment to the team, individual accountability for assigned tasks, and development of inter-personal skills (Katzenbach & Smith, 1999). From a pedagogical standpoint, the development of the team contract provides structure to the learning experience. Development of the contract requires the team to conduct planning to understand the assignment to lay out a plan of action and determine tasks. Anecdotally, we have found that teams that have completed contracts tend to be more organized, more focused, and more efficient overall. We believe that increased efficiency can contribute to a positive team experience by increasing team cohesiveness.

Team contracts can be developed by the team members or supplied by the instructor. The instructor may choose to supply a team contract template and then have the students tailor the contract to their specific needs. Team contracts can vary in the degree of specificity of responsibilities. In a more general contract, the overall responsibilities of all team members are stated. Table 1 provides an example of a more general, student-developed contract used in an advanced accounting course that states overall team member responsibilities. Another example contract is available in Bryant and Albring (2006, p. 252). In general, the contract should mention team member responsibilities such as attending all meetings, being prepared, contributing to the discussions, and following through with an assigned task. Although these responsibilities may seem obvious, these are important requirements that may need reinforcement. By requiring that the team members sign the contract, the team members acknowledge their role in the team and may feel a greater degree of commitment to the team.

Alternatively, a more specific contract typically details the individual responsibilities of each team member for a given project. Some projects could use both general and specific contracts. Where teams are utilized throughout the semester (i.e., maintaining the same cohorts), the team could use one overall general contract for the semester with separate specific contracts for individual projects. Completion of the general contract would be required before work on the first project, while before beginning each individual project, team members would turn in the signed contract

Table 1.   Example Team Contract.

General Responsibilities

General group member responsibilities:
1. Attend every team meeting, be on time and remain throughout the session. If a member cannot be present, inform the other team members in advance of your absence.
2. Be prepared and participate actively in discussions related to the team's assignment. Encourage discussion and participation by all members of the team.
3. Be respectful and considerate of the suggestions presented by each team member.
4. Maintain the confidentiality of any communications of a personal nature presented during the team meeting.
5. Assist in the development of ideas, facts and research needed to complete the assignment.
6. Research, document and disseminate to the other team members the relevant research issues that are discovered in your independent research.
7. Complete all the above-mentioned in a professional and ethical manner, adhering to the University's code of ethical conduct.

Signatures _____   Date _____

regarding the specific responsibilities assigned to them. Table 2 includes two examples of student-developed contracts that describe the specific responsibilities of one team member assigned to coordinating the research and those of a different team member assigned to coordinating the presentation. These contracts were also developed as part of an advanced accounting course. The term *coordinator* is chosen rather than *leader* or some other alternative title to suggest that everyone on the team would contribute and participate in reading researched materials and reviewing the presentation slides. The coordinator is a working member of the team and is the *go to* person for the assigned role. The coordinator is different from a team leader who is responsible for directing a team rather than working as a team member (Wysocki, 2002).

Our experience indicates that team contracts set the tone for the team and establish the norm for acceptable and expected behavior. Feedback from students is that they like the fact that the expectations are defined up front. We have seen fewer team conflicts and more teams taking responsibility for the resolution of issues among themselves as a result of using contracts.

PEER EVALUATIONS

Peer evaluations are one way to hold the students accountable for their performance in a team setting. Beatty et al. (1996, pp. 19–22) discuss how

Table 2. Example Team Contract.

Individual Responsibilities

Individual responsibilities of the research coordinator:

I, the undersigned, _____, agree to take on the responsibility of being the *Research Coordinator*.

My duties will specifically include, but may not be limited to, the following:

1. I will be primarily responsible for overseeing the research necessary to develop our final recommendation for the assignment.
2. I will gather and disseminate to the team members the relevant current accounting literature and press releases that are essential to reaching a supportable recommendation.
3. I will make sure a team consensus is reached based on all relevant financial accounting research before finalizing our recommendation.
4. I will do my best to coordinate, prompt, and participate in discussions related to the team's recommendation for the assignment.
5. All the preceding I will complete in a professional and ethical manner, adhering to my own, as well as this University's, code of ethical conduct.

Signed _____   Date _____

Individual responsibilities of the presentation coordinator:

I, the undersigned, _____, agree to take on the responsibility of being the *Presentation Coordinator*.

My duties will specifically include, but may not be limited to, the following:

1. I will be primarily responsible for synthesizing all the team's research and recommendations into a clear, complete, and appealing PowerPoint format.
2. I will allow adequate time for other team members to comment and proofread the PowerPoint presentation and make timely revisions as necessary.
3. I will come to class prepared with the above-mentioned PowerPoint presentations on a workable computer disk on *date.*
4. I will arrange for a practice presentation session as deemed necessary by a consensus of the members of the team.
5. All the preceding I will complete in a professional and ethical manner, adhering to my own, as well as this University's, code of ethical conduct.

Signed _____   Date _____

peer evaluations can assess each team member's contribution to the team's goals and give each student an opportunity for input. Student input is especially useful for teams that have had problems with free riders or other team problems (Bowes-Sperry, Kidder, Foley, & Chelte, 2005, p. 7). Other problems encountered by teams include attendance at team meetings or responsiveness to E-mails and phone calls. The peer evaluation also increases students' sense of accountability because they know their peers will evaluate them.

To be effective, peer evaluations should require the students to evaluate the performance of others in a professional manner. Studies have shown that peer evaluations improve student attitudes toward teamwork (Pfaff & Huddleston, 2003, p. 43). Peer evaluations can also reduce any perceived lack of unfairness and increase a sense of justice surrounding a team project (Bowes-Sperry et al., 2005, p. 4). In addition, research has shown that the use of peer evaluations can improve the relationship among teammates; more evenly apportion the workload and enhance the quality of results (Chen & Hao, 2004, p. 275; Cook, 1981, p. 50; Druskat & Wolff, 1999, p. 58).

Peer evaluations that are based on a team contract help team members to recognize that they are responsible for their assigned duties and accountable individually for productive collaboration as team members (Bryant & Albring, 2006, p. 251). This is important since peer evaluations provide a mechanism for partially determining grades to individuals within the team (Beatty et al., 1996, pp. 19–20).

Evaluation criteria for peer evaluations vary considerably and have centered on contributions and may include "what are perceived as reasonable expectations of any group member" (Beatty et al., 1996, p. 20). Table 3 contains an example peer evaluation form developed by the authors and used by multiple faculty and students across all levels of accounting courses.[1] Beatty et al. (1996, p. 22) and Bryant and Albring (2006, p. 255) provide additional examples of peer evaluation forms. Beatty et al. use a total of nine items on a separate form required for each team member evaluated. These nine items focus broadly on dependability and availability, input and work quality, and group equity, including the following items on a 7-point Lickert scale (Beatty et al., 1996, p. 22):

- Always attended meetings
- Available when needed
- High-quality ideas
- Dependable
- High-quality work
- Facilitated goal achievement
- Did more than their fair share
- Easy to work with
- Overall evaluation

Table 3. Peer Evaluation of Team Members Assessment Rubric.

Area (Points Possible)	Team Member A	Team Member B	Team Member C	Team Member D	Myself E
Attitude: (25)					
Positive outlook (5)					
Willingness to assume responsibilities (10)					
Ability to work with others (10)					
Attendance: (15)					
To planned meetings (10)					
To communications (5)					
Contributions: (60)					
Involvement during meetings (20)					
Preparation for meetings (20)					
Completion of assigned tasks (20)					
Total points (100 possible)					

Comments to support point allocations:

Bryant and Albring (2006, p. 255) provide a much simpler form using a single page for the entire team, asking for only a percentage rating of contribution for each team member and a place for comments. We believe both simplicity and structure are important. Accordingly, we chose an approach that couples a one-page form for the entire group (similar to Bryant and Albring's evaluation) with a detailed set of criteria (similar to Beatty et al.'s evaluation). Importantly, in our experience, additional structure is especially helpful with undergraduate students who may need more guidance in determining the relevant criteria for rating.

In addition to simplicity and structure, we do recognize, as Beatty et al. (1996, p. 19) suggests that, "no single set of criteria is universally accepted by all instructors or students." As a result, we believe it is important to capture student "attitudes" and we do so in a separate category. This "named factor" is idiosyncratic to our form, but appears to overlap considerably with some subcategories on Beatty et al.'s form (i.e., "willingness to assume responsibilities and ability to work with others").

Our peer evaluation, which appears in Table 3, balances the simplicity of Bryant and Albring's peer evaluation and the intricacy of Beatty et al.'s peer evaluation. That is, our peer evaluation is more comprehensive than Bryant and Albring's. At the same time, in contrast to Beatty et al.'s, it does not require students to make an evaluation – that we believe may be inappropriate for students to make – of the overall quality of each team member's work. Instead, the peer evaluation in Table 3 focuses on team members' inputs that do not require the expertise needed to evaluate the "quality" of other team members' work.

Point Allocation

There is no clear guidance or consensus in the literature on point allocation for peer evaluations. In fact, the peer evaluation information can be used either qualitatively or quantitatively. Beatty et al. (1996, p. 26) acknowledge that with respect to point allocation, there are "no hard and fast rules" that apply. Beatty et al. propose a weighting of at least 25% to achieve a clear distinction in team and individual grades. If the point allocation is too high, students may be reluctant to negatively impact the grade of their peers. If the point allocation is too low, the peer scores will be viewed as unimportant. In the past, we have used the peer evaluations quantitatively, assigning approximately 10% of the points for the team assignment to the total peer score. Although this weighting contradicts the recommendation by Beatty et al. (1996, p. 26) of "at least 25%," instructors often prefer to provide a lower weighting such as this in an attempt to place more emphasis on the team and less on the individual. The risk, of course, is that 10% may admittedly be too low for students to view the peer evaluation as salient, as suggested by Beatty et al. (1996, p. 26). We encourage faculty members to modify the point allocation based on results and their own preferences for teamwork emphasis versus team member accountability. Students should be given a copy of the peer evaluation form in advance and be informed as to how it will be used, so that the evaluation criteria can be clearly understood.

Description of Factors

The description of the factors that comprise the peer scores was developed on the basis of the authors' prior experience with teams and team interactions. These descriptions are how we operationalized these terms in the peer evaluations and are generally consistent with the other peer evaluation forms cited earlier. Because these are the items on which they are evaluated, the students are provided with a description of each factor in an attempt to clarify the criteria and to ensure a common understanding by the students. Attitude, attendance, and contributions comprise the major categories and are described as follows.

A team member's *attitude* includes a *positive outlook* and commitment to the project. Attitude includes overall disposition toward assuming the duties required by the project. Thus, a team member should have a *willingness to assume responsibilities*. Willingness is expressed primarily by the individual's voluntarily effort to help in areas for which they have been designated as responsible as well as assuming joint responsibility for the project overall. A team member should also exhibit the *ability to work with others*. Working with others includes the individual's willingness to collaborate with all members of the group. This includes listening to alternative points of view and respectfully considering the ideas of other teammates. If necessary, this attitude suggests the willingness to resolve conflicts in a mature and productive manner while supporting the achievement of overall team results.

A team member's *attendance* is imperative for the team to function effectively. Attendance includes *attending planned team meetings and scheduled events*. Attendance means being on time and present during project team meetings and at graded events such as a presentation of results or discussions involving the instructor. Also included in attendance is *responsiveness to E-mail and/or phone calls* in a cooperative and timely fashion. Team efforts typically require extensive communication and coordination, thus individuals must be available and responsive to communication with each other. In our experience, inadequate availability and lack of communication are the great banes of effective teamwork. In some environments where it is particularly difficult for students to meet their team members outside of class, instructors may want to consider allocating some class time for teams to meet. Students always appreciate this approach, and this allows the instructor to be present to answer questions and provide additional guidance and clarity to the teams during team discussion.

Contributions include team member involvement in discussion *during the team meetings* to reach consensus on relevant issues. Contributions also include individual preparation for the meetings including an *individual's effort to understand the material and prepare ahead of time* to help the team progress to the completion of the project. Adequate contributions should ultimately be evaluated based on the *completion of the task assigned* per the signed contract. This should include evidence that an adequate effort was made toward completion in an effective and timely manner to attain a high-quality result. In some cases, as the assignment develops and the team achieves a better understanding of required tasks, the team contract may need to be amended. In this event, revisiting the contract for amending individual requirements must be based on a consensual agreement of the members and must be well documented. It almost goes without saying, but any amendments of the team contract should be completed before administering the peer evaluation.

Justification of Evaluation and Self-Scoring

In addition to completing the point allocation on the peer evaluation rubric, the peer evaluator must justify the score assigned to each team member in writing. It is expected that each evaluator will provide a paragraph or two supporting the points assigned in the evaluation. If the evaluation is cursory, the evaluator's grade is penalized for doing an inadequate job. A cursory evaluation is one in which all team members are assigned the same score without justification and/or there is no written support of the assigned scores.

The peer evaluations are due on the next class day after the project due date.[2] Extending the due date of the peer evaluation after the date of the presentation or assignment gives the evaluator time to reflect on how well things went on the day the assignment was due. Dommeyer (2006, p. 24) found that completion of the peer review outside of class resulted in more objective evaluations that included more feedback on open-ended questions. We also believe that completing the evaluation outside of the classroom may put the student more at ease and ensure ample time for reflection is provided for their feedback.

Requiring evaluators to evaluate themselves as well as their teammates forces them to reflect on their own performance relative to the performance of their peers (Haas, Haas, & Wotruba, 1998, pp. 201–202). Overall, prior studies, including Haas et al. (1998, pp. 205–206), found that self-ratings tend to be higher than peer ratings and that males tend to evaluate their own performance more favorably than females. This observation indicates that students often overestimate their own contribution to a team project. Students in general evaluate their own performance significantly differently from how their peers evaluate them, indicating a greater need for self-awareness. For example, some students who are rated as under-performers by their peers may rate themselves much higher. These students are not aware of (or choose to ignore) their lack of performance relative to their peers. Other students who are rated very highly by their peers may rate themselves lower because their internal expectations are very high, or they may be modest. Often the students in the latter group could benefit from increased confidence in themselves. See Smith (2001, pp. 674–676) for a discussion on how self-awareness can be developed to aid learning.

Scoring Peer Evaluations

Peer evaluators can be anonymous or known to those being evaluated. There are pros and cons for anonymity. If the evaluations are anonymous, the student knows only the average peer score assigned to them, not the individual scores. The benefit of true anonymity is that there will be no hard feelings that may carryover if students have to work together on other assignments. We have used anonymous peer scoring for teams of 4–6 students. However, in smaller teams (i.e., 3 students), it may be difficult for the evaluator to be truly anonymous. An obvious motivation for anonymity is to encourage the evaluators to feel comfortable with providing honest feedback, especially negative concerns. An objective of peer evaluation is for the students to learn how to give constructive feedback while supporting their evaluations with facts. If the evaluator does not provide support for their point allocations, the evaluator's score should be penalized. For instance, we assess a 10% penalty upon the average peer evaluation grade of students who fail to provide support for their evaluations.

Table 4 contains an example grid that can be used to summarize peer scores. In the example, Student A allocated points to students A through E at 95, 83, 86, 100, and 94, respectively. Student A received an average score of 96.8. The student's self-evaluation may be included or excluded from the average scores. In this example, the student's self-evaluation is included in the average score. Deeter-Schmelz and Ramsey (1998, p. 88) suggest that a high standard deviation among raters may be an indication of problems with the team dynamics. Although high standard deviations may be one

Table 4.   Example Scoring of Peer Evaluation Rubric.

Points allocated by student → Points allocated to student ↓	A	B	C	D	E	Average
A	95	89	100	100	100	96.8
B	83	93	100	90	70	87.2
C	86	83	100	80	80	82.3−10 = 72.3
D	100	91	100	100	100	98.2
E	94	91	100	100	100	97

indication of problems, we have not examined standard deviations with our use of peer evaluations since we use peer evaluations in a single project (versus repeated or multiple projects).

There may be situations where it may be desirable to choose to calculate a student's average peer score by excluding their own score such as with student C in our example. Student C gave everyone a 100. However, the other team members rated this student consistently with one of the lowest scores. Student C also gave every team member a 100 and provided no written reasons for the allocation. Student C's self-score was not deemed valid. Additionally, student C was penalized 10% because the student's evaluation showed no discretion or thought to the evaluation process. The other students supported their point allocation to their teammates with written comments. In terms of a letter-grade scale, this group provided peer evaluations (after adjustment) that resulted in 3As (student A, D, and E), one B (student B), and one C (student C) for its members. The 10 points allocated to the peer evaluation was part of the 100 points for the team project and therefore was 10% of the project grade.

DISCUSSION AND CONCLUSIONS

During several years of using team contracts and peer evaluations, we have found these tools to be helpful on the whole in encouraging students to take ownership of team tasks and in helping to clarify and structure necessary tasks involved with the various dimensions of teamwork. To assist other faculty who may wish to use these tools, we conclude with a discussion of our experiences and describe the perceptions and comments of students as depicted by a convenience survey taken at the conclusion of the most recent

Table 5. Undergraduate Convenience Survey Means $(N = 15)$[a].

		Means
1.	The use of team contracts increased my sense of responsibility to the team	4.13
2.	The use of team contracts increased team members' overall sense of responsibility to the team	4.13
3.	My performance was improved because of the team contract	3.73
4.	My team's performance was improved because of the team contract	4.07
5.	My satisfaction with the team project was improved because of the team contract	3.87
6.	The team contract increased my sense of accountability to the team	4.13
7.	The following features of teamwork were enhanced by using the team contract	
	Fairness of team process	4.40
	Fairness of team results	4.20
	Sense of overall commitment	4.27
	Task-specific commitment	4.33
	Clarity of expectations	4.47
	Overall effectiveness	4.53
8.	The use of peer evaluations increased my sense of responsibility to the team	4.22
9.	The use of peer evaluations increased team members' sense of responsibility to the team	4.33
10.	My performance was improved because of the peer evaluation	3.33
11.	My team's performance was improved because of the peer evaluation	3.67
12.	My satisfaction with the team project was improved because of the peer evaluation	4.11
13.	The peer evaluation increased my sense of accountability to the team	3.78
14.	The following features of teamwork were enhanced by using peer evaluations	
	Fairness of team process	4.11
	Fairness of team results	4.22
	Sense of overall commitment	4.44
	Task-specific commitment	4.11
	Clarity of expectations	4.11
	Overall effectiveness	4.22

[a]Based on a fully anchored Lickert scale, where 1 = strongly disagree, 2 = moderately disagree, 3 = neutral, 4 = moderately agree, and 5 = strongly agree.

semester. Responses were obtained separately from students in an advanced undergraduate financial accounting course as well as graduate financial accounting students in a Master of Accounting Science (MAS) course. The quantitative results can be found in Table 5 (reflecting undergraduate student responses) and Table 6 (reflecting graduate student responses).

We would encourage readers to examine the data from the two tables in a comparative fashion in an effort to determine the likely differences between using these tools in undergraduate versus graduate classes. According to the

Table 6.   Graduate Convenience Survey Means ($N = 32$)[a].

		Means
1.	The use of team contracts increased my sense of responsibility to the team	3.16
2.	The use of team contracts increased team members' overall sense of responsibility to the team	3.13
3.	My performance was improved because of the team contract	2.44
4.	My team's performance was improved because of the team contract	2.75
5.	My satisfaction with the team project was improved because of the team contract	2.75
6.	The team contract increased my sense of accountability to the team	3.03
7.	The following features of teamwork were enhanced by using the team contract	
	Fairness of team process	3.16
	Fairness of team results	3.09
	Sense of overall commitment	3.31
	Task-specific commitment	3.28
	Clarity of expectations	3.41
	Overall effectiveness	3.09
8.	The use of peer evaluations increased my sense of responsibility to the team	3.68
9.	The use of peer evaluations increased team members' sense of responsibility to the team	3.61
10.	My performance was improved because of the peer evaluation	3.32
11.	My team's performance was improved because of the peer evaluation	3.26
12.	My satisfaction with the team project was improved because of the peer evaluation	3.10
13.	The peer evaluation increased my sense of accountability to the team	3.61
14.	The following features of teamwork were enhanced by using peer evaluations:	
	Fairness of team process	3.71
	Fairness of team results	3.65
	Sense of overall commitment	3.55
	Task-specific commitment	3.48
	Clarity of expectations	3.35
	Overall effectiveness	3.61

[a]Based on a fully anchored Lickert scale, where 1 = strongly disagree, 2 = moderately disagree, 3 = neutral, 4 = moderately agree, and 5 = strongly agree.

data, the undergraduate student respondents perceived the two tools to be more useful than did the graduate student respondents. This appears to be the clearest message to glean from the data. We asked the respondents to measure their perceptions along several dimensions of benefits that may have accrued to the two groups as a result of using the two tools including sense of responsibility and accountability, performance, satisfaction, fairness, task specific commitment, clarity, and overall effectiveness. Both groups found the tools to be beneficial on the margin. However, regardless of the dimension, undergraduates consistently found the team contracts and peer evaluations to be more beneficial than did the graduate students.

Within the graduate student responses (Table 6), there was a slightly higher rating of the perceived usefulness of the peer evaluations (items 8–14) than the perceived usefulness of the team contracts (items 1–7), which was an effect that appeared to be consistent with the written comments provided by the students. This effect was slightly reversed for the undergraduate students per the data in Table 5.[3]

The quantitative data appeared to be consistent with additional feedback supplied by the respondents as well. Undergraduate students provided the following statements in response to the request for other comments on the use of team contracts:

- I would imagine [the team contract] would be very useful when dealing with team members who aren't doing their work, but for good teams it doesn't change much.
- [Team contracts] did help us in setting a timeline of what we wanted to accomplish and when.
- [Team contracts] helped to cement our roles in the team.
- I think [team contracts] helped reassure myself [sic] that other members would put effort in and it ensured no one is free riding.
- Everyone knew that peer evaluations will go back to the teacher, and this reason helped everyone do their best.

Graduate students provided the following comments:

- Overall, our commitment to each other kept us in line more than the contract. That said, I do believe that team contracts can be beneficial, especially when team members are unfamiliar with each other.
- The evaluation has more use than the contract. I've never had to use a contract before and found it to be useless busy work for this project.
- I don't really think the team contract had much impact on the project. The peer evaluation might have had a little bit of impact.
- I was most satisfied with the peer evaluation, not so much the team contract.
- Peer evaluations are always helpful.
- Peer evaluations are a great way for members to share if they had a bad member.
- Peer evaluation is good.
- The peer evaluation made me want to work with other team members with much dedication.

• Peer evaluations are very common but still very effective. Contracts are unnecessary.

Undergraduate respondent comments clearly seemed to reflect perceptions that the team contracts provide benefits, and this is especially true for teams who may have had problems. Graduate student perceptions as reflected in the comments clearly indicate a higher regard for the use of peer evaluations than for team contracts.[4] This result appears consistent with the means in Tables 5 and 6. The comments revealed that these tools seemed to be perceived as working best to prevent problems or where a group was at risk of dysfunctional behavior. This was a result that was not captured by the quantitative data and a situation that was perhaps more likely to be encountered by undergraduate teams.

In conclusion, at their worst, team contracts may be duplicitous or unnecessary for adding structure and encouraging responsibility for team tasks where students are more advanced (e.g., graduate students) or where the students are otherwise intrinsically motivated. From our view, this finding does not greatly distract from using team contracts – even for graduate students. However, given the differences between undergraduate and graduates, instructors may find team contracts unnecessary for graduate courses. In general, this same observation is also true for peer evaluations, although they were incrementally perceived as more useful on the whole to graduate students than were team contracts. For undergraduate students, team contracts appear useful in adding structure, clarifying tasks, and instilling a sense of responsibility by requiring the students to sign their name to a contract and be accountable for their responsibilities to the team. Our view is that undergraduates tend to be more uncomfortable with unstructured tasks than graduate students and also tend to be less intrinsically motivated. Thus, the use of team contracts can be especially useful in the undergraduate context.

Peer evaluations encourage students to objectively and thoughtfully evaluate the contributions of themselves and others to the team results. From the survey comments examined, we find this observation to be true at both the undergraduate and the graduate levels. Graduate students, not surprisingly, often mentioned that the peer evaluations were more useful than the team contracts in motivating effort and clarifying roles.

We see the downside risk of using these tools as very low and feel that the use of team contracts and peer evaluations has not added significant time demands for the instructor. In fact, we feel that using these tools has reduced the amount of refereeing we have had to do to resolve team conflicts. Incremental time requirements for the peer evaluations involve only entering data for scoring using an excel spreadsheet.[5]

Use of peer evaluations and team contracts has benefits and limitations. The benefits are to build a stronger bond and a more corroborative team relationship. However, there are inherent limitations that this chapter does not address. There is the issue of the optimal way to incorporate the peer score into the students' grades. A suggestion for future research would be to ask students about their perception of the percentage allocation to the peer evaluation to determine whether the points allocated to the peer component are adequate to modify behavior. There is also the issue of the impact of using team contracts and peer evaluations during multiple projects throughout the semester or in different courses. A suggestion for future study may be to see whether there is a differential impact on the team performance and/or student perception if team contracts and peer evaluations are used repeatedly in a single course or across courses in the curriculum.

NOTES

1. The peer evaluation form presented in Table 3 is the culmination of input from many students and faculty over a 5-year period. Therefore, the credit for the evaluation form belongs to many individuals who added to its usefulness. Also, the authors do not purport that the peer evaluation has statistical validity and/or reliability. Only anecdotal evidence of the effectiveness and usefulness of this instrument has been obtained from other faculty and students.

2. In our experience, it is more effective to not allow late submissions versus serving a penalty for late submissions. Non-acceptance seems to be a strong deterrent for late submissions.

3. The reader should note that the difference between the means presented may not be statistically significant. Since the difference is derived from a convenience sample involving a very small number of students, we did not calculate a formal statistical analysis for the results presented. Thus, any conclusions presented should be interpreted in light of this limitation.

4. We did not test to see whether the graduate students had used team contracts or peer evaluations as undergraduates. This, perhaps, could have influenced their responses.

5. See Sherwood and DePaolo (2007, pp. 109–120) for discussion of a web-based software to complete the scoring of peer evaluations.

ACKNOWLEDGMENTS

The authors are indebted to numerous graduate and undergraduate students and fellow faculty members at Northern Illinois University for their contributions to the development of these instructional materials. We specifically acknowledge Anita Pedapati for her thoughtful insights on how to evaluate peers. We are also indebted to the participants at the 2005 Colloquium on Change in Accounting Education for helpful insights and feedback and to the editor and two anonymous reviewers at *Advances in Accounting Education.*

REFERENCES

Albrecht, W. S., & Sack, R. (2000). *Accounting education: Charting the course through a perilous future.* Accounting Education Series Vol. 16. Sarasota, FL: American Accounting Association.

Apostolou, B., Watson, S., Hassell, J., & Webber, S. (2001). Accounting education literature review (1997–1999). *Journal of Accounting Education, 19*(1), 1–61.

Association to Advance Collegiate Schools of Business (AACSB). (2007). *Eligibility procedures and accreditation standards for business accreditation.* AACBS: Tampa, FL.

Balkcom, S. (1992). Cooperative learning. *Education research consumer guide.* Office of Research, Office of Educational Research and Improvement of the U.S. Department of Education, June, ED/ OERI 92-38. Available at http://www.ed.gov/pubs/OR/ ConsumerGuides/cooplear.html. Retrieved on September 9, 2008.

Beatty, J. R., Haas, R., & Sciglimpaglia, D. (1996). Using peer evaluation to assess individual performances in group class projects. *Journal of Marketing Education, 18*(2), 17–27.

Bowes-Sperry, L., Kidder, D., Foley, S., & Chelte, A. (2005). The effect of peer evaluations on student reports of learning in a team environment: A procedural justice perspective. *Journal of Behavioral & Applied Management, 7*(1), 4–24.

Bryant, S., & Albring, S. (2006). Effective team building: Guidance for accounting educators. *Issues in Accounting Education, 21*(3), 241–265.

Chen, Y., & Hao, L. (2004). Students' perceptions of peer evaluation: An expectancy perspective. *Journal of Education for Business, 79,* 275–282.

Clinton, B. D., & Kohlmeyer, J. M., III. (2005). The effects of group quizzes on performance and motivation to learn: Two experiments in cooperative learning. *Journal of Accounting Education, 23*(2), 96–116.

Cook, R. W. (1981). An investigation of student peer evaluation on group project performance. *Journal of Marketing Education, 3*(1), 50–52.

Deeter-Schmelz, D., & Ramsey, R. (1998). Student team performance: A method for classroom assessment. *Journal of Marketing Education, 20*(2), 85–93.

Dommeyer, C. J. (2006). The effect of evaluation location on peer evaluations. *Journal of Education for Business, 82*(1), 21–26.

Druskat, V. U., & Wolff, S. (1999). Effects and timing of developmental peer appraisals in self-managing work groups. *Journal of Applied Psychology, 84*(1), 58–74.

Greenberg, J. (1996). *Managing behavior in organizations.* Upper Saddle River, NJ: Prentice Hall.

Haas, A. L., Haas, R. W., & Wotruba, T. R. (1998). The use of self-ratings and peer ratings to evaluate performances of student group members. *Journal of Marketing Education, 20*(3), 200–209.

Hite, P. A. (1996). An experimental study of the effectiveness of group exams in an individual income tax class. *Issues in Accounting Education, 11*(1), 61–75.

Katzenbach, J., & Smith, D. (1999). *The wisdom of teams: Creating the high performance organization.* New York, NY: HarperCollins Publishers, Inc.

Millis, B., & Cottell, P. (1998). *Cooperative learning for higher education faculty.* (American council on education Oryx Press series on higher education). Phoenix, AZ: Oryx Press.

Pfaff, E., & Huddleston, P. (2003). Does it matter if I hate teamwork? What impacts student attitudes toward teamwork. *Journal of Marketing Education, 25*(1), 37–45.

Sherwood, A. L., & DePaolo, C. A. (2007). Student peer evaluations in business education: A web-based administration. *Academy of Educational Leadership Journal, 11*(1), 109–120.

Smith, P. A. (2001). Understanding self-regulated learning and its implications for accounting educators and researchers. *Issues in Accounting Education, 16*(4), 663–700.

Wysocki, R. (2002). *Building effective project teams.* New York: Wiley.

FACTORS AFFECTING INITIAL PLACEMENT OF ACCOUNTING PH.Ds

William W. Stammerjohan, Deborah L. Seifert and Ronald P. Guidry

ABSTRACT

The perceived prestige of the doctoral degree granting institution traditionally has had a major effect on job opportunities available to a new accounting Ph.D. However, given recent shortages of accounting academics, the role of program prestige may have changed. It is possible that individual factors also may now play a role in the initial placement decision. This study examines the effects of both doctoral program prestige and individual factors on the initial placement decision.

While our results indicate that doctoral program prestige still largely dictates the initial placement decision, several other factors are found to be important. New graduates initially placed at higher level institutions report faculty involvement during the application process as well as significant research support by the hiring institution. New faculty placing lower than expected report the mix of teaching and research as well as the quality of life as being significant factors in their employment decision.

Advances in Accounting Education: Teaching and Curriculum Innovations, Volume 10, 103–118
Copyright © 2009 by Emerald Group Publishing Limited
ISSN: 1085-4622/doi:10.1108/S1085-4622(2009)0000010007

Universities that hire new accounting Ph.Ds often cite the tradeoff between hiring the "best athlete" or the "best fit" (Rittenberg, 1998; Mukherji, 1998). Similarly, new accounting Ph.Ds must decide whether to pursue employment with the highest-ranked university possible or to look for a position that best fits one's individual lifestyle. Not surprisingly, doctoral programs want their graduates to place at similar or higher ranked universities to build their reputation and perceived prestige (Fogarty & Ruhl, 1997; Fogarty & Saftner, 1993). Given the current shortage of new accounting Ph.Ds (AAA/AAPLG, 2005; Plumlee, Kachelmeier, Madeo, Pratt, & Krull, 2006), understanding the factors affecting a doctoral student's acceptance of an initial academic position is important. Doctoral program administrators will want to monitor individual factors that might cause their graduates to select a less prestigious placement. Hiring institutions will be interested in any lifestyle factors that might give them a competitive edge in attracting new faculty.

This study examines how both doctoral program prestige and individual factors affect the initial placement decision. We find that doctoral program prestige still largely dictates the initial placement decision. However, several other factors also appear to play a role. Graduates whose faculty send cover letters with their position applications or whose faculty make phone calls on their behalf are placed at higher level institutions. Additionally, higher placed graduates reported receiving extensive other faculty support. Higher placing individuals also indicated receipt of significant research support from their new employer. In contrast, lower placing graduates reported inadequate faculty support. However, for this group, the mix of teaching and research and the quality of life were important factors.

The remainder of this chapter is organized as follows. Next, we develop our research hypotheses. This is followed by a discussion of our research method and variable selection. We then report our results, describe several limitations of the study, and present our conclusions.

RESEARCH HYPOTHESES

The Role of Prestige

We examine doctoral student placements between 1990 and 2001, a period during which the market for new accounting Ph.Ds reversed from a surplus to a shortage position. To determine whether prestige is still a major factor in doctoral student placement, we retest the following hypothesis from Fogarty and Ruhl (1997, p. 31):

H₁. Graduates of higher-status accounting doctoral programs tend to obtain initial faculty positions in higher-status accounting departments.

Individual Factors Affecting Placement

Kida and Mannino (1980) surveyed Ph.D students, faculty at doctoral granting schools, and some faculty from non-doctoral granting institutions. They found that being able to interact effectively with colleagues and the department chair were the most important factors affecting placement. They also found tenure requirements to be important, and research support was significant to those at doctoral granting institutions.

Holland and Arrington (1987) interviewed relocating rather than new faculty. They found that spousal and family happiness, quality of life, and geographic location were the most significant placement factors for faculty relocating to a non-doctoral granting institution. Those moving to a doctoral granting school had more concerns about salary, the department head, and research support.

Eaton and Hunt (2002) examined both new and relocating faculty. They found that teaching load, compatibility with other faculty, and spousal approval of the area were important to both new and relocating faculty, regardless of whether they were joining doctoral or non-doctoral granting institutions. Research support, library facilities, and travel were more important to faculty selecting doctoral granting schools. Geographic location was more important for those taking a position at a non-doctoral granting institution. Promotion and tenure requirements were important to all new faculty, but more so to those at non-doctoral granting schools.

Prior research has not combined the analyses of individual factors with doctoral degree granting program prestige. Therefore, we offer and test the following hypothesis in this study:

H₂. Individual factors will impact the initial placement decision of some new accounting Ph.Ds after controlling for degree granting institution prestige.

RESEARCH METHOD

Sample

Our target population included 1,357 U.S. accounting doctoral program students who met the following criteria: (1) graduated between 1990 and 2001; (2) had initial placement information in Hasselback (1990–2000) and/or Hasselback (2002); (3) started their initial tenure track positions with U.S. institutions, other than their degree granting institutions, within 2 years of graduation (Stammerjohan & Hall, 2002); and (4) had contact information in Hasselback (2002).

We surveyed the target population in two phases. First, we e-mailed each of them an attachment with a web-based version of our survey instrument. This yielded 281 responses (net first e-mail). In the second phase, we attempted to contact the non-respondents by telephone. When contacted we asked each graduate to either respond while on the phone or to complete the web-based survey. This approached generated 123 usable phone responses (net phone call responses) and 28 usable e-mail responses (net second e-mail responses).

Although our survey response rate is only 32 percent, additional analysis indicates that the survey is representative of the target population. For example, the target population (sample survey) includes graduates from 104 (80) degree granting institutions that were initially placed at 473(256) different institutions. Additionally, the target population includes graduates of all 80 degree granting institutions included in Stammerjohan and Hall (2002), while the survey sample includes graduates from 74 of these programs.

Variable Selection

Institutional Prestige

Measuring perceived institution prestige can be a difficult prospect (Fogarty & Saftner, 1993). Several studies have asked subjects about the quality of an accounting program without defining "quality" (Estes, 1970). Other measures have experienced methodological problems such as unrepresentative samples, individual biasing effects, temporal changes, and confounding institutional factors (Rhode & Zeff, 1970; Morton, 1975; Fairweather, 1988).

Other measures of prestige have used publication counts (Bazley & Nikolai, 1975; Andrews & McKenzie, 1978; Windal, 1981; Dyckman & Zeff, 1984; Hagerman & Hagerman, 1989), citation analyses (Brown & Gardner, 1985), or the tallying of editorial board institutional affiliation (Mittermaier, 1991). However, these measures are not without error either (Blair, Cottic, & Wallace, 1986).

Stammerjohan and Hall (2002) developed a more precise ranking of initial placement institutions that relies on *Best Colleges* data and regression analysis to create a single score. Since the current study examines doctoral student placement at all institutions, our study relies on this metric as well as the Hasselback and Reinstein (1995) publication count measure.

We obtained our prestige variables from Hasselback (1990–2000), Hasselback (2002), Hasselback and Reinstein (1995), Stammerjohan and Hall (2002), and U.S. News & World Report (1997) (hereafter *Best Colleges*). The detailed descriptions of our variables follow and is summarized in Table 1.

We use two placement metrics (BCS and HRS) to assess the prestige level of each initial placement institution. The BCS score is our general placement level measure, based on the method developed by Stammerjohan and Hall (2002). They converted the rankings and information reported in *Best Colleges* into numerical scores and used regression analysis to create a single set of scores that cover the entire spectrum of national, regional, specialty, and liberal arts colleges and universities. In addition to the *Best Colleges* ranking itself, their model specifically considers such factors as ACT score, freshman acceptance rate, educational spending per student, freshman retention rate, graduation rate, and alumni giving rate. While the Stammerjohan and Hall (2002) method assigns low numerical scores to higher level institutions, we use linear transformations to assign higher numerical scores to higher level institutions to facilitate interpretation of our findings. These transformations do not affect our results. Finally, we assume that doctoral program graduates prefer employment at institutions with higher BCS scores.

We measure research productivity for each initial placement institution in our study using the HRS score. It is a research productivity decile based on the average number of quality-weighted sole-authored articles per faculty member reported by Hasselback and Reinstein (1995). We assign an HRS score of one to institutions with zero publications and an HRS score of ten to the institutions with the most publications. We exclude institutions not included in Hasselback and Reinstein (1995) from our HRS analyses. Again, we assume that doctoral program graduates prefer employment at more research productive institutions.

Table 1. Variable Definitions.

Measure	Definition
Prestige	
BCS	Stammerjohan and Hall (2002)-based initial placement institution *Best College* score. In addition to the *Best Colleges* ranking itself, it captures factors such as ACT score, freshman acceptance rate, educational spending per student, freshman retention rate, graduation rate, and alumni giving rate
HRS	Hasselback and Reinstein (1995)-based initial placement institution weighted average publication score
DGPHS	Controls for the effects of degree granting institution placement history
DGHRS	Controls for the effects of degree granting institution research productivity level
CHBCS	The difference in Stammerjohan and Hall (2002)-based *Best College* scores between the current institution and initial placement institution for those graduates who changed institutions during our sample period
CHHRS	The difference in Hasselback and Reinstein (1995)-based weighted average publication scores between the current institution and initial placement institution for graduates who changed institutions during our sample period
Individual factors	
ABD	One if the graduate started his or her first tenure track position 1 or 2 years before graduation, zero otherwise
CHANGE	One if the graduate changed institutions, zero otherwise
COVER	One if the graduate's applications were sent under a faculty cover letter, zero otherwise
PHONE	One if the graduate's faculty placed phone calls on behalf of his or her job search, zero otherwise
LETTERS	One if the graduate's faculty either provided cover letters or letters of recommendation in support of his or her job search, zero otherwise
SUBMIT	One if the graduate submitted a resume to the AAA Annual Meeting Placement Center, zero otherwise

We also control for the effects of degree granting institution placement history (DGPHS) and degree granting institution research productivity level (DGHRS). The DGPHS score is based on a weighted average ranking reported by Stammerjohan and Hall (2002, pp. 9–10). We assigned degree granting institutions with weighted average rankings between 61 and 80 a DGPHS score of one. Scores of two, three, and four represent weighted average ranks of 41–60, 21–40, and 1–20 respectively. For degree granting institutions not ranked by Stammerjohan and Hall, we used a DGPHS score of zero to report summary statistics, but excluded them from analyses that include placement history as an explanatory variable.

Similar to the HRS metric, DGHRS scores are based on the average number of quality-weighted sole-authored publications per faculty member reported by Hasselback and Reinstein (1995). We assign DGHRS scores by quartiles where a score of one is assigned to a degree granting institution ranked in the lowest quartile, and a score of four is assigned to degree granting institutions ranked in the highest quartile.

Individual Doctoral Student Factors
We capture individual doctoral candidate information on those who started their first tenure track position at least 1 year before graduation using the ABD indicator variable. ABD is one when the graduates started their first tenure track position at least 1 year before graduation and zero otherwise. We also identify those doctoral students that change institutions after their initial selection using the CHANGE indicator variable (one for a change, zero otherwise). We document the types of faculty support offered to graduates seeking an initial academic appointment using indicator variables as well. COVER is one when the graduate's applications were sent under a faculty cover letter and zero otherwise. PHONE is a one if faculty members made phone calls in support of the graduate's application process and zero otherwise. LETTERS is one if faculty members sent either cover letters and/ or letters of recommendation in support of the graduate's application process and zero otherwise. Finally, the SUBMIT indicator variable is one if the graduate submitted a resume to the American Accounting Association (AAA) Annual Meeting Placement Center and zero otherwise.

Methodology

We test our hypotheses using two sets of ordinary least squares (OLS) regressions. The first set, our *placement level regressions*, explore the significant factors that influence the level of placement after controlling for placement history (DGPHS) and research productivity (prestige) of the degree granting institution (DGHRS). Since DGPHS and DGHRS are highly correlated, we do not include both variables in the same regressions.

Our *change of institution regressions* explore the significant factors that influence whether a graduate changed positions during our sample period (CHANGE) and the difference in the levels between the current and initial placement institutions (CHBCS, CHHRS).

RESULTS

Descriptive Analysis

We report target population means in Table 2 by whether graduates changed institutions, by whether graduates started their first tenure track position at least 1 year before graduation (ABD), and by graduation year. Research sample means appear consistent with those of the target population. Graduates initially placed at more research productive institutions (HRS) appear more likely to have changed institutions. Additionally, doctoral student graduates who started their first tenure track position at least 1 year before graduation (ABD) were more likely to change institutions.

In later years, graduates selected higher level institutions, as measured by the BCS scores, and slightly more research productive institutions, as measured by the HRS scores. While we expected the percentage of graduates changing institutions (CHANGE) to significantly decline in later years

Table 2.   Target Population Means.

	Number	BCS	HRS	CHANGE	ABD
Mean	1,357	6.756	5.457	0.286	0.291
Median	1,357	6.474	5.000	0.000	0.000
Graduate not surveyed	925	6.772	5.403	0.291	0.298
Sample	432	6.721	5.570	0.278	0.275
No institution change	968	6.747	5.289	0.000	0.264
Institution change	389	6.779	5.872	1.000	0.357
Not ABD	962	6.778	5.542	0.260	0.000
ABD	395	6.704	5.252	0.352	1.000
Graduation year					
1990	115	6.941	5.841	0.417	0.409
1991	133	6.184	5.093	0.429	0.286
1992	126	6.755	5.492	0.365	0.413
1993	130	6.353	4.783	0.415	0.346
1994	137	6.580	5.370	0.431	0.343
1995	127	6.755	5.413	0.417	0.291
1996	111	6.836	6.566	0.351	0.279
1997	119	6.465	4.982	0.202	0.261
1998	131	6.851	5.537	0.061	0.176
1999	102	7.360	5.918	0.000	0.176
2000	84	7.380	6.475	0.012	0.179
2001	42	7.475	5.561	0.000	0.262

Note: See Table 1 for variable definitions.

because they should have not had time to change institutions, it is interesting that the percentage of graduates starting their first tenure track position at least 1 year before graduation also declined in the later years (ABD). This suggests that doctoral candidates may be seeing ABD status as a hindrance to meeting the increased tenure requirements at most institutions.

Placement Level Regressions

Table 3 summarizes our placement level regression results. The dependent variables are the two initial placement institution prestige metrics: the BCS score and the HRS measure. Our regression sample included only 374 observations with the DGPHS variable and 381 with the DHHRS variable. All four regressions are highly significant as indicated by the F-statistics and corresponding p-values. The adjusted R^2s range from 0.215 to 0.305. As expected, graduates from degree granting institutions with higher placement history and research productivity scores (DGPHS, DGHRS) are initially placed at higher level institutions (BCS and HRS). Therefore, Hypothesis 1 is supported. Consistent with expectations, all four regressions reflect the positive influence of faculty cover letters (COVER), and at least the marginally positive influence of phone calls (PHONE). Only the HRS regressions indicate that ABD status negatively affects initial placement. Finally, the results suggest that submitting resumes to the AAA Annual Meeting Placement Center does not yield placement at the more prestigious institutions.

Change of Institution Regressions

We report the change of institution regression results in Table 4. The three dependent variables in these regressions are whether graduates changed institutions during our sample period (CHANGE), the difference in *Best College* scores between the current and initial placement institutions (CHBCS), and the difference in research productivity scores between the current and initial placement institutions (CHHRS).

Logistic Regressions
As expected, earlier graduates in target population (graduation year) are much more likely to have changed institutions (CHANGE). Graduates of degree granting institutions with higher placement history scores (DGPHS) and graduates initially placed at more research productive institutions

Table 3.   Placement Level Regressions.

Variable	Expected Sign	BCS		HRS	
Intercept	No prediction	4.3916 12.62 0.0001	4.8205 13.97 0.0001	2.5857 6.75 0.0001	3.2097 8.33 0.0001
DGPHS	+	0.9089 7.73 0.0001		1.0672 8.24 0.0001	
DGHRS	+		0.6864 6.40 0.0001		0.7620 6.37 0.0001
SUBMIT	No prediction	−0.6368 −2.78 0.0057	−0.8834 −3.93 0.0001	−0.5788 −2.30 0.0223	−0.9329 −3.72 0.0002
COVER	+	0.4677 2.02 0.0220	0.5348 2.26 0.0122	0.4334 1.70 0.0449	0.5208 1.97 0.0247
PHONE	+	0.2632 1.20 0.1148	0.3285 1.48 0.0694	1.0286 4.27 0.0001	1.1021 4.46 0.0001
ABD	−	0.0423 0.18 0.5716	−0.0537 −0.22 0.4113	−0.3884 −1.50 0.0666	−0.5006 −1.87 0.0310
Observations		374	381	374	381
Adjusted R^2		0.252	0.215	0.305	0.256
F-Statistic		26.10	21.84	33.67	27.15
$p<$		0.0001	0.0001	0.0001	0.0001

Notes: See Table 1 for variable definitions. The three numbers reported for each independent variable above are the coefficient, t-statistic, and p-value respectively. The p-values for the directionally signed variables (+ or −) are one-tailed, the others are two-tailed.

(HRS) are significantly more likely to have changed institutions. It also appears that those graduates, who started their first tenure track positions at least 1 year before graduation (ABD), are at least marginally more likely to have changed institutions (CHANGE).

OLS Regressions
Later year graduates in the sample appear to have moved to more prestigious institutions; however, on average, graduates move from higher

Table 4.   Change of Institution Regressions.

Variable	Expected Sign	CHANGE		CHBCS	CHHRS
Intercept	No prediction	−0.0114 0.00 0.9607	−0.2137 1.03 0.3113	2.4207 6.45 0.0001	1.2487 2.61 0.0094
Graduation Year	− for CHANGE and no prediction for CHBCS or CHHRS	−0.2546 121.75 0.0001	−0.2561 124.27 0.0001	0.1162 2.63 0.0089	0.1733 2.95 0.0034
DGPHS	No prediction	0.1998 7.46 0.0063		0.8053 6.98 0.0001	
BCS	No prediction	−0.0083 0.71 0.7901		−0.7857 −17.10 0.0001	
DGHRS	No prediction		0.0483 0.51 0.4746		0.2932 2.14 0.0332
HRS	No prediction		0.0851 10.60 0.0011		−0.5420 −10.42 0.0001
ABD	+ for CHANGE and − for CHBCS or CHHRS	0.2285 2.66 0.0514	.02882 4.21 0.0201	−0.0883 −0.43 0.3328	−1.0158 −3.77 0.0001
Observations		1,286	1,300	359	346
Adjusted R^2				0.460	0.317
Likelihood ratio		162.04	170.48	77.28	41.00
$p<$		0.0001	0.0001	0.0001	0.0001

Notes: See Table 1 for variable definitions. The three numbers reported above for each logit (CHANGE) regression independent variable are the coefficient, chi-square, and p-value. The three numbers reported for each OLS (CHPHS or CHHRS) regression independent variable are the coefficient, t-statistic, and p-value. The p-values for the directionally signed variables (+ or−) are one-tailed, the others are two-tailed.

to lower level institutions. In fact, graduates initially placed at higher *Best College* score and more research productive institutions (BCS, HRS) experienced significant negative changes between their current and initial placement institutions (CHBCS, CHHRS). Additionally, higher ranked degree granting institutions (DGPHS, DGHRS) are significantly associated with positive institution changes. Graduates who started their first tenure track position at least 1 year before graduation (ABD) also experienced significant negative changes in research productivity between their current and initial placement institutions (CHHRS).

Individual Factors Sub-Sample Results

To further examine individual factors affecting placement in the first academic position, we analyzed a sub-sample (79 useable responses) of the original 432 survey respondents to look for individual factors affecting the initial placement decision. The sub-sample is composed of those individuals who placed at a higher or lower university than would be expected given the ranking of their doctoral degree granting institution.

We administered a follow-up survey to the sub-sample that asked questions such as "What factors lead you to accept your first academic position?" and "Was your initial placement typical of your doctoral granting institution?". We also solicited information about faculty support in the placement process. These were the only questions that yielded significant differences between the graduates who placed higher than expected and those that placed lower than expected.

The sub-sample respondents listed many factors that influenced their initial placements (e.g., location, collegial environment, research support, salary, doctoral program, teaching and research balance, and quality of life). Only three of these factors were significantly different between those placing higher than expected and those that placed lower than expected. Chi-square tests confirmed that those placing higher than expected chose a school based on research support while those placing lower than expected chose an institution based on the teaching and research mix, or the quality of life. Therefore, Hypothesis 2 is supported. Individual factors did influence the initial placement of some accounting Ph.Ds after controlling for degree granting institution prestige.

As to whether respondents thought that their initial placement was typical for their doctoral granting institution, those placing lower than expected were more accurate than those placing higher than expected. Chi-square tests reveal that 21/32 of the low group and 13/44 (three missing responses) of the high group believed they placed below their peers ($p = 0.020$). In the high group, 31/44 thought that they placed about equal to their peers versus 11/32 in the low group ($p = 0.037$). In the low group, 4/32 versus zero in the high group believed that normal placement was more research oriented ($p = 0.019$). Also in the low group, 2/32 versus zero in the high group believed that they placed lower than what their faculty wanted and that most of their peers had higher placements ($p = 0.097$).

Finally, faculty support was much more evident in the initial placement of the higher than expected group. Chi-square tests indicate that 10/30 in the low group versus 3/45 in the high group (four missing responses) received no faculty assistance with their placement ($p = 0.007$). For the high group, 22/45 versus 6/30 for the low group benefited from faculty phone calls and personal contacts during the placement process ($p = 0.045$).

Limitations

Our change in institution results are obviously understated since the latest graduates have not had time to change institutions and because we only capture change when a graduate moves from one U.S. institution to another U.S. institution. Additionally, our research design does not capture graduates who may have taken either foreign academic positions or left academia. We also may underreport the number of graduates starting initial tenure track positions before graduation since we are not able to capture this factor if the graduate completes his or her degree in the same calendar year. Additionally, we do not include any graduates who completed their degrees more than 2 years after starting their initial tenure track positions. Finally, we are constrained to observable factors and cannot control for the specific desires, strengths, and weakness of each graduate.

CONCLUSIONS AND IMPLICATIONS

Consistent with prior research, we find that graduates of degree granting institutions with better placement histories and higher research productivity (i.e., high prestige) tend to be placed at higher level (high prestige) institutions. We find this result even as the market for new accounting Ph.Ds has shifted to a high demand position.

We also find that the effect of starting the initial tenure track position before graduation is significantly associated with a less research productive initial placement and a higher likelihood of changing institutions. This result is especially important if doctoral granting institutions are considering sending their doctoral students out ABD to conserve funding. While the shortage of doctoral candidates may be increasing the incentives for students to leave programs early, our findings confirm that starting ABD may have significant career costs.

While faculty cover letters appear to be a common practice among the higher ranked degree granting institutions, this practice seems rare at less prestigious degree granting institutions. Faculty phone calls also appear to be less common among the lower ranked degree granting institutions. We hope these findings may encourage faculty to increase their support to doctoral program graduates to include both application cover letters and phone calls.

Our finding that some individuals were able to place at higher prestige institutions than should have been possible based on their degree granting program may be due to the current supply shortage of candidates. This suggests opportunity at high prestige institutions for those doctoral program graduates interested in research, which otherwise might not have been available. For those individuals placing lower than expected, the mix of teaching and research and the quality of life were important. The current high demand market may have provided these graduates with an opportunity to take a position for personal "fit," as opposed to one based on prestige.

Our study contributes to the current literature by combining prestige information with individual placement factors. In the current high demand market, doctoral granting institution prestige still drives most of the initial academic placements; yet, individual factors also play a role. The large number of available academic positions may cause doctoral program graduates to trade off higher prestige placements for less prestigious institutions where lifestyle decisions are accommodated.

ACKNOWLEDGMENTS

We thank our anonymous reviewer and our editor, Anthony H. Catanach Jr., for their helpful comments and suggestions on this manuscript.

REFERENCES

AAA/AAPLG – American Accounting Association/The Accounting Programs Leadership Group. (2005). *Supply and demand for accounting Ph.D.s.* Sarasota, FL: American Accounting Association.

Andrews, W., & McKenzie, P. (1978). Leading accounting departments revisited. *Accounting Review, 53*(1), 135–138.

Bazley, J., & Nikolai, L. (1975). A comparison of published accounting research and qualities of accounting faculties and doctoral programs. *Accounting Review, 49*(3), 605–609.

Blair, D., Cottic, R., & Wallace, M. (1986). Faculty ratings of major economics departments by citations: An extension. *American Economic Review, 76*(1), 264–267.

Brown, L., & Gardner, J. (1985). Applying citation analysis to evaluate the research contributions of accounting faculty and doctoral programs. *Accounting Review, 59*(3), 262–277.

Dyckman, T., & Zeff, S. (1984). Two decades of the journal of accounting research. *Journal of Accounting Research, 22*(1), 225–297.

Eaton, T. V., & Hunt, S. C. (2002). Job search and selection by academic accountants: New and relocating faculty. *Journal of Accounting Education, 20*, 67–84.

Estes, R. (1970). A ranking of accounting programs. *Journal of Accountancy, 130*(1), 86–90.

Fairweather, J. (1988). Reputational quality of academic programs: The institutional halo effect. *Research in Higher Education, 28*(4), 345–355.

Fogarty, T. J., & Ruhl, J. M. (1997). Institutional antecedents of accounting faculty research productivity: A LISREL study of the "best and brightest". *Issues in Accounting Education, 12*(1), 27–48.

Fogarty, T. J., & Saftner, D. V. (1993). Down the up staircase: US academic accounting prestige and the placement of doctoral students. *Accounting Education, 2*(2), 93–110.

Hagerman, R., & Hagerman, J. (1989). Research promotion standards at selected accounting programs. *Issues in Accounting Education, 4*(2), 265–279.

Hasselback, J. R. (1990–2000). *Accounting faculty directory: 1990–2001.* Upper Saddle River, NJ: Prentice Hall.

Hasselback, J. R. (2002). *Accounting faculty directory: 2002–2003.* Upper Saddle River, NJ: Prentice Hall.

Hasselback, J. R., & Reinstein, A. (1995). A proposal for measuring scholarly productivity of accounting faculty. *Issues in Accounting Education, 10*, 269–306.

Holland, R. G., & Arrington, C. E. (1987). Issues influencing the decision of accounting faculty to relocate. *Issues in Accounting Education, 2*, 55–71.

Kida, T. E., & Mannino, R. C. (1980). Job selection criteria of accounting Ph.D. students and faculty members. *The Accounting Review, 55*, 491–500.

Mittermaier, L. (Ed.) (1991). Representation on the editorial boards of academic accounting journals: An analysis of accounting faculties and doctoral programs*Issues in Accounting Education, 6*(2), 221–238.

Morton, J. (1975). A new ranking of accounting faculties and doctoral programs. *Journal of Accountancy, 139*(2), 103–105.

Mukherji, A. (1998). Hiring faculty: The "best fit" or "best athlete". *Issues in Accounting Education, 13*(3), 721–723.

Plumlee, R. D., Kachelmeier, S. J., Madeo, S. A., Pratt, J. H., & Krull, G. (2006). Assessing the shortage of accounting faculty. *Issues in Accounting Education, 21*(2), 113–125.

Rhode, J., & Zeff, S. (1970). A ranking of accounting programs. *Journal of Accountancy, 130*(4), 92–95.

Rittenberg, L. (1998). Hiring faculty: The "best fit" or "best athlete". *Issues in Accounting Education, 13*(3), 717–719.

Stammerjohan, W. W., & Hall, S. C. (2002). Evaluation of doctoral programs in accounting:
    An examination of placement. *Journal of Accounting Education, 20,* 1–27.
U.S. News & World Report. (1997). *America's best colleges.* Washington, DC: U.S. News &
    World Report Inc.
Windal, F. (1981). Publishing for a varied public: An empirical study. *Accounting Review, 56*(4),
    653–658.

STUDENTS' ETHICAL AND PROFESSIONAL PERCEPTIONS OF EARNINGS MANAGEMENT

Daryl M. Guffey, D. David McIntyre and
Jeffrey J. McMillan

ABSTRACT

We examine the influence of two treatments on students' perceptions of earnings management. We find that student reading assignments on earnings management and professionalism topics followed by individual testing do not alter student-reported beliefs. However, when the same students process and report their beliefs about earnings management practices in a group setting, the results are different from their initially reported individual beliefs. These statistically significant results suggest that a group dynamic that involves students in the learning process, may be effective in influencing the ethical judgments and perceptions of our future business professionals.

Prior research (Bruns & Merchant, 1990, p. 23; Rosenzweig & Fischer, 1994, p. 31) suggests that business persons view improving short-term earnings via accounting methods as less ethically acceptable than manipulating operating procedures. A logical extension of this line of inquiry is whether students

Advances in Accounting Education: Teaching and Curriculum Innovations, Volume 10, 119–129
Copyright © 2009 by Emerald Group Publishing Limited
All rights of reproduction in any form reserved
ISSN: 1085-4622/doi:10.1108/S1085-4622(2009)0000010008

perceive earnings management differently from professionals, and whether simple educational interventions can shift students' ethical perceptions.

Several studies have examined students' perceptions of earnings management (Geiger & O'Connell, 1999, p. 227; Clikeman, Geiger, & O'Connell, 2001, p. 389). Other research has explored alternative methods of incorporating ethics education in accounting education. Hiltebeitel and Jones (1991, p. 262) found that students revised the manner in which they resolved professional ethical dilemmas after completing ethics modules in accounting courses. Beets (1993, p. 59) found that role-playing enhanced student understanding of professional ethics. Green and Weber (1997, p. 777) reported that auditing students reasoned at a higher level of ethical development after exposure to the American Institute of Certified Public Accountants Code of Professional Conduct. Mintz (1995, p. 247) argued that case analysis, role-playing, and collaborative learning are pedagogical techniques one can use to teach virtue to accounting students. However, Ponemon (1993, p. 185) found that ethics instruction did not foster accounting students' moral development as measured by the Defining Issues Test (DIT).

Based on Mintz's (1995) assertions, we investigate the impact of group dynamics on the ethics learning process. We find that testing students after they completed required readings on earning management and professionalism topics did not alter students' beliefs. However, requiring students to discuss the readings in a group setting did result in a statistically significant change in how students perceived various earnings management practices.

HYPOTHESES AND RESEARCH METHOD

We specifically examine ethics education in the first intermediate accounting course. The first ethics intervention required students to complete readings on earnings management and professionalism topics, after which each student was individually tested. These readings provided arguments for both the need for some form of earnings management, as well as problems inherent in managing earnings. The students did not receive any guidance from the instructor, thus decreasing the likelihood that instructor bias affected student ratings. Our first hypothesis is

H_1. Required earnings management and professionalism readings and individual testing alone will not alter students' perceptions of the ethical acceptability of earnings management practices.

After students had completed and taken the readings test, a second ethics intervention required students to discuss each scenario as a group, and arrive at a consensus opinion. Therefore, our second hypothesis is

H₂. Required earnings management and professionalism readings and individual testing followed by group discussion will not alter students' perceptions of the ethical acceptability of earnings management practices.

Participants

Students enrolled in three sections of the first intermediate accounting course at a large public university served as the subject pool for the study. As an incentive to participate and complete the study, students earned an opportunity to improve their semester grades. Participating students created a unique and anonymous identification code that helped preserve the confidentiality of their individual responses. Ninety-eight students began the study, however, 12 were dropped due to nonattendance during one phase of the research study. The final sample of 86 students was composed of 4 sophomores, 62 juniors, 19 seniors, and one graduate student. Accounting majors comprised 28 percent of the sample. Ages averaged 20.9 years and ranged from 19 to 27. Thirty-one females (36 percent) and 55 males (64 percent) participated in the study. Almost 35 percent of the sample group had previously completed an ethics course. The average grade point average (GPA) for the sample was 2.96 (on a 4.0 scale). Forty-seven percent of sample students had a GPA over 3.12 and 17 percent reported a GPA over 3.62.

Tasks and Treatments

We conducted the experiment over five consecutive 50-min Monday, Wednesday, and Friday class periods. On day one, students provided basic demographic information: class year, gender, age, GPA, and major. Next, students evaluated the ethical acceptability of actions portrayed in 13 earnings management scenarios (Bruns & Merchant, 1990). They rated the actions using the following five-point Likert scale:

(1) Ethical practice.
(2) Questionable practice. Would not say anything to the manager, but it makes me uncomfortable.

(3) Minor infraction. The manager should be warned not to do it again.
(4) Serious infraction. The manager should be severely reprimanded.
(5) Totally unethical. The manager should be fired.

Students then rated the professionalism demonstrated in the same 13 scenarios using the following five-point Likert scale:

(1) Totally professional
(2) Mildly unprofessional
(3) Somewhat unprofessional
(4) Quite unprofessional
(5) Totally unprofessional

At the end of the first day, students received readings packets on earnings management and professional responsibility to study for the next class meeting (Table 1). In addition to discussing the general concept of earnings management, these readings explored specific positive and negative viewpoints associated with earnings management from both the "preparer" and "regulator" perspectives.

On the second day of the experiment, students completed a test on the readings. The mean score was 84.29 percent (high of 98, low of 64) and the median score was 85, suggesting that students studied the readings. On the third day of the study, students again individually evaluated the same 13 business scenarios. Before leaving for the day, students formed groups of four for the next phase of the experiment. On the fourth day, students used

Table 1. Listing of Educational Readings.

DeChow, P. M., and Skinner, D. J. (2000). Earnings management: Reconciling the views of accounting academics, practitioners, and regulators. *Accounting Horizons 14*(2): 235–250 (students provided pages 238–242)

Parfet, W.U. (2000). Accounting subjectivity and earnings management: A preparer perspective. *Accounting Horizons 14*(4): 481–488. Article provides a preparer's perspective and argues that business managers have responsibility to promote the company's best interest through considering all available options

Remarks by Chairman Arthur Levitt, Securities and Exchange Commission, The "Numbers Game". September 28, 1998. Article provides a regulator's perspective and explains why financial reporting was under intense pressure. He outlines a financial community response to the problem

Mautz, R. K. (1988). Public accounting: Which kind of professionalism. *Accounting Horizons 2*(3): 121–125. The article advances two types of professionalism: "Expert-Competitor" and "Concern for the Public Interest" the entire 50-min class period to discuss the readings among themselves within their group. Each group then evaluated the same 13 earnings management scenarios. Each group completed one survey instrument so that all students on a team received the same "group" perception rating score.

On day five, the participants individually completed an exit survey that collected their individual student identification numbers and readings tests scores. Each student also answered the following open-ended questions:

- Did the assigned readings change your perception of professionalism and/or ethical behavior as it relates to earnings management? If so, how?
- Did considering the survey scenarios with a group change your perception of professionalism and/or ethical behavior as it relates to earnings management? If so, how?
- If none of the activities above changed your perception of professionalism and/or ethical behavior as it relates to earnings management, what would? If you do not believe anything would change your perception, why do you feel that way?

Research Measures

Merchant and Rockness (1994, p. 79) argue that ethical acceptability depends on the intent of management as well as the type, direction, and materiality of the earnings manipulation. Accordingly, we adopt their measures as follows.

Accounting Manipulations
Accounting manipulations (ACC) involve altering the recording of existing accounting transactions. These actions involve departures from generally accepted accounting principles (GAAP).

Operating Manipulations
Operating manipulations (OPER) relate to the timing of year-end transactions and operating decisions so that revenues and expenses are reported in a desired accounting period. Managers decide to accelerate/delay the undertaking of an operating activity to move revenues/expenses from one accounting period to another.

Type
The type (TYPE) measure captures whether subjects feel stronger about one form of earnings manipulation than another. TYPE equals ACC minus OPER. A positive value suggests that students perceive accounting manipulations as more serious violations than operating manipulations, whereas a negative value suggests the contrary. In addition, the greater the spread between the two manipulations, the greater the perceived ethical disparity.

Direction
The direction variable (DIR) assesses whether subjects feel differently about earnings manipulation practices that increase earnings versus those that decrease earnings. DIR is the difference between two scenarios that involve the manipulation of a discretionary expenditure. In one scenario managers delay an expenditure to increase current earnings, whereas in the other they accelerate the expenditure to decrease current earnings.

Materiality
Materiality (MAT) captures whether the magnitude of an earnings manipulation affects subjects' ratings. MAT is the difference between two scenarios that are identical except for the amount of an unrecorded liability.

Intent
The intent variable (INTENT) measures whether subjects will assign different acceptability ratings to earnings manipulation practices for "good" versus "bad" reasons. INTENT is the difference between two scenarios. In one, the manager wishes to meet a divisional profit target (i.e., bad reason), whereas in the other, the manager improves earnings to obtain funding for important product development projects (i.e., good reason).

RESULTS AND ANALYSIS

We recorded the evaluation scores for each of the six dependent variables at three stages during the research project: (1) before any intervention activities (pretest); (2) after completing the "readings" test (first intervention); and (3) after the group activity (second intervention). Our analysis included responses only from juniors and seniors that successfully completed the project ($n = 81$) to yield a more homogeneous sample.

Earnings Management Findings

Table 2 presents mean and standard deviations for each variable during the pretest, after the first intervention, and after the second intervention. The pretest results are consistent with those reported for practitioners (Rosenzweig & Fischer, 1994), and for students (Clikeman et al., 2001). The responses from all three intervals suggest that students viewed accounting manipulations less acceptable than operating manipulations (i.e., TYPE variable), just as did practitioners. Similarly, the magnitude and positive direction of the MAT and DIR variables suggest that the students rated larger earnings and increasing income manipulations more unfavorably. Again, these results are consistent with those of Rosenzweig and Fischer (1994) for practitioners.

We used a one-way ANOVA, repeated-measures design, to assess the significance of the treatment (interventions) on the respondents' mean scores. The results appear in Table 3. The analysis revealed a significant main effect for the overall treatment for all variables except INTENT. Planned contrasts showed no significant differences between pretest scores and scores after the first intervention. However, the contrasts did reveal a

Table 2. Perceived Ethical Acceptability Factors.

Variable	Practitioners Mean[a]	Pretest Mean (Std Dev)	First Intervention Mean (Std Dev)	Second Intervention Mean (Std Dev)
ACC	3.5	2.87	2.90	3.17
		(0.68)	(0.71)	(0.52)
OPER	1.51	2.16	2.13	1.99
		(0.48)	(0.49)	(0.36)
TYPE	1.99	0.71	0.77	1.18
		(0.70)	(0.66)	(0.56)
DIR	0.70	2.47	2.28	2.62
		(1.11)	(1.05)	(0.81)
MAT	0.91	1.11	1.10	1.35
		(0.76)	(0.74)	(0.88)
INTENT	0.21	0.41	0.59	0.68
		(0.97)	(1.09)	(0.72)

Notes: ACC, accounting manipulations; OPER, operating manipulations; TYPE, ethical disparity based on the type of manipulation; DIR, direction of manipulation; MAT, materiality; and INTENT, intent of the manager.
[a]Means for practitioners found by Rosenzweig and Fischer (1994) are rescaled for comparative purposes. They did not present standard deviations (std dev) in their study.

Table 3. Ethics-One-Way ANOVA Repeated Measures Results
($n = 81$).

Variable	Treatment F-Value	Planned Contrasts F-Values	
		Pretest vs. First intervention	Pretest vs. Second intervention
ACC	7.50***	0.17	10.46***
OPER	4.53*	0.27	5.78*
TYPE	16.12***	0.46	22.10***
DIR	3.08*	2.22	1.01
MAT	3.48*	0.02	4.32*
INTENT	2.31	0.48	4.43*

Notes: ACC, accounting manipulations; OPER, operating manipulations; TYPE, ethical disparity based on the type of manipulation; DIR, direction of manipulation; MAT, materiality; and INTENT, intent of the manager.
*$p < .05$; **$p < .01$; ***$p < .001$.

significant difference between pretest scores and scores after the group (second) intervention for ACC and TYPE ($p<.001$), as well as OPER, MAT, and INTENT ($p< .05$). The significant main effect of the treatment seems to be captured only when the students gather and subsequently report their assessment as a group.

Professionalism Findings

Table 4 presents professionalism perception score means and standard deviations for each variable during the pretest, as well as after the first and second interventions. Across the three measurement intervals, the ratings mirror those of the ethical acceptability ratings.

We again used a one-way ANOVA, repeated-measures design to assess the significance of the treatment (interventions) for the professionalism variables. Table 5 reports the results. The analysis revealed a significant main effect for the TYPE ($p<.001$), ACC ($p<.01$), and OPER ($p<.01$) variables. Planned contrasts for these three variables revealed no significant differences between pretest scores and scores after the first intervention. However, our planned contrasts did indicate a significant difference between the pretest scores and scores after the group intervention for TYPE ($p<.001$), ACC ($p<.05$), and OPER ($p<.05$). Again, the results suggest that the group dynamic was solely responsible for the difference between the individual participant ratings and the final consensus group rating.

Table 4. Perceived Professionalism Factors.

Variable	Pretest Mean (Std Dev)	First Intervention Mean (Std Dev)	Second Intervention Mean (Std Dev)
ACC	3.03	2.92	3.24
	(0.73)	(0.73)	(0.55)
OPER	2.29	2.25	2.08
	(0.58)	(0.50)	(0.44)
TYPE	0.74	0.67	1.16
	(0.71)	(0.72)	(0.55)
DIR	2.48	2.26	2.43
	(1.09)	(1.19)	(0.79)
MAT	0.96	0.91	1.11
	(0.93)	(0.84)	(1.05)
INTENT	0.44	0.49	0.67
	(0.94)	(1.04)	(0.71)

Notes: ACC, accounting manipulations; OPER, operating manipulations; TYPE, ethical disparity based on the type of manipulation; DIR, direction of manipulation; MAT, materiality; and INTENT, intent of the manager.

Table 5. Professionalism-One-Way ANOVA Repeated Measures Results ($n = 81$).

Variable	Treatment F-Value	Planned Contrasts F-Values	
		Pretest vs. First intervention	Pretest vs. Second intervention
ACC	6.42**	1.75	4.55*
OPER	5.65**	0.46	6.90*
TYPE	17.70***	0.68	18.94***
DIR	1.47	3.08	0.12
MAT	1.27	0.23	1.15
INTENT	1.63	0.15	2.96

Notes: ACC, accounting manipulations; OPER, operating manipulations; TYPE, ethical disparity based on the type of manipulation; DIR, direction of manipulation; MAT, materiality; and INTENT, intent of the manager.
$^*p < .05; ^{**}p < .01; ^{***}p < .001$.

Prior studies indicate that gender, academic major, and completion of an ethics course may cause the observed differences for earnings management and professionalism. Therefore, we analyzed separate ANOVAs to ascertain the possible effects of these factors on the control variables. Our review suggests that the second treatment (specifically the group intervention) was successful in both cases (earnings management and professionalism) when controlling for these three individual differences.

Our statistical tests suggest that individual readings alone did not have a significant effect on the students' perceptions of the ethical acceptability of the listed practices. The information captured through the open-ended questions found somewhat contrary evidence. When asked whether the assigned readings changed their perception of professionalism and/or ethical behavior as it relates to earnings management, over 83 percent of students replied affirmatively. Therefore, it does appear that the required readings did have some influence on students' opinions about earnings management related matters. These results leave us to speculate about how specific group interactions manipulated individual judgments to yield statistically significant different group responses.

LIMITATIONS

In this study, we first tested for differences between students' initial responses and their responses after they had completed the required readings and the subsequent individual testing. Then we compared the same initial responses for these students versus their responses after completing the required readings followed by individual testing and a required group session. It is possible that the group activity in and of itself caused a difference to occur. We are unable to draw such a conclusion. A research design that allows only one condition to change may provide additional insight into the benefits of the group activity.

Additionally, it is plausible that an ordering effect occurred. That is, the results may have differed if the order of the interventions were reversed, group intervention first and then readings.

CONCLUSION

Our results suggest that students' perceptions of earnings management practices were not affected by having them review text material and articles on which they were subsequently tested. However, requiring students to discuss these same materials in groups did yield ratings that were significantly different from the students' individual pretest assessments.

These results suggest that a group process helped students better internalize and thoughtfully consider moral and ethical reasoning issues.

We also find that students in the first intermediate course perceive earnings management in much the same manner as practitioners. That is, they perceive accounting manipulations as a more serious ethical dilemma than operating manipulations. This suggests that early ethics training intervention may be warranted in the accounting curriculum.

ACKNOWLEDGMENT

We thank an anonymous reviewer and Anthony H. Catanach Jr. (co-editor) for their helpful comments and suggestions.

REFERENCES

Beets, S. D. (1993). Using the role-playing technique in accounting ethics education. *Accounting Educators' Journal*, 5(Fall), 46–65.

Bruns, W. J., Jr., & Merchant, K. A. (1990). The dangerous morality of managing earnings. *Management Accounting*, 71(August), 22–25.

Clikeman, P. M., Geiger, M. A., & O'Connell, B. T. (2001). Students' perceptions of earnings management: The effects of national origin and gender. *Teaching Business Ethics*, 5(4), 389–410.

Geiger, M. A., & O'Connell, B. T. (1999). Accounting student ethical perceptions: An analysis of training and gender. *Teaching Business Ethics*, 2(3), 227–233.

Green, S., & Weber, J. (1997). Influencing ethical development: Exposing students to the AICPA code of conduct. *Journal of Business Ethics*, 16(8), 777–790.

Hiltebeitel, K., & Jones, S. (1991). Initial evidence on the impact of integrating ethics into accounting education. *Issues in Accounting Education*, 6(Fall), 262–275.

Levitt, A. J. (1998). The numbers game. Remarks delivered at the New York University Center for Law and Business, New York, September 28. Available at http://www.sec.gov/new/speech/speecharchive/1998/spch220.txt

Mautz, R. K. (1988). Public accounting: Which kind of professionalism? *Accounting Horizons*, 2(3), 121–125.

Merchant, K. A., & Rockness, J. (1994). The ethics of managing earnings: An empirical investigation. *Journal of Accounting and Public Policy*, 13, 79–94.

Mintz, S. M. (1995). Virtue ethics and accounting education. *Issues in Accounting Education*, 10(2), 247–267.

Ponemon, L. A. (1993). Can ethics be taught in accounting? *Journal of Accounting Education*, 11(2), 185–209.

Rosenzweig, K., & Fischer, M. (1994). Is managing earnings ethically acceptable? *Management Accounting*, 75(March), 31–34.

ACCOUNTING CERTIFICATE PROGRAMS: SERVING THE NEEDS OF STUDENTS WHILE BENEFITING YOUR UNIVERSITY AND ACCOUNTING DEPARTMENT

Janet A. Samuels, D. Jordan Lowe and Catherine A. Finger

ABSTRACT

The supply of accounting majors has not kept pace with the increasing demand for accounting graduates. One way of increasing the number of qualified accountants, while maintaining desired quality, is through a non-degree program such as the Post-Baccalaureate Certificate in Accountancy. A certificate program addresses the needs of students who already have a bachelor's degree in another discipline and want to gain accounting knowledge. The purpose of this chapter is to assist accounting administrators and faculty in deciding whether a similar program would be feasible and beneficial for their school. We describe the benefits of a certificate program, which include the potential for increased enrollments and an enhanced learning environment. We discuss design alternatives and

Advances in Accounting Education: Teaching and Curriculum Innovations, Volume 10, 131–149
Copyright © 2009 by Emerald Group Publishing Limited
All rights of reproduction in any form reserved
ISSN: 1085-4622/doi:10.1108/S1085-4622(2009)0000010009

implementation issues in terms of our program and other certificate programs in the United States. We also discuss the needs and characteristics of certificate students currently enrolled in our program.

The Sarbanes-Oxley Act of 2002, economic factors, and the expansion of business in the United States and globally have resulted in an increased demand for accounting graduates (Arens & Elder, 2006, p. 349; Bureau of Labor Statistics, 2007; McTague, 2007, p. 16). However, although demand has increased, enrollment of accounting majors has not kept pace (AICPA, 2008, pp. 8–9; Billiot, Glandon, & McFerrin, 2004, p. 464). In addition, there is some concern that accounting is not attracting "the best and the brightest" students (Frecka & Nichols, 2004, p. 175; Reckers, 2006, p. 39). In fact, there have been several discussions regarding how to increase the supply of accountants without sacrificing quality (Billiot et al., 2004, pp. 464–465; Leslie, 2007; Turley, 2007).

One way an accounting department can attract students and increase enrollments is by offering a non-degree accounting certificate program to individuals who already have a *non-accounting* bachelor's degree. Arizona State University at the West Campus (ASUWC) has such a program called the Post-Baccalaureate Certificate in Accountancy ("certificate program").[1] A certificate program addresses the needs of students who already have a bachelor's degree in another discipline and want to enter the accounting profession and/or enhance their accounting knowledge and skills. In addition, a certificate program can benefit an accounting department and university by increasing enrollment of high-quality students.

Although certificate programs offer many benefits to multiple stakeholders, we identified only 25 traditional universities in the United States with certificate programs. One reason for the scarcity of certificate programs may be that some administrators and accounting educators are not aware of the benefits of these programs.

This chapter provides information about accounting certificate programs (at ASUWC and other schools) and data on the characteristics of accounting certificate students (at ASUWC). The objectives of the chapter are to (1) describe a certificate program, (2) explain the benefits of a certificate program to the institution, (3) explain the benefits of this program for students including advantages over obtaining a Master's in accounting or second undergraduate degree, and (4) providing design issues that schools should address.

SURVEY AND DATA SOURCES

This section describes the sources we used to obtain data. First, we conducted an exhaustive online search for universities with certificate programs. This process consisted of searching the Internet (through Google) using various combinations of the key words "certificate," "accounting," "post-bac," "post-baccalaureate," and "accountancy." Additionally, we identified some schools through discussions with other academics.[2] Our search located 25 traditional universities in the United States with certificate programs in accounting (Table 1). Through subsequent phone calls and

Table 1. U.S. Schools Identified as Offering an Accounting Certificate Program[a].

State	Name of University	City
Arizona	Arizona State University at the West Campus	Glendale
California	Golden Gate University	San Francisco
	Santa Clara University	Santa Clara
	University of San Diego	San Diego
Georgia	Georgia State University	Atlanta
Illinois	DePaul University[b]	Chicago
Indiana	Indiana University Kokomo	Kokomo
	Indiana University–Purdue University Fort Wayne	Fort Wayne
	Indiana University Southeast	New Albany
	University of Southern Indiana	Evansville
Iowa	Grand View College	Des Moines
Kentucky	Bellarmine University	Louisville
	The University of Northern Kentucky	Highland Heights
Massachusetts	University of Massachusetts Dartmouth	North Dartmouth
Pennsylvania	Robert Morris University	Moon Township
Oregon	Portland State University	Portland
	Oregon State University	Corvallis
	Southern Oregon University	Ashland
Texas	University of Houston	Houston
Virginia	George Mason University	Fairfax
	University of Mary Washington	Fredericksburg
	Virginia Commonwealth University	Richmond
Washington	Seattle University	Seattle
	University of Washington-Tacoma	Tacoma
	Washington State University-Vancouver	Vancouver

[a]We included a school only if it was in the United States and offered an accounting certificate for students with non- accounting undergraduate degrees.
[b]DePaul University calls their program "Accounting Studies."

further online analysis, we were able to gather information on 22 of the 25 universities' certificate programs.

Second, we obtained data about ASUWC's current undergraduate and certificate students through an anonymous survey administered electronically on the Blackboard Academic Suite™ in Spring 2007. We asked students to participate in this study and sent them two follow-up e-mails.[3] One hundred and eighteen undergraduate students responded to the survey from a total of 363 currently enrolled (33% response rate). Correspondingly, 71 of 144 certificate students completed the survey (49% response rate).

Third, we obtained access to certain ASUWC student records to supplement our analysis. We compare the educational performance of certificate students with undergraduate accounting degree students ("undergraduate students"). At ASUWC, we treat certificate and undergraduate students the same throughout their accounting education. That is, both the student groups have comparable entrance requirements, take classes together, have the same grading criteria, and are held to the same overall standards. Given these similarities, we believe comparisons between these two student groups are meaningful.

BENEFITS AND COSTS OF A CERTIFICATE PROGRAM TO AN ACCOUNTING DEPARTMENT AND UNIVERSITY

Increased Revenue and Cost Implications

A certificate program can benefit an institution by increasing the revenue (and/ or cost savings) in three ways. First, the addition of a certificate program can help fill upper division accounting courses and add a significant number of student credit hours to the accounting department. Some universities have relatively large accounting certificate programs. For example, ASUWC, Portland State University, University of Houston, and Golden Gate University all have more than 100 accounting certificate students. During the past five semesters (up to and including Spring 2007), ASUWC had on average 148 certificate students and 336 undergraduate accounting students enrolled. Although most of these students are enrolled part-time, they still generate significant credit hours for our accounting department. At ASUWC, from 2004 to 2006, certificate students averaged 1,574 student credit hours per semester as compared to 3,044 for the undergraduate students.

Second, in certain situations, the university may receive a higher tuition per credit hour from certificate students. That is, certificate students are not enrolled in an undergraduate degree program but instead are in a non-degree program. At ASUWC, the current program design requires certificate students to pay graduate-level tuition. Therefore, although certificate students attend undergraduate classes, they pay graduate-level tuition. Alternatively, certificate students could be required to pay additional fees to enroll in undergraduate accounting courses. At ASUWC, we are considering decreasing tuition to undergraduate rates but adding a fee for certificate students to enroll in courses. The department would benefit from the additional fees and the university would still retain tuition dollars.

Third, institutions may be able to achieve cost savings (on a per-student basis) as the college services utilized by certificate students are often less than those consumed by traditional undergraduate students. Traditional undergraduates rely on career placement services, health and counseling centers, and the center for resident life, whereas certificate students are much less apt to do so. In addition, certificate students do not typically participate in extra-curricular activities.

There are also additional costs associated with a certificate program. Marketing is a large incremental cost associated with the program. At ASUWC, this includes brochures that are sent to prospective students, design and maintenance of a webpage describing the program, and radio and other advertising costs. The program requires a staff to answer inquiries from prospective students. At ASUWC, the accounting administrative assistant is able to handle these inquiries in addition to her regular duties. Additionally, the accounting administrative assistant fills out an official "Certificate" form for each graduating certificate student. These are signed by the dean and mailed to students after program completion. Certificate students do consume incremental resources for required services such as admissions, financial aid, and advising. The admission process for certificate students requires additional work as transcripts and paper applications must be reviewed by an accounting staff to ensure the student meets the pre-requisite requirements. However, financial aid and advising resources are the standard services required for all students, and special processes are not required for certificate students.

Raising the Bar

Another benefit to an institution is that certificate students can "raise the bar" in accounting classes. According to Table 2, certificate students are significantly older, have more full-time work experience and more actual accounting experience than undergraduate students. Prior education research has found that older, non-traditional students have better time management skills, study habits, motivation, and commitment to learning (Delvin, 1996, p. 57; Trueman & Hartley, 1996, p. 206; Wynd & Bozman, 1996). In fact, our data indicate that certificate students spend an average of 7.8 hours on homework per accounting class per week as compared to 6.7 hours for undergraduate students (Table 3). Thus, certificate students can bring their higher level of maturity, their varied backgrounds, and work experience (including "real world" accounting work experience) to the classroom and enhance the overall learning experience.

Table 2.   Certificate and Undergraduate Student Demographics.

	Certificate Students	Undergraduate Students
Sample size	71	118
Age	36.7***	29.5
Gender (% female)	61	66
Marital status – married (%)* *(remaining percentage are unmarried)*	48	34
Number of children under 18 at home	0.5	0.6
In-state students (%)	93	92
Current job type (%)		
Accounting related	56	40
Other business related	23	26
Non-business related	7	16
No Job	14	18
Mean full-time work experience (in years)		
Accounting related	3.9	3.1
Other business related	6.2**	2.9
Non-business related	2.9	2.1
Total	13.0**	8.1

*Distribution of certificate and undergraduate student data differ with $p<0.06$.
**Using a t-statistic, certificate and undergraduate student data differ with $p<0.01$.
***Using a t-statistic, certificate and undergraduate student data differ with $p<0.001$.

Table 3. Educational Performance.

	Certificate Students	Undergraduate Students
Mean hours per week spent on school work (outside of class) for each accounting class	7.8	6.7
Actual grade performance[a]		
GPA in intermediate I	2.72*	2.14
GPA in junior level accounting classes	2.98*	2.58
GPA in senior level accounting classes	3.03*	2.81
Overall accounting GPA	2.99*	2.63

*Distribution of certificate and undergraduate student data differ with $p < 0.001$.
[a]Information determined from actual data rather than self-reported data averaged over a three-year period (2004 through 2006). A gradepoint of 4.0 corresponds with a grade of "A."

Certificate students also "raise the bar" in accounting classes by achieving better grades than undergraduate students. Data from the last three years indicate that our certificate students' grades were significantly higher than undergraduates for their junior level accounting classes, senior level accounting classes, and overall during this three-year period (Table 3). The largest difference was for Intermediate Accounting I in which the difference across student groups was more than half a grade (.58). However, it appears that over time undergraduates were able to adjust and raise their educational performance although still not performing quite as well as certificate students. Other schools were not able or willing to share actual grade data with us because of the proprietary nature of this information.

Accreditation Requirements

There are no additional accreditation requirements that need to be considered when schools add a certificate program. Only the degree-granting process is subject to accreditation; therefore, non-degree certificate programs are not subject to additional accreditation restrictions. This exception can be especially beneficial for schools that are currently undergraduate-only schools. A certificate program can allow them to serve additional students without needing to meet higher accreditation requirements applicable to schools with masters programs.

BENEFITS OF A CERTIFICATE PROGRAM
FOR STUDENTS

The 30-credit-hour non-degree certificate program at ASUWC is targeted at students who have a non-accounting undergraduate degree but who now want an accounting education. For example, some students have accounting-related jobs but lack the requisite accounting background to succeed at their current positions. Other individuals are interested in gaining accounting knowledge to change careers to accounting. Regardless, most of these students want the option of obtaining a CPA license and thus want a program that offers the necessary classroom hours and accounting knowledge. In fact, 90% of ASUWC certificate students want to obtain a CPA license (which is similar to the 89% of our undergraduates who want to obtain their CPA license). These students want the accounting knowledge and classes and are not concerned about obtaining a degree or even a certificate.[4]

One option that these students may consider is obtaining a second undergraduate degree with a major in accounting. Often this will require students to take several general education and/or non-accounting business requirements. A typical student with an undergraduate degree from another school may need between 45 and 55 additional credits to obtain a second undergraduate degree. These credits, added to the credits already earned for the first undergraduate degree, would likely total to much more than the 150 credit hours required to sit for the CPA exam. Thus, a second undergraduate degree may be less attractive than a certificate program as the undergraduate degree is often more time consuming and expensive due to transfer limits and/or requirements for additional general education and/or business-related courses.

Alternatively, these students might consider obtaining a Master's degree in accounting rather than a certificate. Frecka and Nichols (2004, p. 185) note that the majority of master's in accounting programs emphasize technical skills that build on the "core" accounting courses (such as intermediate accounting) that are typically included in undergraduate accounting degree programs. Some masters programs require students to take core accounting courses before admission, but do not offer these courses to students (e.g., Arizona State University at the Tempe campus and Marquette University). Thus, students without undergraduate accounting courses would not be able to enroll in these programs until they completed these core courses at another institution.

Another option for these students is to obtain a master's degree from a program that allows them to take core courses as part of the master's program (e.g., Michigan State University; University of Texas at Austin; Clemson University; University of Colorado, Denver; and University of Nevada, Las Vegas). However, because these students would need to take the "core" courses either before admission or during the master's program, the length of the master's program for these individuals could extend well beyond a typical time frame. Therefore, a student combining a non-accounting undergraduate degree with an accounting master's degree would have, in total, much more than the 150 credit hours required for a CPA. Moreover, some students may already have a master's degree (e.g., approximately 20% of ASUWC certificate students have an M.B.A.) and do not feel the need to obtain another master's degree. Consequently, many students may prefer a certificate program over a master's in accounting.

Students may also obtain an accounting certificate from other sources such as online or non-traditional schools (e.g., University of Phoenix or DeVry University) or executive/continuing education programs offered by a university or a university extension (e.g., UC Berkeley Extension, University of Minnesota College of Continuing Education). Drawbacks to these programs include higher costs (e.g., University of Phoenix can be more costly than in-state tuition for a public university), lack of accounting courses (e.g., UC Berkeley Accounting Certificate program offers approximately 15 credit hours of upper-division accounting courses) and no requirement for an undergraduate degree (e.g., neither UC Berkeley nor University of Minnesota College of Continuing Education requires an undergraduate degree). Although a limited number of accounting courses and no requirement for an undergraduate degree may not sound like drawbacks, these are requirements for obtaining a CPA.

A large majority of certificate students want to obtain their CPA, and many want a career change. Before the student survey, we had reasoned that certificate students, being older with more work experience, might be less inclined to aspire to a career in public accounting compared to undergraduate students. However, our results indicate that about a third of the students in each group indicated a preference for public accounting, with industry accounting being a close second choice (Table 4).[5]

Taken together, the primary needs of these students are to gain a "base" of accounting knowledge to support their career goals and to obtain that knowledge as quickly as possible (regardless of whether they obtain another degree).

Table 4. Career Expectations.

	Certificate Students (%)	Undergraduate Students (%)
Panel A: Accounting job aspirations		
Consulting	16	8
External audit	19	18
General accounting	17	22
Internal audit	9	13
Tax	14	13
Other accounting job	7	3
Not sure	18	21
Desire non-accounting job	0	2
Panel B: Type of company desired		
Public accounting (national or regional firm)	22	21
Public accounting (local firm)	14	13
Industry	33	25
Government/not-for-profit	11	20
Other	7	4
Not sure	13	17

CERTIFICATE PROGRAM DESIGN AND CONSIDERATIONS

This section of the chapter discusses issues that educators might want to consider when designing a new certificate program or revising an existing accounting certificate program. This discussion is based on characteristics of 22 certificate programs across the United States (including ASUWC). Design decisions made for these programs appear in Table 5 and are the basis for the following discussion.

Entrance and Tuition Requirements

When ASUWC created its certificate program, it wanted to meet the student needs described earlier. It also wanted to ensure that the certificate program would make a positive contribution to the accounting department's mission and goals. ASUWC uses admission and program requirements as one method of maintaining the desired quality of the certificate program.

Table 5. Summary of Design Choices by Certificate Programs[a].

	Percentage of Schools
Admission and certificate requirements:	
Degree requirements for admission	
Any non-accounting undergraduate degree	70
Undergraduate *or* graduate business degree	22
Undergraduate business degree	4
Other	4
Minimum incoming GPA requirement?	
Yes	73
No	27
Credit hours required:	
Upper-division total credit hours required for the certificate	33.6 hours (range: 15–49 hours)
Upper-division accounting credit hours required for the certificate	23.8 hours (range: 12–40 hours)
Tuition:	
Undergraduate tuition	62
Graduate tuition	29
Other	9
Certificate students:	
Certificate students are primarily	
Part-time students	61
Full-time students	17
Evenly divided between part-time and full-time	22
Classes:	
Undergraduate and certificate students in the same upper-division accounting classes?	
Yes	88
No	12
Masters degrees available:	
Accounting department offers a master's in accounting degree	
Yes	50
No	50
Business school offers other master's programs (e.g., MBA)	
Yes	91
No	9

[a]Some schools did not respond to all of the questions.

Certificate students are classified as non-degree graduate students and are subject to several admission requirements. One of the first admission considerations is the type of degree that certificate students have completed. At ASUWC, they must possess a four-year non-accounting baccalaureate degree from a regionally accredited university or college.

Including all non-accounting majors provides for interesting class discussions given the wide variety of backgrounds represented. This inclusive requirement also increases the number of students who are qualified to enter the program. Another alternative would be to require a *business* degree (either undergraduate or graduate) as some schools do (e.g., Seattle University and Indiana University Southeast). Although this alternative would ensure that students already have the requisite introductory business core classes, this requirement would limit the number of students eligible to apply to the program. Accordingly, Table 5 indicates that 70% of the certificate programs have no restriction on the type of undergraduate or graduate degree students need for admission.

Other admission requirements may include incoming grade point average (GPA) and completion of specific coursework. ASUWC requires that certificate students have a minimum incoming GPA of 2.50 (on a 4.0 scale) and have completed certain lower-division business classes. Seventy-three percent of schools with a certificate program have an incoming GPA requirement. However, only half of the schools we contacted require certain lower-division courses as a pre-requisite to the program (with the most common requirement being introductory accounting courses). ASUWC certificate students who need lower-division business classes typically elect to take them at a low-cost community college. Schools in areas without community colleges may need to consider whether there is enrollment space in lower-division business courses for the certificate students.

Finally, schools must decide what tuition to charge certificate students. Sixty-two percent of programs charge undergraduate tuition. Public institutions may have rules in place that determine the type of tuition that students must pay, and therefore, this decision may not be entirely under the control of the department or even the institution.

Completion Requirements

The AACSB does not regulate non-degree programs such as the certificate program, and therefore, these programs can include as many credit hours as a school desires. ASUWC's certificate program requires 30 credit hours, including six general business credits. This design allows students with a 120-hour undergraduate degree to obtain the hours needed for the CPA exam. In addition, the state of Arizona requires "related courses" such as other business courses for CPA certification. Therefore, the requirement for six general business credits helps students gain the required credits for CPA certification. Other schools require between 15 and 49 total credit hours for the certificate with accounting courses making up the majority of these credits (12–40). These differences may reflect different CPA requirements for various states. Since many certificate students enroll in the program to get the credit hours for CPA licensure, schools considering adding a certificate program should determine whether certificate students can obtain the necessary credits needed for their specific state's CPA requirements.

Once in the program, certificate students focus on accounting and business courses. Our certificate program requires six accounting classes: intermediate accounting I and II, cost management, income tax accounting, accounting information systems, and accounting technology. Certificate students must take a minimum of two accounting electives and two business electives. Of course many students take more than these minimum course requirements to meet the 150-hour certification requirements as they may need additional business courses or other specific courses required by the state licensing board.

Certificate students already have earned an undergraduate degree that presumably included general education credits. Therefore, the certificate program does not have any general education requirements. By focusing strictly on accounting and business classes, certificate students can accelerate their accounting education (rather than obtaining another degree).

Finally, after ASUWC students complete the necessary requirements, they receive a "certificate" and are invited to "walk" during convocation/graduation. The transcripts provide notation of the completion of the certificate which is verifiable to potential employers.[6]

Class Design

The majority of our students are working adults who need night classes to fit their work schedules. As shown in Table 6, ASUWC certificate students work significantly more hours per week compared to undergraduate students (35 hours per week versus 28 hours, respectively; $p < 0.01$). It is likely due to the greater work demands of the certificate students that they only average about 5.4 credit hours per semester as compared to undergraduates who average a 10.9–credit-hour load. Given their higher workload and lower average credit hours per semester, certificate students tend to prefer evening classes. In fact, actual university data indicate that 77% of the classes taken by ASUWC certificate students are evening classes.

Table 6. Class and Work Management.

	Certificate Students	Undergraduate Students
Hours per week working while going to school	35**	28
Percentage of students working 40 hours or more per week	70***	37
Credit hours currently enrolled in	5.4***	10.9
Average commute to campus	41 minutes***	29 minutes
What times of the day do you prefer for classes? (%)[b]		
Morning classes	13***	42
Afternoon classes	24*	42
Evening classes	80***	54
Saturday classes	26	14
No preference	3	3
What types of classes do you prefer? (%)[b]		
Classes that meet once a week	81**	60
Classes that meet twice a week	30***	62
Classes that meet three times a week	6	6
No preference in how often a class meets	0	1
What is the most number of days you want to be on campus for all classes? (%)****		
1 day a week	17	3
2 days a week	50	31
3 days a week	21	33
4 days a week	7	26
5 days a week	1	2
No preference	3	5
Percentage of classes taken that are night classes[a]	77	51

*Using a t-statistic, certificate and undergraduate student data differ with $p < 0.05$.
**Using a t-statistic, certificate and undergraduate student data differ with $p < 0.01$.
***Using a t-statistic, certificate and undergraduate student data differ with $p < 0.001$.
****Distribution of certificate and undergraduate students data differ with $p < 0.001$.
[a]Information determined from actual data rather than self-reported data.
[b]Amounts do not add to 100% as participants could check multiple items.

Eighty-one percent of certificate students prefer classes that are offered once a week, and most do not want to be on campus more than twice a week for all of their classes combined. ASUWC accommodates certificate students by offering each required accounting class at night (as well as during the day) for every semester. Although 61% of schools indicate that their certificate students are primarily part-time students, there are also full-time certificate students.

Another consideration is whether to have certificate students and undergraduate students take classes together. ASUWC reasoned that combining these two student groups would be beneficial as class sizes would grow and the incremental costs would be minimized. Additionally, certificate students' diverse backgrounds can potentially lead to a higher quality of classroom discussion and "raise the bar" of the undergraduate students. Our data indicate that 88% of schools offering a certificate program have a similar design of combining undergraduate and certificate students in the same classes (Table 5). However, certificate students (paying graduate tuition) in the same classes as undergraduate students can create concerns about differential tuition. Another design consideration, especially for schools that struggle with meeting accreditation requirements, would be to create separate classes for the two student groups. Accreditation requirements do not apply to certificate programs or any courses that are only for certificate students (AACSB, 2008). Administrators should be aware that if certificate students are co-mingled with undergraduate students, then the class needs to be counted in the accreditation calculations for Academically Qualified (AQ) and Professionally Qualified (PQ) percentages. However, if separate classes are established for certificate students, then these class sections do not need to be considered when reporting AQ and PQ percentages to the AACSB.

Finally, if a school decides to enroll certificate and undergraduate students in the same classes, another consideration is whether to require the same coursework for both sets of students. All the schools we contacted required the same coursework for certificate and undergraduate students in the same course. Alternatively, a certificate program could require certificate students to complete an extra paper or project. Although this requirement may result in more work for instructors, it may also alleviate certificate student concerns about paying graduate-level tuition.

Other Considerations

An important aspect of a successful program is attracting qualified students. To attract certificate students, ASUWC sends information packets to its non-accounting business students while receiving their undergraduate degrees. Mailings are targeted to business students because they have the

Table 7. Career Expectations.

	Certificate Students (%)	Undergraduate Students (%)
Plan to stay at current employer upon graduation		
Yes	44	40
No	40	41
Don't currently have a job	16	19
Plan to use career services		
Yes	28	43
No	36	22
Don't know	36	35

necessary prerequisites for the certificate program. In addition, advertisements are carried on the radio and the business section of local newspapers on an annual basis to reach a broader market. ASUWC's website explains the certificate program in detail.

In terms of career plans, 44% of ASUWC certificate students stated that they intended to stay with their present employer (Table 7). Although certificate students do not have a background in accounting, some of them may still have an accounting-related job at their current employer or want to change employment status within their present firm. It is likely because of their desire to stay at their present firm that only 28% of ASUWC certificate students plan on using career services (compared to 43% of undergraduate students). Thus, increasing student population by certificate students does not require similar career services resources as required by undergraduate students.

Another consideration is that certificate students typically take most of their classes at night and, therefore, tend not to be as involved in campus activities (such as Beta Alpha Psi) and may not feel a part of the campus. This is also a problem for universities with undergraduate students who work full-time and do not live in campus.

Certificate students also tend to take evening classes during the summer sessions as a means of finishing their program as soon as possible. In fact, our current data suggests that more than 40% of our summer accounting classes consist of certificate students. The certificate student enrollment has resulted in medium to large classes during the summer sessions. Schools should anticipate that certificate students will want several summer classes offered and that faculty will be needed to cover these classes.

Finally, schools should analyze the effect that a new certificate program would have on existing programs. Schools with a master's in accounting program, which allow non-accounting undergraduate students to take "core" accounting courses as part of their education, may want to carefully consider the ramifications of a certificate program as it will compete with the existing programs. However, a certificate program could be designed such that it is complementary to a master's in accounting program.

SUMMARY

In summary, we feel that the ASUWC certificate program provides a valuable service to the accounting profession, the community, the students, and the university. Overall, we believe that the following characteristics have contributed to the success of the ASUWC certificate program: (1) Our campus is in a large metropolitan area and many potential students are within commuting distance; (2) the competition for this program is minimal, as there is no similar program in the area and the program meets many students' needs; (3) when the program was created, existing classes could accommodate both the undergraduate program and the certificate program students; (4) night classes that met once per week were already being offered; and (5) ASU is a public university that charges public school tuition, which is significantly less than private school tuition.

Educators who want to introduce a new certificate program, or who want to revise an existing one, should consider many things to achieve a "win-win" situation. Is their university located in a large metropolitan area or a rural one? Would a certificate program complement existing offerings or compete with them? How does current enrollment in accounting courses compare with desired enrollment? What are the needs of students and faculty? A certificate program would not be an ideal fit for all accounting departments, but for many it can do much to meet the needs of students while increasing student quality, enrollment, revenue, and student credit hours for an accounting department and its university.

NOTES

1. Some certificate programs (e.g., The University of Illinois at Champaign Urbana and The University of West Florida) require entering students to have an undergraduate degree in *accounting* and are offered for the specific purpose of

providing the additional hours students need to sit for the CPA exam. These professional accounting certificate programs, as they are often called, are not included in our "certificate program" designation and are not discussed in this chapter.

2. A search was necessary because non-degree programs such as certificate programs are not tracked by either the AACSB or the AICPA. We did not include non-traditional schools such as online programs and executive education programs in our results.

3. Three lottery prizes totaling $100 were awarded to encourage participation. Using Blackboard Academic Suite™, we could see who participated although we could not identify responses with specific participants.

4. According to a summary provided by Stacey Grooms of the National Association of State Boards of Accountancy, Inc., in July 2007, it appears that students in all states can earn a CPA license *without* having an undergraduate accounting degree. Although a few states provide language that indicates that an undergraduate accounting degree is required, they also provide other options that substitute classes and thus provide for an equivalent education without a degree.

5. A study performed in a job market familiar with the certificate program found that public accounting recruiters had no hiring preferences between certificate and undergraduate students but do favor masters' degrees over undergraduate degrees and accounting certificates (Almer & Christensen, 2008).

6. Some students drop out of the certificate program after they obtain the necessary classes they need for the CPA license but before completing all the certificate requirements. This is another indicator that students are not necessarily interested in obtaining the certificate as much as the accounting courses.

ACKNOWLEDGMENTS

This chapter has benefited from the helpful comments of Elizabeth Almer, Charles Bailey, Steve Kaplan, Sue Ravenscroft, John Sweeney, and Bruce Baldwin (who was instrumental in creating and implementing the ASUWC certificate program). We also appreciate the insights provided by our colleagues William Duncan, Barbara Muller, and Michael Del Valle (the Student Support Coordinator and advisor). We thank Siddhartha Rudrarajo for research assistance.

REFERENCES

Almer, E. D., & Christensen, A. (2008). Revisiting hiring decisions by public accounting firms: The impact of academic qualifications, age and gender on new-hire evaluations. *Advances in Accounting Education, 9,* 77–94.

American Institute of Certified Public Accountants (AICPA). (2008). *2008 trends in the supply of accounting graduates and the demand for public accounting recruits – 2008*. New York: AICPA.

Arens, A. A., & Elder, R. J. (2006). Perspectives on auditing education after Sarbanes-Oxley. *Issues in Accounting Education, 21*(4), 345–362.

The Association to Advance Collegiate Schools of Business (AACSB). (2008). *Eligibility procedures and standards for accounting accreditation*. Section 1, 9: AACSB.

Billiot, M. J., Glandon, S., & McFerrin, R. (2004). Factors affecting the supply of accounting graduates. *Issues in Accounting Education, 19*(4), 443–467.

Bureau of Labor Statistics. (2007). Available at http://www.bls.gov/oco/ocos001.htm#outlook. Retrieved on December 12, 2007.

Delvin, M. (1996). Older and wiser? A comparison of learning and study strategies of mature age and younger teacher education students. *Higher Education Research and Development, 15*, 51–60.

Frecka, T. J., & Nichols, W. D. (2004). Characteristics of master's in accounting degree programs. *Issues in Accounting Education, 19*(2), 165–188.

Leslie, D. W. (2007). Testimony before the United States treasury advisory committee on the auditing profession. Washington D.C., December 3, 2007.

McTague, J. (2007). Go east, young accountant. *Barron's, 87*(16), 16.

Reckers, P. M. J. (2006). Perspectives on the proposal for a generally accepted accounting curriculum: A wake-up call for academics. *Issues in Accounting Education, 21*(1), 31–43.

Trueman, M., & Hartley, J. (1996). A comparison between time management skills and academic performance in mature and traditional entry university students. *Higher Education, 32*(2), 199–215.

Turley, J. S. (2007). Testimony before the United States treasury advisory committee on the auditing profession. Washington D.C., December 3, 2007.

Wynd, W. R., & Bozman, C. S. (1996). Student learning style: A segmentation strategy for higher education. *Journal of Education for Business, 71*(4), 232–237.

ACCOUNTING DEPARTMENT CHAIRS' PERCEPTIONS OF THE IMPORTANCE OF COMMUNICATION SKILLS

Jacqueline J. Schmidt, Brian Patrick Green and Roland Madison

ABSTRACT

Employers state that their major concern with accounting graduates is their inadequate skills in reading, writing, speaking, and listening (Kranacher, 2007, p. 80). Yet, the American Institute of Certified Public Accountants (AICPA) and some state boards of accountancy have minimized the importance of these skills on professional certification exams. This conflict creates a mixed message. The purpose of our study is to determine accounting department chairs' perceptions of the importance of writing, speaking, listening, interpersonal, and technological communication skills for both the accounting and the business curricula and where in the curriculum these skills are taught. In our study, we surveyed 122 accounting administrators from the largest North American accountancy programs. Survey respondents report that most required communication courses are in the general business curriculum and, to a lesser extent, as a required course in the accounting major. Consistent across demographics, respondents also indicate that all communication

Advances in Accounting Education: Teaching and Curriculum Innovations, Volume 10, 151–168
Copyright © 2009 by Emerald Group Publishing Limited
All rights of reproduction in any form reserved
ISSN: 1085-4622/doi:10.1108/S1085-4622(2009)0000010010

skills are important, but writing skills followed by technological skills are the most valued for the accounting curriculum, while writing and speaking skills are most important in the business curriculum. Implications for the curriculum are discussed.

There continues to be conflict between employers' assessment of students' inadequate communication skills and the perceived efforts by business schools to improve those skills. Employers persist in stating that their major concern with accounting graduates is their inadequate skills in reading, writing, speaking, and listening (Bunn, Barfit, Cooper, & Sandifer, 2005, pp. 154–163; Kranacher, 2007, p. 80).

Professional organizations also support communication skills. Historically, both the *Accounting Education Change Commission* (AECC, 1990, pp. 307–312) and the *American Institute of Certified Public Accountants* (AICPA) *Vision* statement for the profession (AICPA, 1998) include a communication emphasis. The *Association for the Advancement of Collegiate Schools of Business* (AACSB) *International* (AACSB, 2008, pp. 1–78) also continues to support the importance of communication skills for graduates.

Most accounting educators' research has assessed how to improve specific communication skills in the classroom, such as public speaking (Ameen, Guffey, & Jackson, 2000, pp. 85–105) or writing (Stout & DaCrema, 2005, pp. 307–328; Christ, 2002, pp. 41–57). There are no recent studies that investigate where communication skills are taught in business and accounting programs, or how those who control curricula design view the current importance of communication skills. Our study is motivated by this critical dearth of published information on the value of and where communication competencies are taught. One further motivation emerges from the reluctance of the AICPA and some state agencies to make communication competency an important part of professional certification exams. The question remains how can practitioners' communication needs be met if we are unsure of what is being done or needs to be changed.

The purpose of our study is twofold. First, we determine how chairs of accounting programs perceive the skills of speaking, writing, listening, interpersonal communication, and technological communication for *both* the accounting and the business curricula. Are some skills more important for the business than for the accounting curriculum? Second, we also determine wherein the curriculum communication skills are taught, if they are required, and measure the chairs' perceptions of how much class time *ideally* should be spent on these skills.

We organize the remainder of this chapter as follows. The first section of this chapter reviews the relevant literature. The second section sets out our study's research method and questions. The third section discusses the findings and results. We end the chapter with conclusions, recommendations for future research, and implications for the profession.

PRIOR LITERATURE

Studies of practitioners continue to reinforce the importance of communication skills for success in the field. Demonstrating effective communication skills is one factor that contributes to a student's success in a job interview (Eberhardt, McGee, & Mosey, 1997, pp. 293–296; Rosa, 2006, pp. 7–8) and in their professional advancement (Dirk & Buzzard, 1997, pp. 3–7).

A survey of public accounting firms confirmed the need for improved communication skills to advance in the field (Stowers & White, 1999, pp. 23–40). Lee and Blaszczynski (1999, pp. 104–107) asked Fortune 500 executives what skills entry-level accountants would need in 2002. Executives felt that the importance of communication, computer, and group skills would increase while accounting knowledge would decrease. A 2006 survey of 1400 CFOs at U.S. companies with more than 20 employees asked the CFO's if written and verbal communications skills were more or less important than they were 5 years ago. On a five-point scale with five much more important and one much less important, 43% of the respondents felt communication skills were much more important and 37% felt they were somewhat more important than they were 5 years ago (Laff, 2006, pp. 20–22).

In a 2003 study, practitioners identified 15 non-traditional accounting skills as being important enough for both in- and out-of-class activities, even if it required sacrificing some course content to learn them. At the top of the list of professional skills were analytical/critical thinking, written communication, and oral communication (Burnett, 2003, pp. 129–134). Other studies continue to emphasize practitioners' perceptions of the importance of these skills for accountants (Nellermore, Weirich, & Reinstein, 1999, pp. 41–60), for management accountants, (Siegel, 2000, pp. 75–76; Hassall, Joyce, Montaño, & Anes, 2005), for the growing market of women accountants (Duffy, 2004, pp. 39–42), and for internal auditors (Smith, 2005, pp. 513–519).

The profession's message on the value of communication skills is mixed. Recently, the Editor-in-Chief of *The CPA Journal* stated that "employers say their major concern with today's accounting graduates is their ... lack of adequate communication skills: reading, writing, listening, and speaking" (Kranacher, 2007, p. 80). However, as of April 5, 2004, the AICPA instituted a computer-based CPA Examination that assessed research and communication skills. The exam asked candidates questions whose answers required the candidate's use of presentation and spreadsheet skills but reduced the AICPA's emphasis on traditional communication skills.

Accounting educators also recognize the importance of communication skills. Tan, Fowler, and Hawkes (2004, pp. 51–67) found that both practitioners and academics placed high importance on thinking, problem solving, listening, and quantitative skills for management accountants. Elizabeth Rosa (2006, p. 7) argues "to be successful, CPA's need to be competent in both written and oral communication ... and the education of every accounting major should include the development of these skills."

However, little research examines the value of or where these skills are in the curriculum. Knight (1999, pp. 10–29) found in a survey of 52 top-ranked undergraduate business schools that 50 schools had lower division (first and second year) writing requirements and 17 had similar oral communication requirements often housed outside the business school. A total of 36 schools had an upper division writing requirement, while many writing requirements are stressed throughout the business curriculum. Universities' most frequently offered course is a sophomore or junior-level business commu-nication, usually taught to fulfill the mandates set by accrediting agencies such as AACSB (Wardrope, 2002, pp. 60–72). Much of the research on business school communication training centers on this course, which although covers a wide range of topics, historically focuses on written communication (Wardrope & Bayless, 1999, pp. 33–41).

Many educators argue that communication training must be integrated into the accounting curriculum. Albin and Crockett (1991, p. 325) contend "skills can be properly developed only within an accounting context, which means that they must be integrated into accounting classes." Friedlan (1995, pp. 47–63) found that when students were taught "other" skills within an accounting class, they perceived the "other" skills as being more important than when the skills were taught either independently or in other courses. Sneed and Morgan (1999, p. 25) concur that if "these skills are not stressed in accounting courses, majors may perceive that they are unimportant for their selected career." Lee and Blaszczynski (1999, pp. 104–107) also argue that teaching such skills in accounting classes will be more effective than simply adding more communication or computer classes. Not only integration but timing of skill development is important. There is concern that a business communication course has limited effect on student skills when taken late in a student's academic career (Ashbaugh, Johnstone, & Warfield, 2002, pp. 123–148).

We surveyed accounting programs in North America to determine the importance and location of communication in the accounting and the business curricula. Our analysis may provide a framework for examining how communication education currently operates within accounting and business curricula. The results are descriptive, not prescriptive, but provide a basis for academics to review their own programs.

METHOD

We surveyed department chairs using the communication skills of writing, speaking, listening, interpersonal, and technological identified by previous researchers. Our purpose was to assess how current educators perceive the importance of communication and determine where universities teach communication skills in the accounting and the business curricula. We pretested two alternative forms of the survey, varied by the order of the questions. Faculty outside of the authors' universities reviewed the final forms. In 2006, we summarized and analyzed survey data from 530 chairpersons of accounting programs in North America with at least five full-time accounting instructors. We received 122 usable responses for a return rate of 23%.

Of the schools responding, 85 were private, 36 were public; 74 were AACSB-accredited and 48 were not. One institution did not indicate its accreditation status. We used a two-factor analysis of variance mixed design on the five areas of instructional skills: speaking, writing, interpersonal, listening, and technological. The independent factor was the type of institution (either public versus private or AACSB-accredited versus non-AACSB-accredited), with the repeated measures factor as the type of program (accountancy versus business). We asked the department chairs the following research questions:

1. What level of importance do chairs assign for instruction of individual communication skills?
2. Where in an accounting/business program are communication skills taught?
3. How much class time should be ideally allocated for each individual communication skill in a required communication course?

RESULTS

Demographics

The majority of the 122 responding chairs were from private (70%), AACSB (62%) institutions (Table 1). All institutions offered a bachelor's degree with an accounting major and about one-half offered MBAs (48%) and/or an accounting-related master's degree (52%). An equal number of institutions offered a Master's in Taxation (11%) and/or PhDs in accounting (12%). Three-fourths of the respondents were male, with the majority of chairs over 50 years old (76%). Nearly all chairs were tenured (91%) and had the rank of at least associate professor (89%). There were no significant differences in faculty demographics between private to public or AACSB to non-AACSB institutions.

Importance of Communication Skills

In the first question, we asked accounting department chairs to rate the importance of five categories of communication skills using a five-point Likert scale, where 1 indicates "no importance" and 5 indicates "maximum importance." Each chair rated the importance of speaking, writing, listening, interpersonal communication, and technological communication in both the accounting and the business curricula. *All* communication skills received over a 4 on the five-point scale.

We performed a one-factor repeated measures analysis for group differences among the five communication skills within the accounting and the business curricula. The Mauchly's test of sphericity was significant in both analyses, and therefore, a Greenhouse–Geisser adjustment was used in testing the within group mean differences. Table 2, panel A, presents our results and a visual ranking of importance for the five communication skills in the accounting curriculum. The visual order indicates that chairs perceive *writing* (4.37) as the most important communication skill in the accounting curriculum, being significantly more important than *speaking* (4.16) skills (p-value of .001) and *listening* (4.13) and *interpersonal* (4.17) skills (p-value of .01). *Technology* (4.28), though ranked second, was not significantly different from the other four skills.

Table 2, panel B, presents our results and a visual ranking of importance for the five communication skills in the business curriculum. Again, the visual order illustrates chairs' perception of *writing* (4.34) as the most

Table 1.   Sample Demographics.

	Frequency	Percent
Panel A: Institutional Demographics (n = 122)		
Public	36	30
Private	85	70
AACSB	74	62
Non-AACSB	48	39
Degrees offered		
Bachelors	122	100
MBA	58	48
MS/MA/MPA	64	52
Masters in Tax	14	11
Doctorate	15	12
Panel B: Chair Demographics		
Gender (n = 117)		
Male	87	74
Female	30	26
Age (n = 119) (years)		
30–39	1	1
40–49	27	23
50–59	73	61
60+	18	15
Rank (n = 121)		
Instructor/clinical	6	5
Assistant	7	6
Associate	34	28
Full	74	61
Tenured (n = 121)		
Tenured	110	91
Non-tenured	11	9

important skill within the business curriculum, significantly more important than *listening* (4.04) and *technology* (4.09) skills (*p*-value of .001) and *interpersonal* (4.14) skills (*p*-value of .01). *Speaking* (4.27), ranked second, was significantly more important than *listening* skills (*p*-value of .05). While *speaking* was rated higher than *technology* and *interpersonal* skills, the difference was not significant. Chairs ranked s*peaking* as relatively equal in importance with *listening* and *interpersonal* skills in the accounting curriculum. Unlike accounting, *speaking* is not grouped with *interpersonal*

Table 2.   Ranked Importance within Groups.

	Speak	Write	Listen	Interpersonal	Technological
Panel A: Within Accounting Group, p-Values					
Speaking	.000	1.000	1.000		1.000
Writing		.002	.002		.504
Listening			1.000		.714
Interpersonal					1.000
Technological					

Listen	Speak	Interpers	Techno	Write
4.13	4.16	4.17	4.28	4.37

	Speak	Write	Listen	Interpersonal	Technological
Panel B: Within Business Group, p-Values					
Speaking	.833	.024	.215		.057
Writing		.000	.007		.000
Listening			1.000		1.000
Interpersonal					1.000
Technological					

Listen	Techno	Interpers	Speak	Write
4.04	4.09	4.14	4.27	4.34

and *listening* skills in the business curriculum. Within the business
curriculum, *speaking* is ranked above *interpersonal* skills and is significantly
more important than *listening*. It is important to note that in both curricula,
chairs ranked *writing* as the most important and *listening* as the least
important communication skill.

Chairs rated *writing* as the most important communication skill for both
the accounting (4.37) and the overall business (4.34) curricula (Table 3,
panel A). Chairs also rated *listening* as the least important skill for
accounting (4.13) and overall business (4.04). Chairs perceived all skills but

Table 3. Ranked Importance of Communication Instruction.

Panel A: Importance of Communication Instruction in All Institutions

	Accounting	Business	Paired *n*	*p*-value*
Speaking	4.16	4.27	116	.028*
Writing	4.37	4.34	115	.452
Listening	4.13	4.04	116	.025*
Interpersonal	4.17	4.14	116	.417
Technological	4.28	4.09	116	.000***

Panel B: Importance of Communication Instruction: Private versus Public Institutions

	Private (*n* = 85)		Public (*n* = 36)	
	Accounting	Business	Accounting	Business
Speaking*	4.17	4.29	4.18	4.27
Writing	4.41	4.41	4.28	4.22
Listening	4.16	4.13	4.06	3.88**
Interpersonal	4.21	4.21	4.12	4.03
Technological**	4.30	4.13	4.21	4.03

Panel C: Importance of Communication Instruction: AACSB versus Non-AACSB Institutions

	AACSB-accredited (*n* = 74)		Non-AACSB-accredited (*n* = 48)	
	Accounting	Business	Accounting	Business
Speaking	4.10	4.27	4.26	4.26
Writing	4.39	4.38	4.35	4.28
Listening	4.07	3.96*	4.22	4.17
Interpersonal	4.17	4.14	4.17	4.13
Technological**	4.30	4.10	4.24	4.07

*Significant difference at a *p*-value of .05.
**Significant difference at a *p*-value of .01.
***Significant difference at a *p*-value of .001.

speaking as a communication skill more important for accounting than general business. *Speaking* was significantly more important for the business (4.27) than the accounting curriculum (4.16) at the .05 level. However, chairs perceived *listening* as a skill significantly more important (*p*-value of .05) for accounting (4.13) than business (4.04). *Technological* communication skills showed the greatest significant difference at the .001 level, as more

important for accounting (4.28) than business (4.09). Nearly all significant
differences between the accounting and the business curricula were mirrored
when grouped by private versus public institutions (see Table 3, panel B).
However, for public institutions, *listening* skills are valued significantly
(*p*-value of .01) higher by chairs for accounting (4.06) than business (3.88).
This result is replicated for *listening* in panel C for AACSB-accredited
institutions.

Required Courses in Communications

In the second question, we asked department chairs if their programs
included a required communication course and if the required course is
taught as part of the overall business or accounting curriculum (Table 4).
Significantly more programs (*p*-value of .001) had a required communication course taught as a part of the general business curriculum (61%) than
the accounting curriculum (42%). At the beginning of the project, we

Table 4. Proportion of Schools that have a Required Communication
Course in the Business or Accounting Curriculum.

Panel A: Aggregate Sample[a]

	Yes	No	*n*
% Having a required course in accounting curriculum	42% (51)	58% (71)	122
% Having a required course in business core curriculum	61% (74)	39% (48)	122

Panel B: Private versus Public/Accredited versus Non-Accredited[a]

	Private (*n* = 85)	Public (*n* = 36)	Accredited (*n* = 74)	Non-accredited (*n* = 48)
% Having a required course in accounting curriculum	43% (36)	42% (15)	39% (29)	46% (22)
% Having a required course in business core curriculum	67% (57)	47% (17)	57% (42)	67% (32)

[a]Using a McNemar test for the paired responses, the percent of business programs that have a
required communication course is significantly greater than accounting programs over all
comparisons, at a *p*-value of .001.

predicted that both percentages would have been higher, given the public focus on communication skills of business students in general and the specific industry call for accounting graduates with excellent communication skills. Private universities had a significantly higher proportion (p-value of .001) of communication courses taught in the business core (67%) than the accounting program (47%). Private schools had a higher proportion of required communication courses in both accounting and business core programs than public schools. Surprisingly, although AACSB stresses the importance of communication courses, non-AACSB schools had a higher proportion of required communication course in both the accounting and the business core programs.

Additional Courses in Communication

As a follow-up question for chairs in programs with a required communication course in their business or accounting curriculum, we asked how many communication courses (not necessarily required) were offered in their curriculum (Table 5). In the aggregate programs with a required course in accounting, 57% offered one additional course, 31% offered two, and 12% offered three. For programs with a required course in the business curriculum, 77% offered one additional course, 18% offered two, and 5% offered three additional courses. Overall, in both accounting and business curricula, private and AACSB-accredited institutions offered more additional courses in communication.

Institutions with No Required Communication Course

We also asked chairs whose institutions did not have a required communication course in either the accounting or the business curriculum to indicate if communication skills were not taught at all, taught as part of the accounting courses, taught as part of business core courses, or taught outside of the accounting and the business curricula. Chairs were allowed to choose as many options as applicable. Only 38 chairs responded, of which 23 were private and 15 were public institutions, while 24 were AACSB-accredited and 14 were non-AACSB-accredited institutions. The most frequent option for teaching communication skills outside of a required class was to have skills taught as part of courses in the accounting program (73% private, 80% public, 71% AACSB, and 86% of non-AACSB). The

Table 5.   Additional Courses in Communication Besides Required.

Panel A: Aggregate Accounting and Business Courses Required plus Additional
Communication Courses

	Required in accounting (%) (n = 35)	Required in business (%) (n = 49)
% Offering one course	57	77
% Offering two courses	31	18
% Offering three courses	12	5

Panel B: Required Courses in Accounting plus Additional Courses

	Private (%) (n = 27)	Public (%) (n = 8)	AACSB (%) (n = 21)	Non-AACSB (%) (n = 14)
% With one course	52	75	48	71
% With two courses	33	25	33	29
% With three courses	15	0	19	0

Panel C: Required Courses in Business plus Additional Courses

	Private (%) (n = 39)	Public (%) (n = 10)	AACSB (%) (n = 30)	Non-AACSB (%) (n = 17)
% With one course	72	100	70	90
% With two courses	23	0	27	10
% With three courses	5	0	3	0

second most frequently selected option was to include communication skills
as part of other courses in the general business core (73% private, 67%
public, 67% AASCB, and 79% non-AASCB). Third was to have
communication skills taught outside of the accounting and the business
programs (53% private, 73% public, 58% AASCB, and 57% non-AASCB).
There were no significant differences based on institutional charter or
accreditation standards.

Emphasis on Communication Skills in the Required Course

As a further follow-up question, we asked chairs from institutions that
required communication courses in either their accounting or business
curriculum to indicate the approximate percentage of class time they believe

should ideally be spent on the various communication skills in a required communication course (Table 6). All chairs would ideally spend about 60% or more time on writing and speaking activities. Listening skills were least stressed in the chair responses under any institutional, accreditation, or curriculum demographic sub-sample.

Table 6. Proportion of Perceived Ideal Time for Teaching Skills in a Communication Course.

Panel A: Accredited versus Non-Accredited

Skill	AACSB-accredited		Non-AACSB-accredited		Interaction	Main accredited	Main curriculum
	Accounting	Business	Accounting	Business			
Speaking	34.04 (9)	32.36	25.08 (14)	24.87	.659	.073[a]	.659
Writing	31.05 (10)	42.56	29.28 (14)	30.30	.110	.031[a]	.052[a]
Interpersonal	9.60 (8)	9.12	16.16 (14)	16.07	.463	.226	.463
Listening	7.18 (9)	6.37	15.00 (14)	14.23	.862	.032[a]	.426
Technological	18.14 (8)	9.59	14.48 (13)	14.53	.260	.531	.296

Panel B: Private versus Public

	Private		Public		Interaction	Main Institution	Main Curriculum
	Accounting	Business	Accounting	Business			
Speaking	29.10 (19)	28.47	28,78 (4)	26.25	.801	.657	.801
Writing	28.83 (20)	35.85	38.29 (4)	38.72	.685	.958	.329
Interpersonal	13.33 (18)	12.92	12.36 (4)	12.47	.278	.702	.885
Listening	11.42 (19)	10.37	10.94 (4)	11.28	.154	.643	.742
Technological	17.32 (17)	12.39	9.63 (4)	11.28	.515	.329	.827

Notes: Table entries represent proportion ideal time spent on a skill in a communication skill. Numbers in parenthesis are cell sample sizes.
[a]Cell sizes are relatively small to reliably measure significance.

There were statistically significant differences between AACSB-accredited and non-AACSB-accredited schools in ideal time spent on listening (p-value of .032) and writing skills (p-value of .031) although the small sample sizes reduce the reliability of the achieved significance. Chairs in non-AACSB programs would ideally want more course time on listening skills in both business and accounting curricula, while AACSB chairs would ideally want more time on writing skills in both business and accounting curricula. No other significant differences were measured. AACSB accounting chairs want to ideally spend more time on technology skills (18%) in the accounting course than in business communication courses (10%).

CONCLUSION AND LIMITATIONS

The purpose of our study was to understand accounting department chairs' perception of the importance of communication skills in the business and the accounting curricula, determine where these skills are taught in the curriculum, and the chairs' perception of ideal proportion of time spent on each communication skill in a required course. Department chairs perceived writing, speaking, listening, interpersonal, and technological skills as important in *both* the business and the accounting curricula. They perceived writing as the most important communication skill for both the accounting and the overall business curricula, while listening was the least important of this group. While chairs rank technological skills as second in accounting, they rank speaking skills as second in the overall business curriculum. In general, chairs perceive communication skills as *more important* for the accounting curriculum than for general business, specifically listening and technological skills.

Most programs had a required communication course taught as a part of the general business curriculum, with a lesser number of chairs reporting it being taught specifically in the accounting curriculum. Most schools that do not require a communication course in either their accounting or business curriculum teach communication skills by integrating them within courses in their accounting or business program, while a fewer number of institutions rely on coursework outside of the business program.

Chairs had few differences in perceptions of communication skills value based on institutional charter or accreditation. Public and AACSB-accredited schools perceived listening as significantly more valuable for the accounting curriculum. Public and private schools both perceived speaking as more valuable for the business curriculum, while AACSB and non-AACSB schools did not perceive this difference. Private schools *did* require and offer more communication courses than public institutions. AACSB-accredited institutions did offer more additional communication courses than non-AACSB schools, but non-AACSB-accredited schools had more required communication courses.

Limitations and Future Research

While our study provides a description of the importance of and where communication skills are taught in the curriculum, it has some limitations that provide opportunities for further research in this area. We did not ask chairs at schools without a required course in which courses in the accounting and the business curricula are communication skills taught. It would be important to know what skills are taught and what percentage of class time they allot to communication instruction. We also did not ask chairs at schools that have a required course if, in addition to the required course, they integrate communication skills into other accounting or business courses in their curriculum, and if so, which courses and what communication skills. We recommend additional research include this information as it would be very helpful in providing a more complete picture of how departments are teaching communication within their programs

It might also be helpful to obtain information on programs' additional courses' topics or content, or the frequency in which the courses are actually taught, and student registration numbers for the optional course offerings. The small sub-sample in some cells limited our ability to measure some significant differences. Expanding the sample size may assist researchers in answering additional questions. Finally, future studies might expand the communication skills categories studied, particularly technological communication.

Implications for the Curriculum

Given the debate on the value of integration and learning voiced by Albin and Crockett (1991, pp. 325–327), Sneed and Morgan (1999, pp. 22–27), and Lee and Blaszczynski (1999, pp. 104–107), programs should consider whether these skills be taught primarily in stand-alone courses or integrated throughout the curriculum. Burnett also contends that skills need to be throughout the curriculum rather than in just one or two courses (Burnett,

2003, pp. 129–134). This is a critical question for the curriculum and reflects the field's overall commitment to these skills

Using our findings, departments should also review their course offerings in communication to determine what communication skills they are emphasizing. For example, our study finds writing is a major component in communication courses, particularly the business communication course. However, practitioners especially after Sarbanes-Oxely are emphasizing the need for more public speaking and interpersonal skills (Watkins, 2005, pp. 57–61) and listening (Green, Callahan, & Madison, 2008). A universities' curriculum emphasis should reflect current needs of the profession.

Additionally, the profession might want to identify more specific guidelines for communication competencies and requirements for accountancy and business programs to ensure a more uniform student experience independent of institutions. Perhaps, the limited differences between public and private and AACSB-accredited and non-AACSB-accredited institutions reflect the influence of earlier statements by the profession. Finally, the profession should begin to think about ways to evaluate communication skills in professional exams. The professions inclusion of these skills in the exam will send a strong message both to academics and to students about their importance.

ACKNOWLEDGMENTS

The authors acknowledge the skills and assistance of Professor Jerry Moreno from John Carroll University and an anonymous reviewer, whose comments and suggestions were greatly appreciated.

REFERENCES

AACSB – American Assembly of Collegiate Schools of Business. (2008) *Eligibility procedures and accreditation standards for business accreditation* (pp. 1–78). AACSB.

AECC – Accounting Education Change Commission. (1990). Objectives of education for accountants: Position statement number one. *Issues in Accounting Education, 5*(2), 307–312.

AICPA – American Institute of Certified Public Accountants. (1998). CPA vision project identifies top five issues for the profession. *The CPA Letter, 1*(12).

Albin, M. J., & Crockett, J. R. (1991). Integrating necessary skills and concepts into the accounting curriculum. *Journal of Education for Business, 66*(6), 325–327.

Ameen, E. C., Guffey, D. M., & Jackson, C. M. (2000). Silence is not golden: Further evidence of oral communication apprehension in accounting majors. *Advances in Accounting Education* (3), 85–105.

Ashbaugh, H., Johnstone, K. M., & Warfield, T. D. (2002). Outcome assessment of a writing-skill improvement initiative: Results and methodological implications. *Issues in Accounting Education, 17*(2), 123–148.

Bunn, P. C., Barfit, L. A., Cooper, J., & Sandifer, L. B. (2005). CPAs in Mississippi: Communication skills and software needed by entry-level accountants. *Delta Pi Epsilon Journal, 47*(3), 154–163.

Burnett, S. (2003). The future of accounting education: A regional perspective. *Journal of Education for Business, 78*(3), 129–134.

Christ, M. Y. (2002). Developing intermediate accounting students' analytical and communi-cation skills through the annual report project. *Advances in Accounting Education* (4), 41–57.

Dirk, R., & Buzzard, J. (1997). What CEOs expect of employees hired for international work. *Business Education Forum, 51*(4), 3–7.

Duffy, M. N. (2004). Tips for working with female clients. *Journal of Accountancy, 197*(4), 39–42.

Eberhardt, B. J., McGee, P., & Mosey, S. (1997). Business concerns regarding MBA education: Effects on recruiting. *Journal of Education for Business, 72*(5), 293–296.

Friedlan, J. M. (1995). The effects of different teaching approaches on students' perceptions of the skills needed to success in accounting courses and by practicing accountants. *Issues in Accounting Education, 10*(1), 47–63.

Green, B. P., Callahan, M. & Madison, R. (2008). The maturation effect of professional internships on student perceptions and values. Paper presented at the American Accounting Association 2008 National Convention. Anaheim, CA.

Hassall, T., Joyce, J., Montaño, J. L., & Anes, J. A. (2005). Priorities for the development of vocational skills in management accountants: A European perspective. *Accounting Forum, 29*(4), 379–394.

Knight, M. (1999). Writing and other communication standards in undergraduate business education: A study of current program requirements, practices, and trends. *Business Communication Quarterly, 62*(1), 10–29.

Kranacher, M. (2007). The problem with communication. *The CPA Journal, 204*(1), 80.

Laff, M. (2006). Wanted: CFOs with communications skills. *T+D, 60*(12), 20–22.

Lee, D., & Blaszczynski, C. (1999). Perspectives of 'Fortune 500' executives on the competency requirements for accounting graduates. *Journal of Education for Business, 75*(2), 104–107.

Nellermore, D. A., Weirich, T. R., & Reinstein, A. (1999). Using practitioners' viewpoints to improve accounting students' communications skills. *Business Communication Quarterly, 62*(2), 41–60.

Rosa, E. (2006). Be demanding: Require exceptional communication skills. *Pennsylvania CPA Journal, 77*(1), 7–8.

Siegel, G. (2000). Management accounts: The great communicators. *Strategic Finance, 82*(6), 75–76.

Smith, G. (2005). Communication skills are critical for internal auditors. *Managerial Auditing Journal, 20*(5), 513–519.

Sneed, J., & Morgan, D. A. (1999). Evaluating the verbal, quantitative, and problem-solving skills of students entering the accounting curriculum. *Management Research News, 22*(4), 22–27.

Stout, D. E., & DaCrema, J. J. (2005). A writing-improvement model for accounting education. *Advances in Accounting Education* (7), 307–328.

Stowers, R. H., & White, G. T. (1999). Connecting accounting and communication: A survey of public accounting firms. *Business Communication Quarterly, 62*(2), 23–40.

Tan, L. M., Fowler, M. B., & Hawkes, L. (2004). Management accounting curricula: Striking a balance between the views of educators and practitioners. *Accounting Education, 13*(1), 51–67.

Wardrope, W. J. (2002). Department chairs' perceptions of the importance of business communication skills. *Business Communication Quarterly, 65*(4), 60–72.

Wardrope, W. J., & Bayless, M. L. (1999). Content of the business communication course: An analysis of the coverage. *Business Communication Quarterly, 62*(4), 33–41.

Watkins, K. J. (2005). Will they throw eggs. *Journal of Accountancy, 199*(4), 57–61.

THE INFLUENCE OF MOTIVATION ON CHEATING BEHAVIOR AMONG ACCOUNTING MAJORS

Kenneth J. Smith, Jeanette A. Davy and Donald L. Rosenberg

ABSTRACT

This study uses structural equation modeling to examine the influence of academic motivation on reported prior cheating behavior, neutralization tendencies, and likelihood of future cheating among accounting majors. It also investigates the impact of prior cheating on neutralization of cheating behaviors and the likelihood of future cheating, as well as the potential mediating effects of neutralization on future cheating behavior. Our results support differentiation of the theoretical constructs within the specified process model, and also show significant positive associations between an amotivational orientation and prior cheating, neutralization, and the likelihood of future cheating.

Academic dishonesty on college campuses has received considerable attention in recent years from the media, administrators, and researchers. In fact, evidence that cheating among college students is becoming more prevalent is cited as a "contributing factor to the failed ethical conduct of our corporate executives and professional accountants" (Burke, Polimeni, &

Advances in Accounting Education: Teaching and Curriculum Innovations, Volume 10, 169–188
Copyright © 2009 by Emerald Group Publishing Limited
All rights of reproduction in any form reserved
ISSN: 1085-4622/doi:10.1108/S1085-4622(2009)0000010011

Slavin, 2007, p. 58). Studies have found that students who cheat in school will cheat in the workplace (Nonis & Swift, 2001, pp. 74–75; Granitz & Loewy, 2007, p. 293) and that those who have cheated in the past are likely to cheat again in the future (Davis & Ludvigson, 1995, p. 120; Nonis & Swift, 1998, p. 197).

Much of the research conducted on student cheating over the past 30 years has focused on identifying the characteristics of students who cheat and what can be done to stop them (Jordan, 2001, p. 233). Studies involving demographic factors that might identify cheaters, such as age and gender, have not provided consistent results (Whitley, 1998, pp. 239–242). For academicians to better understand why students cheat and what might be done to reduce their propensity to cheat, it is necessary to expand the search for predictors of cheating behavior.

This study examines the role that academic motivation plays in predicting cheating behavior among accounting majors. Barkoukis, Tsorbatzoudis, Grouios, and Sideridis (2008, p. 39) note that motivation is "thought to be one of the most important aspects of human behavior ..." and that it may be associated with a number of factors including academic performance. With respect to performance, studies have shown that students with lower grade point averages, lower course grades, and lower SAT/ACT scores are more likely to cheat (Crown & Spiller, 1998, pp. 686–687; Whitley, 1998, pp. 242–243). Thus, a more reliable determination of the interrelations between motivational factors and academic performance and the resulting influence on student cheating could facilitate the development of more powerful intervention strategies to limit student cheating and to promote professional attitudes among future members of the accounting profession (Jordan, 2001, p. 234).

This study will address the dearth of research to assess the influence of amotivation, as well as extrinsic and intrinsic motivation on key educational outcomes. This will provide an empirical test of Deci and Ryan's (2000, p. 237) conceptualization of amotivation as an anchor on one side of their posited motivational continuum, and assess its contribution to the hypothesized cheating dynamic and the potential ramifications for development of cheating mitigation strategies.

To more fully explore the role of motivation in cheating behavior, this study uses structural equation modeling to test a modified version of the (Smith, Davy, Rosenberg, & Haight, 2002, p. 48) cheating model. We find significant positive associations between amotivation and prior cheating, likelihood of cheating, and neutralization. Positive relationships between the following factors also are noted: intrinsic motivation and academic performance, external-identified regulation and prior cheating, prior cheating and neutralization, and neutralization and likelihood of cheating. Our study also shows negative associations between the following factors: external-identified regulation and academic performance, amotivation and academic performance, and academic performance and neutralization.

MODEL DEVELOPMENT

We modify the Smith et al. (2002, p. 48) cheating model by replacing alienation with academic motivation as the attitudinal construct potentially associated with cheating behaviors. We also use Vallerand et al.'s, (1992, p. 1013) Academic Motivation Scale (AMS). The AMS is a 28-item psychometric instrument which contains seven subscales, each designed to assess a differential state along a continuum that is anchored on the left by amotivation, proceeds through extrinsic motivation, and is anchored on the right by intrinsic motivation (Deci & Ryan, 2000, p. 237).

Amotivation is the absence of motivation to pursue an activity due to its lack of value to a person, or that person's feeling of incompetence or inability to obtain a desired outcome (Ryan & Deci, 2000, pp. 60–61). Fortier, Vallerand, and Guay (1995, p. 260) conclude that, "When people are in such a state, they perceive their behavior as caused by forces out of their control; they are neither intrinsically motivated nor extrinsically motivated ... "

Extrinsic motivation, as measured by the AMS, is considered increasingly self-determined as it moves through a set of ordered categories from left to right termed external regulation, introjected regulation, and identified regulation (Deci & Ryan, 2000, pp. 235–236). Behaviors that are externally regulated are intentionally directed at either obtaining a positive outcome or avoiding a negative outcome. Introjected behaviors are regulated somewhat internally, and identified regulation entails attributing personal value to a behavior, while still being extrinsically motivated.

Intrinsic motivation is the "drive to pursue an activity simply for the pleasure or satisfaction derived from it" (Fairchild, Horst, Finney, & Barron, 2005, p. 332). Vallerand et al. (1992, pp. 1005–1006) broke down this construct into three self-explanatory types of intrinsic motivation: intrinsic motivation to accomplish, intrinsic motivation to experience stimulation, and intrinsic motivation to know.

Smith, Davy, and Rosenberg (in press) noted inconsistencies in prior research on the factor structure of the AMS, prompting their re-examination of the factorial breakdown of the scale. Exploratory and confirmatory factor analyses on two large scale independent samples supported a four factor conceptualization of academic motivation which suggested single "states" for intrinsic motivation and for amotivation, and two distinct "states" for extrinsic motivation, external-identified regulation and integrated regulation. That finding prompted our use of a similar conceptualization of academic motivation in the current study as illustrated in Fig. 1.

Prior studies of the relationship between motivation and cheating typically differentiate between intrinsic (mastery) goals, extrinsic goals, and performance goals (Jordan, 2001, p. 235). The evidence suggests that students who have a desire to master subject matter are more likely to be able to demonstrate that knowledge, thereby reducing any need to cheat (Baker, 2004, p. 190). Students who are motivated to obtain valued outcomes or to avoid negative outcomes (extrinsic motivation) may see the potential for gain by engaging in dishonest behaviors. However, those who are intrinsically motivated by a desire to learn or to engage in an activity are not helped in achieving these desires by cheating. Though intrinsic motivation has been found to contribute positively in learning, there is evidence that extrinsic motivation impairs learning, resulting in poorer performance and increasing the need to cheat (Baker, 2004, p. 190).

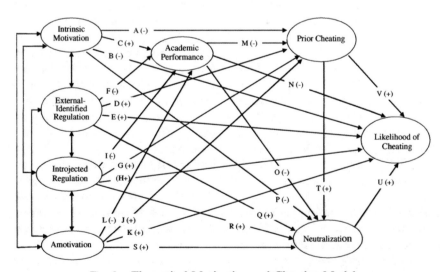

Fig. 1. Theoretical Motivation and Cheating Model.

Paths A and B in our model predict that intrinsic motivation has significant negative relationships with the two cheating constructs (i.e., prior cheating and cheating likelihood), whereas path C predicts a significant positive relation with academic performance. Conversely, paths D and E predict significant positive relationships between external-identified regulation and the two cheating constructs, whereas path F predicts a significant negative relation with academic performance. Paths G and H predict significant positive relationships between integrated regulation and the two cheating constructs, and path I predicts a significant negative relation with academic performance.

Finally, based on Deci and Ryan's (2000, p. 237) construction of motivation as a continuum from positive to negative, the impact of amotivation on cheating behavior should be similar, if not stronger than for either of the extrinsic motivation constructs. Thus, paths J and K predict significant positive relationships between amotivation and the two cheating constructs, whereas path L predicts a significant negative relation with academic performance. Since numerous studies document a negative relationship between academic performance and cheating proclivities (Rakovski & Levy, 2007, p. 473; Crown & Spiller, 1998, p. 689), paths M and N predict a negative relationship between academic performance and the two cheating constructs.

Prior research has shown neutralization to actually facilitate cheating behavior (Smith et al., 2002, p. 59). Neutralization represents the rationalizations and justifications for unethical/dishonest behavior used to deflect self-disapproval or disapproval from others after violating an accepted social norm (Sykes & Matza, 1957, p. 666). This allows students to cheat without feeling inherently dishonest, thereby eliminating a sense of guilt for the dishonest action (Nonis & Swift, 1998, p. 190). Often cited rationalizations for cheating include subject matter difficulty and time constraints (Daniel, Blount, & Ferrell, 1991, p. 716). Intuitively, there is less reason to neutralize when there is less of a need to cheat, supporting the notion that those who perform better are less likely to neutralize (path O). Given that intrinsic motivation is positively linked in learning (thus lowering the need to cheat and to rationalize dishonest behavior), path P predicts a negative relation between this construct and neutralization. Davy, Kincaid, Smith, and Trawick (2007, p. 297) reported a positive relationship between extrinsic motivation and neutralization, thus prompting our inclusion of paths Q and R. Again, Deci and Ryan's (2000, p. 237) continuum concept suggests that amotivation also is positively related to neutralization since amotivated individuals need to rationalize their negative behaviors (path S).

Since neutralization appears to be a means of justifying dishonest behavior, we predict a positive relation between prior cheating and neutralization (path T). Also, we propose path U since neutralization can be used to rationalize future behavior. Neutralization may have a positive influence on the likelihood of cheating and a mediating effect on the relation between prior cheating and likelihood of cheating. Since prior cheating is a good predictor of future cheating (Nonis & Swift, 1998, p. 190; Davis & Ludvigson, 1995, p. 120), path V predicts a positive relation between prior cheating and the likelihood of cheating.

RESEARCH METHOD

Latent variables with multiple indicators and structural equation modeling are used to test the hypothesized relationships depicted in Fig. 1.

Sample

Accounting majors from three AACSB-accredited universities, two on the East Coast and one in the Midwest, provided data for this study. Questionnaires were administered in classes. The instructors were not present and the students were assured of anonymity. This sample generated 714 responses, 13 of which were returned incomplete or blank, yielding 701 as usable for our analysis. Six hundred twenty-two (89 percent) of the respondents came from the East Coast universities, whereas 79 (11 percent) were from the Midwest university. We reviewed the data for demographic differences across the three samples. Average age, gender composition, marital status, and year in school were similar across all three sample schools.

Sophomores ($n = 119$), juniors ($n = 247$), and seniors ($n = 262$) comprised 17 percent, 35 percent, and 37 percent of the sample, respectively, and 37 masters degree students also were represented. Ages ranged from 18 to 59 years with a median of 21 ($\mu = 22.57$, $\sigma = 5.12$). Females comprised 49 percent ($n = 339$) of those reporting, and 87 percent of respondents ($n = 612$) were unmarried.

Measures

To test the theoretical model, we used the following measures:

Academic performance was captured by each student's self-reported score on: (a) how they rated their overall academic performance on a five-point scale ranging from 1 = *very poor* to 5 = *very good* and (b) how they rated their own academic performance as compared to that of their peers (perceived academic performance) on a five-point scale ranging from 1 = *very poor* to 5 = *very good* (Nonis & Swift, 1998, pp. 192–193). We used self-reported academic performance as a surrogate measure for grade point average (GPA) since the data collection design (i.e., student anonymity) precluded the collection of objective GPA information on the sample.

Neutralization was measured using a scale developed by Ball (1966, pp. 22–23) and later utilized by Haines, Diekhoff, LaBeff, and Clark (1986, p. 347). We asked students to "Please indicate the extent to which you agree that a student is justified in cheating in each of the following circumstances". Responses were made on a five-point Likert-type scale ranging from 1 = *strongly disagree* to 5 = *strongly agree* for each of the 11 items. In an exploratory factor analysis which assessed the multidimensionality of the items comprising this scale, Smith et al. (2002, pp. 53–54) found two underlying subscales, difficulty (six items) and access (five items). As in that study, we summed the items on each subscale to create two composite indicators of neutralization to allow for a better estimate of the random error associated with this construct and facilitate the subsequent latent variable tests.

Prior cheating was assessed using an 8 item version of a 12-item scale adapted from Tom and Borin (1988, p. 155). We asked students to "Think of all the exams you have taken in college. How often have you participated in each of the activities during exams?" In response, students reported the frequency with which they engaged in each of the eight cheating behaviors on a five-point Likert type scale ranging from "never" to "very often." Our eight items are identical to those utilized by Smith et al. (2002, p. 54) based on their exploratory factor analysis findings which indicated the presence of two subscales, overt (four items) and covert (four items). Again, as in that study, we summed the items on each subscale to create two composite indicators of prior cheating to facilitate the ensuing latent variable tests.

Likelihood of cheating was evaluated using the 12 item version of Tom and Borin's (1988, p. 155) scale reworded to assess future cheating proclivities.

The preface to these items read "You are taking a course that is difficult but important and there is a possibility that you may or may not make the desired grade if you do not cheat. Please indicate how likely or unlikely you are to cheat under the following conditions." Students responded on the following five-point scale ranging from 1 = *very unlikely to cheat* to 5 = *very likely to cheat*.

Smith et al. (2002, p. 52) found that the items on this scale were unidimensional, that is, they loaded on a single factor. Therefore, we combined the items on this scale into two composite indicator variables based on the matched composites procedure described by Bentler and Wu (1995, pp. 201–202). This procedure is appropriate when it is not expected that any of the composites would be different from one another, "and each composite should measure the same construct, or combination of constructs, as measured by a single composite of all of the original scores" (Bentler & Wu, 1995, p. 201).

Smith et al. (2002, p. 56) report favorable psychometric properties for the aforereferenced measures, prompting their adoption for the present study. Their research (2008, pp. 6–7) also supports a four factor conceptualization of academic motivation as measured on the AMS. Based on these findings, this study adopted the following measures for academic motivation:

Intrinsic motivation was assessed using four items on the subscale from intrinsic motivation to experience stimulation, summed to one indicator, and two items on the subscale from intrinsic motivation to know, summed to one indicator. We summed the items on each subscale to create two composite indicators to allow for a better estimate of the random error associated with this construct and facilitate the subsequent latent variable tests. For each item, students were asked to "indicate the extent to which each response is similar to your own." They responded on a five-point Likert scale ranging from 1 = *does not correspond at all* to 5 = *corresponds exactly*.

External-identified regulation was captured using four items from the external regulation subscale and two items from the identified regulation subscale. Again, we summed the item scores for each subscale to two composite indicators to facilitate the subsequent latent variable analyses. Student response options were identical to those for the intrinsic motivation factor.

Finally, *amotivation* was measured using the four items that comprise the amotivation subscale, and *introjected regulation* was assessed using the two items from the introjected regulation subscale.

Statistical Analysis

We conducted a confirmatory factor analysis on the sample data to independently test the construct and discriminant validity among the constructs represented by the measures. By doing so, we were able to assess whether the factors would load on their respective underlying theoretical constructs. To test the complete measurement model, we used maximum likelihood estimation procedures in EQS Version 6.1 (Bentler, 2006, p. 65) with Satorra and Bentler's (2001) scaling corrections, which allowed us to calculate the Satorra–Bentler χ^2 value (SBχ^2). We selected the Satorra–Bentler rescaled estimate because of non-normal data issues with items on the amotivation subscale. Table 1 presents the items comprising each latent variable to be tested along with the mean score for each predicted latent variable.

We next conducted EQS structural modeling tests to evaluate the theoretical model. We then dropped statistically nonsignificant parameters from the model based on the output of Wald tests applied to the full model. For both the measurement model and structural model tests, we examined model fit using a variety of measures as there is no one definitive index of model fit (Fogarty, Singh, Rhoads, & Moore, 2000, pp. 44 and 46). To measure overall fit, we used the SBχ^2 statistic, the SBχ^2/df ratio, the robust normed fit index (NFI), the comparative fit index (CFI), and the adjusted root mean squared error of approximation (RMSEA) for non-normal conditions. An acceptable cutoff value for the SBχ^2/df ratio is 3.00 according to (Grouzet, Otis, & Pelletier, 2006, p. 82). NFI and CFI values of at least .90 are considered indicative of good model fit (Bentler & Bonnett,

Table 1. Factors for Measurement Model Tests.

Latent Construct	Number of Observed Indicators	Model Test Results[a]
Intrinsic motivation	2	$\mu = 2.873$, $\sigma = 0.880$, $\alpha = .790$
External-identified regulation	2	$\mu = 4.150$, $\sigma = 0.656$, $\alpha = .726$
Amotivation	4	$\mu = 1.593$, $\sigma = 0.920$, $\alpha = .785$
Introjected regulation	2	$\mu = 3.378$, $\sigma = 1.078$, $\alpha = .752$
Academic performance	2	$\mu = 3.575$, $\sigma = 0.714$, $\alpha = .874$
Prior cheating	2	$\mu = 1.314$, $\sigma = 0.427$, $\alpha = .673$
Neutralization	2	$\mu = 1.999$, $\sigma = 0.882$, $\alpha = .907$
Cheating likelihood	2	$\mu = 1.545$, $\sigma = 0.783$, $\alpha = .973$

[a]Cronbach's alpha reliability computed to index the internal consistency of the measure. Values exceeding 0.70 are considered satisfactory (Nunnally, 1978).

1980, p. 600). Finally, RMSEA values of .08 or less are considered acceptable (Hu & Bentler, 1999, p. 27).

Our final analyses consisted of tests of an a priori sequence of nested models against the reduced theoretical model. This nested sequence of models provided direct tests of the hypotheses that the relevant motivational factors are related to academic performance and/or one or more of the key cheating outcomes (as determined by significant path coefficients measured in the reduced structural model). The nested sequence also facilitates a direct examination of the mediating effects of prior cheating and neutralization. The simultaneous estimation of both direct and mediating effects provide a more complete understanding of the roles each construct might play.

We compared the nested structural models using the scaled difference χ^2 test ($\Delta SB\chi^2$; Satorra & Bentler, 2001, p. 511). A significant χ^2 difference value indicates a significant loss-of-fit by constraining a path to zero, indicating that the path should be retained in the model. A nonsignificant χ^2 difference indicates the path could be dropped with no significant loss of model fit.

RESULTS

Tables 2 and 3 present the measurement model test results. Table 2 indicates that the path coefficients from each latent construct to its manifest indicator is significant at $p < .01$. The goodness-of-fit summary presented in Table 3 indicates that the model provides a good fit to the data. The NFI is above .90 and the CFI is above .95. In addition, the RMSEA of .05 falls within its standard of acceptance. The $SB\chi^2/df$ ratio of 2.50 is also below the upper threshold of acceptance.

Table 4 provides goodness-of-fit statistics for the tests of the theoretical model. The NFI and CFI are .930 and .956, respectively, indicating good model fit. In addition, the RMSEA of .51 and the $SB\chi^2/df$ ratio of 2.56 are below their respective maximum thresholds for acceptance.

Table 5 presents the results from testing the a priori sequence of nested models against the reduced theoretical model. As indicated, the model which constrained the path from amotivation to neutralization resulted in a significant loss of model fit ($\Delta SB\chi^2_{diff} = 4.96$; $df = 1$, $p < .05$), indicating that this path should remain in the model. The third model constrained the path from external-identified regulation to academic performance to zero. Again, the $\Delta SB\chi^2$ test indicates that this path should remain ($\Delta SB\chi^2_{diff} = 7.09$; $df = 1$, $p < .01$). As is also apparent, the $\Delta SB\chi^2$ difference tests for each of

Table 2. Standardized Measurement Model Coefficients for the Construct Indicators.

Latent Constructs and Indicators	Standardized Coefficient	t-Value[a,b]
Intrinsic motivation		
Intrinsic motivation to know	.876	–
Intrinsic motivation to experience stimulation	.754	14.223
External-identified regulation		
External regulation	.659	–
Identified regulation	.848	9.375
Amotivation		
Amotivation$_1$	.746	–
Amotivation$_2$	.716	15.682
Amotivation$_3$	.825	14.462
Amotivation$_4$	.875	16.847
Introjected regulation		
Introjected regulation$_1$	.745	–
Introjected regulation$_2$	.781	13.184
Performance		
Academic performance	.965	–
Perceived academic performance	.806	7.179
Prior cheating		
Overt	.646	–
Covert	.915	7.045
Neutralization		
Difficulty	.910	–
Access	.919	24.912
Cheating likelihood		
Cl$_1$	.959	–
Cl$_2$	.994	34.133

[a]Each of the reported t-values is significant at $p < .01$.
[b]Structural equation modeling procedures require that one measure of each construct be fixed to 1.0 to establish the scale of the latent construct.

the five successive constrained models also indicate that the respective constrained paths should remain in the model.

Table 6 presents the estimated maximum likelihood structural coefficients and significance test results for each of the 22 hypothesized paths. Eleven of these paths are significant. Fig. 2 illustrates the significant paths.

Intrinsic motivation has a significant positive relation with academic performance (.217). External-identified regulation has a significant negative relation to academic performance (−.165) and a significant positive relation to prior cheating (.122). Amotivation has a significant negative relation

Table 3.   Goodness of Fit Summary[a].

	Satorra–Bentler Scaled Results	Standard for Acceptance
Statistical tests		
χ^2	299	NA
df	120	NA
p-value	.00	> .05
$\chi^2/\mathrm{d}f$	2.50	< 3.0
Fit indices		
NFI	.931	> .90
CFI	.957	> .90
Residual analysis		
RMSEA	.050	< .08
90% Confidence interval of RMSEA	(.043–.057)	

NFI, Normed Fit Index. Higher values indicate better fit; CFI, Comparative Fit Index. Higher values indicate better fit; and RMSEA = Root Mean Squared Error of Approximation. Lower values indicate better fit.

[a]The measurement model reflects the release of 13 factor covariances as determined by examination of the multivariate Wald test output from the test of the full model. The dropped covariances were: (1) Cheating likelihood – intrinsic motivation; (2) Prior cheating – intrinsic motivation; (3) Neutralization – intrinsic motivation; (4) Amotivation – intrinsic motivation; (5) Academic performance – external-identified regulation; (6) Prior cheating – external-identified regulation; (7) Academic performance – introjected regulation; (8) Prior cheating – introjected regulation; (9) Introjected regulation – amotivation; (10) Neutralization – external-identified regulation; (11) Neutralization – introjected regulation; (12) Cheating likelihood – introjected regulation; and (13) Cheating likelihood – academic performance. By dropping these covariances, the degrees of freedom increased from 107 for the full model to 120 for the reduced model.

to academic performance (−.274) and significant positive relation with prior cheating (.337), neutralization (.095), and likelihood of cheating (.144). Prior cheating has a significant positive influence on neutralization (.632) and likelihood of cheating (.390). Finally, neutralization has a significant positive influence on likelihood of cheating (.269). The remaining hypotheses were not supported.

DISCUSSION

Consistent with the hypothesized model, intrinsic motivation had the posited relation with academic performance. Further, intrinsic motivation had an indirect negative relation (through academic performance) on

Table 4. Theoretical Model Goodness of Fit Test Results.

	Satorra–Bentler Scaled Results	Standard for Acceptance
Statistical tests		
χ^2	307	NA
df	120	NA
p-value	.00	$>.05$
χ^2/df	2.56	<3.0
Fit indices		
NFI	.930	$>.90$
CFI	.956	$>.90$
Residual analysis		
RMSEA	.051	$<.08$
90% Confidence interval of RMSEA	(.044–.058)	

NFI, Normed Fit Index. Higher values indicate better fit; CFI; Comparative Fit Index. Higher values indicate better fit; and RMSEA and Root Mean Squared Error of Approximation. Lower values indicate better fit.

Table 5. Nested Model Comparison Test Results.

Model	Satorra–Bentler Scaled χ^2	df	χ^2/diff[a]
Trimmed Theoretical Model[b]	307.23	120	NA
Path from amotivation to neutralization constrained to zero	311.94	121	4.96*
Path from external-identified regulation to performance constrained to zero	313.96	121	7.09**
Path from amotivation to cheating likelihood constrained to zero	318.52	121	7.87**
Path from external-identified regulation to prior cheating constrained to zero	313.28	121	8.59**
Path from intrinsic motivation to performance constrained to zero	318.89	121	12.23***
Path from amotivation to prior cheating constrained to zero	340.72	121	15.81***
Path from amotivation to performance constrained to zero	333.82	121	35.99***

[a]The χ^2/diff statistics reported in this column were calculated manually using a procedure developed by Satorra and Bentler (2001, p. 511).
[b]The final theoretical model reflects the release of 11 nonsignificant parameter estimates as determined by examination of the multivariate Wald test output from the test of the full model. The full model test specified covariances among all of the independent factors as depicted in Fig. 1.
*$p<.05$; **$p<.01$; ***$p<.001$.

Table 6. Structural Equations Results and Estimated Standard Coefficients for the Hypothesized and Trimmed Models[a].

Hypothesized Relationship		Full Model			Trimmed Model		
Independent variable	Dependent variable	Standard coefficient	t-value	p-value	Standard coefficient	t-value	p-value
Intrinsic Motivation	*Academic performance*	*.178*	*3.046*	*<.01*	*.217*	*3.849*	*<.01*
External-identified regulation	*Academic performance*	*-.171*	*-2.814*	*<.01*	*-.165*	*-2.664*	*<.01*
Amotivation	*Academic performance*	*-.289*	*-5.759*	*<.01*	*-.274*	*-5.189*	*<.01*
Introjected regulation	Academic performance	.014	0.228	NS	NA	NA	NS
Intrinsic motivation	Prior cheating	-.137	-1.473	NS	NA	NA	NS
External-identified regulation	*Prior cheating*	*.141*	*2.140*	*<.05*	*.122*	*2.619*	*<.05*
Amotivation	*Prior cheating*	*.344*	*5.723*	*<.01*	*.327*	*3.495*	*<.01*
Introjected regulation	Prior cheating	.104	1.556	NS	NA	NA	NS
Academic performance	Prior cheating	-.060	-1.301	NS	NA	NA	NS
Intrinsic motivation	Neutralization	-.046	-0.922	NS	NA	NA	NS
External-identified regulation	Neutralization	.071	1.337	NS	NA	NA	NS
Amotivation	*Neutralization*	*.139*	*2.872*	*<.01*	*.095*	*2.107*	*<.05*
Introjected regulation	Neutralization	-.020	-0.373	NS	NA	NA	NS
Academic performance	*Neutralization*	*-.048*	*-1.277*	*NS*	*-.076*	*-2.098*	*<.05*
Prior cheating	*Neutralization*	*.612*	*11.742*	*<.01*	*.632*	*6.193*	*<.01*
Intrinsic motivation	Cheating likelihood	-.006	-0.135	NS	NA	NA	NS
External-identified regulation	Cheating likelihood	-.073	-1.488	NS	NA	NA	NS
Amotivation	*Cheating likelihood*	*.126*	*2.839*	*<.01*	*.144*	*2.897*	*<.01*
Introjected regulation	Cheating likelihood	.031	0.632	NS	NA	NA	NS
Academic performance	Cheating likelihood	.052	1.518	NS	NA	NA	NS
Prior cheating	*Cheating likelihood*	*.391*	*6.913*	*<.01*	*.390*	*4.411*	*<.01*
Neutralization	*Cheating likelihood*	*.281*	*5.286*	*<.01*	*.269*	*3.707*	*<.01*

NA, not applicable and NS, nonsignificant parameter.
[a]The italicized lines of information represent statistically significant paths.

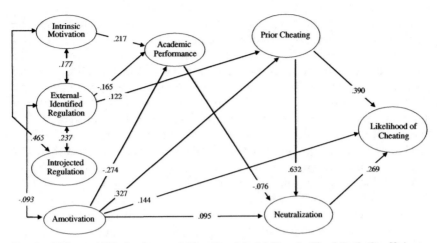

Fig. 2. Trimmed Motivation and Cheating Model Standardized Path Coefficients.

neutralization. These results support the argument that those who are intrinsically motivated (e.g., those who want to learn the material) are better performers and are less likely to engage in neutralizing behaviors. Lower levels of neutralizing behaviors are related to lower levels of cheating behaviors. These types of behaviors will not meet the needs of those intrinsically motivated. As a result, they have less of a need to engage in neutralizing and cheating behaviors.

We argue that amotivation is actually the extreme form of extrinsic motivation. The posited paths to the three cheating constructs were supported. Fairchild et al. (2005, p. 339) hypothesize and support a positive correlation between amotivation and motivation to avoid failure. They argue that amotivated people would be more likely to avoid achievement situations. But what if amotivated people find themselves in just such a situation, such as when they are in college? The need to avoid failure is arguably an extrinsic motivation, that is, there is a need to pass the class. As a result, amotivated students may choose to cheat as a means to avoid failure. Fairchild et al. (2005, p. 339) also argue for and support a positive correlation between amotivation and work avoidance. Work avoidance has been defined as the desire to do as little as possible in an achievement situation (Brophy, 1983, p. 211). One means of avoiding, or at least reducing work, is to cheat.

Although the intrinsic motivation, external-identified regulation, and amotivation results were consistent with the hypotheses, introjected regulation failed to demonstrate any of the posited relations. This may be due to the size of the covariances between introjected regulation and both intrinsic motivation (.465) and external-identified regulation (.237). Even with these large covariances, all three of these constructs have been shown to be distinct through exploratory and confirmatory factor analysis reported by Smith et al. (in press), and the confirmatory factor analysis in this study. Both intrinsic motivation and external-identified regulation had the posited relationships with academic performance and external-identified regulation had a direct relation with prior cheating and an indirect relation with likelihood of cheating. Given the size of the covariances between these two constructs and introjected motivation, they may have negated the latter's effects. That is, the explanatory power of introjected motivation may have been subsumed by these two constructs.

The larger covariance between introjected motivation and intrinsic motivation may be explained by looking at their respective definitions. Introjected regulation is defined as being externally driven. Activities are undertaken to achieve some valued outcome and these activities are fully endorsed by the individual. Intrinsic motivation is defined as internally driven. Activities are undertaken because of pure interest in the activities for their own sake (Deci, Vallerand, Pelletier, & Ryan, 1991, p. 330). One must assume the activities undertaken as a result of intrinsic motivation are also fully endorsed by the individual. It seems reasonable to conclude that activities directed at obtaining a valued outcome (e.g., earning an A) would be similar to the activities undertaken due to pure interest (e.g., the desire to understand accounting). Both sets of activities would be consistent with better academic performance. Thus, there may be overlap between the two constructs, driving force notwithstanding.

Finally, prior cheating was also positively related to neutralization, further supporting arguments that the more individuals engaged in unethical/dishonest behaviors, the greater was their need to rationalize and justify those behaviors. Neutralization, in turn, enhanced the prospect of future cheating. Also consistent with previous research, prior cheating appears to be a good predictor of future cheating.

LIMITATIONS

All of the data was self-reported, introducing the possibility of response bias and under reporting of cheating behavior and neutralization. The issue of response bias is addressed when testing the measurement model. A confirmatory factor analysis did not indicate a significant response bias effect. Additionally, surveys were completed without the faculty member present. The proctors explained that students' responses were completely anonymous. They also explained that only aggregate results would be reported. Since we relied on self-reported performance data to guarantee anonymity, we could not collect the information necessary to gather objective data (e.g., GPA). Given that this study did not focus on mean values, but rather on the interrelationships among the proposed constructs within the proposed model, these limitations are of minimal concern (Smith et al., 2002, p. 62).

The Wald test that we used to drop nonsignificant parameters from the theoretical model is a post-hoc procedure that capitalizes on particular sample data (i.e., it is not theory-driven). To determine whether the relations uncovered in this study hold, replication with another sample is needed.

A final limitation is the cross-sectional nature of the data. Though causal paths are implied in the structure of the model, strong causal statements cannot be made.

IMPLICATIONS AND CONCLUSIONS

The earlier limitations notwithstanding a number of important implications for educators can be drawn from viewing the relationships depicted in Fig. 2. Previous research has presented profiles of people who are more likely to cheat but has done little to suggest what can be done to reduce cheating occurrences, or more importantly, the desire to cheat. This study moves us toward that goal. The impact of intrinsic motivation, external-identified regulation, and amotivation on cheating behaviors is clearly significant.

External-identified regulation and amotivation both had negative direct relations with academic performance and positive relations with prior cheating. Amotivation also had direct positive relations with neutralization and likelihood of cheating. These results bring into question past definitions of amotivation, which argue that behaviors are a result of external forces, not individual choice (Fortier et al., 1995, p. 260; Ryan & Deci, 2000, pp. 60–61). Thus, people in this state do not intentionally decide to engage in behaviors. Initially the direct relationships between amotivation and the two cheating constructs might be argued to be consistent with these definitions (i.e., external forces cause them to cheat). But the definitions do not explain the relationship between amotivation and neutralization. If cheating is a result of forces outside an individual's control, there is no need to neutralize. As a result, past conceptualizations of amotivation need to be revisited. At least some level of decision taking appears to be taking place. Our amotivation measures seem to focus on uncertainty over why one is involved in school/college. This seems to be quite different from not having control. One could choose to drop out. There may be many reasons why one chooses to remain in school, not all external.

External-identified regulation is indirectly related to neutralization and likelihood of cheating through prior cheating. Also, intrinsic motivation and amotivation each have an indirect relationship with neutralization through academic performance. These mediated effects add to our understanding of cheating behavior.

If we can increase the number of students who are intrinsically motivated, we may reduce their desire to justify cheating and, thus, reduce the occurrence of cheating. It is incumbent on educators to search for ways to motivate student interest in the subject matter and its relevance. These efforts may take a variety of forms but arguably must engage students at a deeper level and promote the acquisition and enhancement of multiple skills that students see as valuable in and of their own sake. If we can enhance students' intrinsic motivation to learn and understand in academic settings, there is the potential long-term impact of lessening the need or desire to engage in unethical behaviors in the workplace.

ACKNOWLEDGMENT

The authors would like to acknowledge the valuable comments and suggestions received from the co-editor, Anthony H. Catanach Jr., and two anonymous reviewers.

REFERENCES

Baker, S. R. (2004). Intrinsic, extrinsic, and amotivational orientations: Their role in university adjustment, stress, well-being, and subsequent academic performance. *Current Psychology, 23*(3), 189–202.

Ball, R. (1966). An empirical exploration of neutralization. *Criminologica, 4,* 22–23.

Barkoukis, V., Tsorbatzoudis, H., Grouios, G., & Sideridis, G. (2008). The assessment of intrinsic and extrinsic motivation and amotivation: Validity and reliability of the Greek version of the Academic Motivation Scale. *Assessment in Education: Principles, Policy and Practice, 15*(1), 39–55.

Bentler, P. M. (2006). *EQS 6 structural equations program manual.* Encino, CA: Multivariate Software, Inc.

Bentler, P. M., & Bonnett, D. G. (1980). Significance Tests and Goodness of Fit in the Analysis of Covariance Structures. *Psychological Bulletin, 88*(3), 588–606.

Bentler, P. M., & Wu, J. C. (1995). *EQS for Windows user's guide.* Encino: Multivariate Software.

Brophy, J. E. (1983). Conceptualizing student motivation. *Educational Psychology, 18,* 200–215.

Burke, J. S., Polimeni, R. S., & Slavin, N. S. (2007). Academic dishonesty: A crisis on campus. *CPA Journal, 77*(5), 58–65.

Crown, D. F., & Spiller, M. S. (1998). Learning from the literature on college cheating: A review of empirical research. *Journal of Business Ethics, 17,* 683–700.

Daniel, L. G., Blount, K. D., & Ferrell, C. M. (1991). Academic misconduct among teacher education students: A descriptive-correlational study. *Research in Higher Education, 32,* 703–724.

Davis, S. F., & Ludvigson, H. W. (1995). Additional data on academic dishonesty and proposal for remediation. *Teaching of Psychology, 22,* 119–121.

Davy, J. A., Kincaid, J. F., Smith, K. J., & Trawick, M. A. (2007). An examination of the role of attitudinal characteristics and motivation on the cheating behavior of business students. *Ethics & Behavior, 17*(3), 257–278.

Deci, E. L., & Ryan, R. M. (2000). The "what" and "why" of goal pursuits: Human needs and the self-determination of behavior. *Psychological Inquiry, 11,* 227–268.

Deci, E. L., Vallerand, R. J., Pelletier, L. G., & Ryan, R. M. (1991). Motivation and education: The self-determination perspective. *Educational Psychologist, 26,* 325–346.

Fairchild, A. J., Horst, S. J., Finney, S. J., & Barron, K. E. (2005). Evaluating existing and new validity evidence for the Academic Motivation Scale. *Contemporary Educational Psychology, 30,* 331–358.

Fogarty, T. J., Singh, J., Rhoads, G. K., & Moore, R. K. (2000). Antecedents and consequences of burnout in accounting: Beyond the role stress model. *Behavioral Research in Accounting, 12,* 31–67.

Fortier, M. S., Vallerand, R. J., & Guay, F. (1995). Academic motivation and school performance: Toward a structural model. *Contemporary Educational Psychology, 20,* 257–274.

Granitz, N., & Loewy, D. (2007). Applying ethical theories: Interpreting and responding to student plagiarism. *Journal of Business Ethics, 72,* 293–306.

Grouzet, F. M., Otis, N., & Pelletier, L. (2006). Longitudinal cross-gender factorial invariance of the Academic Motivation Scale. *Structural Equations Modeling, 13*(1), 73–98.

Haines, V. J., Diekhoff, G. M., LaBeff, E. E., & Clark, R. E. (1986). College cheating: Immaturity, lack of commitment, and the neutralizing attitude. *Research in Higher Education, 25,* 257–266.

Hu, L., & Bentler, P. M. (1999). Cutoff criteria for fit indexes in covariance structure analysis: Conventional criteria versus new alternatives. *Structural Equation Modeling, 6,* 1–55.

Jordan, A. E. (2001). College student cheating: The role of motivation, perceived norms, attitudes, and knowledge of institutional policy. *Ethics & Behavior, 11*(3), 233–247.

Nonis, S. A., & Swift, C. O. (1998). Cheating behavior in the marketing classroom: An analysis of the effects of demographics, attitudes, and in-class deterrent strategies. *Journal of Marketing Education, 20*(3), 188–199.

Nonis, S. A., & Swift, C. O. (2001). An examination of the relationship between academic dishonesty and workplace dishonesty: A multicampus investigation. *Journal of Education for Business, 77*(2), 69–76.

Nunnally, J. (1978). *Psychometric theory* (2nd ed.). New York: McGraw-Hill.

Rakovski, C. C., & Levy, E. S. (2007). Academic dishonesty: Perceptions of business students. *College Student Journal, 41*(2), 466–481.

Ryan, R. M., & Deci, E. L. (2000). Intrinsic and extrinsic motivations: Classic definitions and new directions. *Contemporary Educational Psychology, 25*, 54–67.

Satorra, A., & Bentler, P. M. (2001). A scaled difference chi-square test statistic for moment structure analysis. *Psychometrika, 66*(4), 507–514.

Smith, K. J., Davy, J. A., & Rosenberg, D. L. (in press). A re-examination of the factor structure of the academic motivation scale. Under review at *Psychological Reports.*

Smith, K. J., Davy, J. A., Rosenberg, D. L., & Haight, G. T. (2002). A structural modeling investigation of the influence of demographic and attitudinal factors and in-class deterrents on cheating behaviors among accounting majors. *Journal of Accounting Education, 20*, 45–65.

Sykes, G., & Matza, D. (1957). Techniques of neutralization: a theory of delinquency. *American Sociological Review, 22*, 664–670.

Tom, G., & Borin, G. (1988). Cheating in academe. *Journal of Education for Business, 63*(4), 153–157.

Vallerand, R. J., Pelletier, L. G., Blais, M. R., Briere, N. M., Senecal, C., & Vallieres, E. F. (1992). The academic motivation scale: A measure of intrinsic, extrinsic, and amotivation in education. *Educational and Psychological Measurement, 52*, 1003–1017.

Whitley, B. E. (1998). Factors associated with cheating among college students: A review. *Research in Higher Education, 39*(3), 235–274.

INTRODUCTORY ACCOUNTING: PRINCIPLES OR FINANCIAL?

Robert L. Braun and Pierre L. Titard

ABSTRACT

Introductory accounting courses have the dual objectives of teaching the fundamentals of financial and managerial accounting and creating the environment in which students develop positive attitudes toward the discipline. This study examines the extent to which there are differences in effectiveness in attaining each of these objectives under the financial accounting approach to introductory accounting versus a principles of accounting approach. We analyzed attitudes and quiz scores for non-accounting majors in a managerial accounting class as during the period of a curriculum change. Results indicate that student attitudes toward accounting as a discipline were largely unaffected. Student attitudes toward accounting as a factor affecting their careers after graduation were significantly more positive. There were no differences in quiz scores in the managerial accounting course. These findings suggest that although the financial accounting approach is more efficient, it is equally effective with respect to content delivery and more effective with respect to promoting the importance of accounting to careers.

In its *Position Statement No. Two*, the Accounting Education Change Commission (AECC) emphasized that the first course in accounting should

Advances in Accounting Education: Teaching and Curriculum Innovations, Volume 10, 189–203
Copyright © 2009 by Emerald Group Publishing Limited
ISSN: 1085-4622/doi:10.1108/S1085-4622(2009)0000010012

be "a rigorous course focusing on the relevance of accounting information to decision-making (use) as well as its source (preparation)" (AECC, 1992, p. 3). In the decade-and-a-half since the issuance of the AECC's position statement, many accounting programs have changed the introductory accounting course structure, offering a course that provides balanced instruction on uses and preparation of financial accounting information, presumably in response to AECC recommendations (e.g., Abdelmohammadi, Brown, Feldmann, Gujarathi, & Haselkorn, 1998; Deberg, Adams, & Lea, 1998). These courses are typically called "financial accounting" courses rather than "principles of accounting." Financial accounting courses are often associated with a user orientation.

A principles approach typically covers both financial and managerial concepts using a preparer orientation over two semesters. In general, the first semester and about one-third of the second semester cover the financial portion. The financial approach encapsulates the financial content in a one-semester course. Normally, a separate managerial course follows. This chapter examines differences in learning outcomes and attitudes toward accounting associated with both approaches to introductory accounting. As there are approximately 650,000 students taking introductory accounting annually, 260,000 of whom are enrolled in principles of accounting courses (Monument Information Resource, 2008), examination of the efficiency and effectiveness of the introductory accounting curriculum may be of considerable importance.

Two primary objectives of introductory accounting are 1) for students to learn key concepts in financial and managerial accounting and 2) to foster a positive attitude toward accounting as a discipline and as a factor affecting their profession (e.g., Stice, Swain, & Worsham, 1997, p. 55). This study provides information to educators regarding the extent to which the financial accounting approach achieves each of these two objectives as compared to the principles of accounting approach.

The study assessed student learning by analyzing a quiz on managerial accounting topics administered at the beginning of a managerial accounting course for non-accounting majors. We also assessed student attitudes at the beginning of the same managerial accounting course. Taken as a whole, the results indicate that the type of approach was not associated with more positive student attitudes toward accounting as a discipline but was associated with more positive student attitudes toward the importance of accounting to their careers after graduation. Results also suggest that students who had managerial accounting under the principles approach did not show evidence that knowledge gained in the course was retained; their scores on a quiz of managerial topics were not significantly higher than students who had no managerial accounting under a financial accounting approach. These results may be of interest to those considering the efficiency and effectiveness of introductory accounting instruction.

We organized the remainder of the chapter as follows. The next section discusses the motivation for the study. Next, we present the hypotheses and the basis for them. We then discuss the method of inquiry. The next section presents the results. Finally, we offer discussion and implications.

MOTIVATION

Significant increases in demand for accounting professionals have occurred in the years following the implementation of the Sarbanes–Oxley Act of 2002. The American Institute of Certified Public Accountants (AICPA) reports that although the number of accounting majors is up 19 percent nationwide in 2006–2007 as compared to 2003–2004, the number of new hires by CPA firms is up 83 percent over the same period (AICPA, 2008, p. 7). The profession is looking toward accounting programs to help satisfy the growing need for accountants. Although there has been some variation in the trend and it is possible that the most recent numbers are related to a post-Sarbanes–Oxley spike, it appears that the demand for accountants continues to outpace the supply of accounting graduates. The implication is that recruitment of students to the accounting major and the accounting profession remains a matter of considerable importance.

As such, investigations of factors affecting student recruitment to the accounting major have examined characteristics of the accounting student (Nelson, Vendrzyk, Quirin, & Allen, 2002), student perceptions of the profession (Saemann & Crooker, 1999), the 150-hour rule (Boone & Coe, 2002; Allen & Woodland, 2006), the role of introductory accounting in major selection (Mauldin, Crain, & Mounce, 2000; Stice et al., 1997), and student attitudes (Shaftel & Shaftel, 2005). Other studies have examined various factors in attempting to model accounting career choice (Chen, Jones, & McIntyre, 2006; AICPA Lewis/Mobilo Research, Wunderman, 2003; AICPA Taylor Research and Consulting Group, Inc, 2000). Cumulatively, these studies suggest that career choice is a complex decision involving many factors and that fostering positive attitudes in the introductory course enhances the ability to recruit students.

Several studies that have examined the accounting major selection have identified curricular issues as important factors (Boone & Coe, 2002, p. 266; AICPA Taylor Research and Consulting Group, Inc, 2000). The AICPA's commissioned study on the various means of attracting students to the accounting major identified the introductory accounting class as an important factor influencing choice of accounting major for some students (AICPA Taylor Research and Consulting Group, Inc, 2000, p. 4). Indeed, in discussing their finding that the introductory accounting class was the most significant factor influencing major selection among all the factors studied, Chen et al. (2006, p. 16) note the significant implications that this finding has for the profession:

> For the full sample and for the seniors-only sample, the quality of experience in the first accounting course becomes the most important factor in distinguishing major choice between accounting and nonaccounting students. The results may have important policy and educational implications. In the absence of exposure to high school accounting, the first accounting course in college may be the best opportunity to attract students. While it is an important foundational course for disseminating technical knowledge, the importance of the course as a recruiting tool is even further underscored in this study. Without sufficient focus on informing students as to the variety of opportunities available in the field and the dynamic nature of the profession, any preexisting negative perceptions may persist and the profession may lose promising practitioners.

Chen et al.'s (2006) findings underscore the importance of the first course in forming student attitudes toward accounting while maintaining a focus on learning. This study addresses the issue by examining whether student attitudes toward accounting were improved when a financial accounting course was employed rather than a principles of accounting approach and by assessing student learning of managerial accounting material.

HYPOTHESES

The issue addressed by this study is whether a financial accounting approach affects student attitudes and learning outcomes. Albrecht and Sack (2000, p. 29) suggest that traditional introductory accounting courses can foster negative attitudes as they listed, "Introductory accounting courses that give students the impression that accounting is a narrow field and that accountants are only scorekeepers" as one of four reasons why students lack information that would help them choose accounting as a major. Comments of the AECC and others (e.g., Hock & Bloch, 2008, p. 6) suggest that the more user-oriented financial accounting approach helps foster positive attitudes compared to the more preparer-oriented principles of accounting approach.

To our knowledge, these claims are based more on intuition and experience rather than empirical evidence. As such, this study attempts to provide insight into this topic by testing the following hypothesis, stated in the null:

$H_{attitude}$. There will be no significant difference in attitudes toward accounting as a discipline and accounting as a factor affecting careers after graduation between students taking a financial accounting course and students taking a principles of accounting course sequence.

In addition to examining student attitudes toward accounting, this study attempts to assess student knowledge of managerial accounting concepts. Because managerial accounting topics often receive reduced attention in a two-semester course sequence, it is possible that student learning of the material is not retained as knowledge by those students who take the principles course sequence. We examine the following hypothesis, as stated in the null:

$H_{learning}$. There will be no significant difference in scores on a managerial accounting quiz between students who have taken a financial course and students who have taken a principles course sequence.

By examining the two primary objectives of the introductory accounting course, the learning of course material and student attitudes toward accounting, this study gives accounting programs information that is important to curriculum design.

METHOD

To analyze the hypotheses, we measured student attitudes and student learning in a managerial accounting course for non-accounting majors, over three semesters encompassing a period of curriculum change. The study employed a survey instrument measuring student attitudes and a quiz assessing learning of managerial accounting topics. For this study, we refer to the semesters as Semester 1, Semester 2, and Semester 3. We denote the first semester in which the students took financial accounting as Semester 1. Consequently, all students enrolled in Managerial Accounting had completed the two-course principles sequence. Students enrolled in the

Table 1.   Distribution of Student Attitude and Learning Data
by Semester.

	Principles ($N = 380$)	Financial ($N = 563$)	Total ($N = 943$)
Panel A: Attitudinal Survey			
Semester 1	136	–	136
Semester 2	165	309	474
Semester 3	79	254	333
	Principles ($N = 228$)	Financial ($N = 254$)	Total ($N = 482$)
Panel B: Quiz Data			
Semester 1	96	–	96
Semester 2	90	102	192
Semester 3	50	144	194

managerial course in subsequent semesters might have had either the financial or principles approach.

The original curriculum for non-accounting majors included a two-course sequence in principles of accounting that employed the traditional two-thirds financial and one-third managerial coverage. The switch involved a change in orientation of the course from a preparer focus in the principles course to a more user-oriented focus in the financial course. Although the required textbook changed, the same author team wrote both texts. The same set of instructors taught the courses in both sequences. The change occurred at a large regional university in the South with more than 3,500 students enrolled in the college of business.

Table 1 details the number of students participating in the attitudinal survey and the quiz during the three semesters. In all, 943 students responded to the attitudinal survey.

Panel A displays the number of students responding to the survey per semester under each of the introductory accounting approaches. Students self-reported the classes they had taken. Panel B displays the distribution of the learning results by semester as measured by the quiz.

The method of analysis is similar to that employed by Daroca and Nourayi (1994) in that we use both attitudinal and learning data to examine the effects of different types of instruction in introductory accounting. While Daroca and Nourayi examine the delivery of instruction (i.e., instructor delivery or self-study), our study is concerned with the nature of the curriculum as it pertains to introductory accounting. The means of assessing student attitudes and learning differ as well.

Assessment of Student Attitudes

By soliciting information on interest, importance, relevance, value, usefulness, and meaningfulness, we measured student attitudes toward accounting as a discipline and accounting as a factor affecting their careers after graduation. We used a semantic differential instrument with a 5-point Likert scale where opposing terms were situated at the endpoints (e.g., boring/interesting, unimportant/important, irrelevant/relevant, worthless/valuable, useless/useful, and meaningless/meaningful). The assessment instrument appears in Appendix A. We administered the attitude assessment survey during the second class period in the managerial accounting class. As such, attitudes should not have been influenced by their attitudes toward the particular instructor of the managerial course. Although some commentators have suggested that the first course is an opportunity to promote the accounting major and the profession (AECC, 1992; Geiger & Ogilby, 2000; Chen et al., 2006), there was no departmental initiative to "sell" the accounting profession in the financial accounting course.

Assessment of Student Learning

We used a quiz covering managerial accounting topics to assess student learning of managerial accounting concepts. The quiz included questions on selected managerial accounting topics that the managerial portion of the principles course sequence covered at the university involved in the study. The quiz appears in Appendix B. Instructors administered the quiz during the second class period of the semester. Instructors informed students that their scores would not count toward their course grade. We measured learning of managerial concepts in a principles of accounting class by comparing the scores of students who had taken the second principles class to scores of students who had only a financial accounting course. Instructors administered the quiz on the second day of the managerial accounting class.

RESULTS

Assessment of Student Attitudes

The results of the student attitude assessment indicate that although attitudes toward accounting as a discipline were largely unaffected by the introductory accounting approach, students taking financial accounting generally viewed accounting as a factor affecting their careers after graduation more positively than students who took principles of accounting. Attitudinal results appear in Table 2. One of the six factors examined was significant with regard to accounting as a discipline. Students taking principles found accounting to be significantly more valuable than students taking financial accounting ($p \leq 0.51$). Interestingly, with the exception of the boring/interesting factor, students viewed accounting as a discipline favorably on all dimensions (e.g., all means were at or above 4.00, indicating general agreement with the more positive conceptualization of the discipline).

Student attitudes toward accounting as a factor affecting their careers after graduation were significantly more positive for students having taken financial accounting. More specifically, non-accounting majors who had taken financial accounting found accounting to be more important ($p \leq 0.088$), relevant ($p \leq 0.006$), valuable ($p \leq 0.034$), useful ($p \leq 0.016$), and meaningful ($p \leq 0.020$) to their careers after graduation than non-accounting majors who had taken principles of accounting. Taken as a whole, the results of the attitudinal assessment of non-accounting majors suggest that the financial accounting approach is associated with a more positive outlook toward accounting, especially as a factor affecting careers after graduation.

Table 2. Assessment of Student Attitudes.

	Financial ($N = 563$)	Principles ($N = 380$)
As a discipline, accounting is:		
Boring/interesting	2.73	2.65
Unimportant/important	4.23	4.24
Irrelevant/relevant	4.07	4.16
Worthless/valuable	4.21	4.32[a]
Useless/useful	4.19	4.27
Meaningless/meaningful	4.02	4.00
In my career after graduation, accounting will be:		
Boring/interesting	2.92	2.80
Unimportant/important	3.86	3.74[a]
Irrelevant/relevant	3.88	3.71[b]
Worthless/valuable	4.03	3.89[c]
Useless/useful	4.02	3.87[c]
Meaningless/meaningful	3.90	3.76[c]

[a]Difference is significant at the .10 level.
[b]Difference is significant at the .01 level.
[c]Difference is significant at the .05 level.

Table 3. Assessment of Student Learning Analysis of Quiz Scores.

	Mean Quiz Score	N
Principles of accounting students	4.65[a]	228
Financial accounting students	4.68[a]	254

[a]$t = 0.190$, df $= 480$, $p \leq 0.849$.

Assessment of Student Learning

Results associated with the quiz administered to students at the start of their managerial accounting class suggest that there were no statistically differences in knowledge of managerial accounting concepts between students who had been exposed to managerial concepts at the end of a principles of accounting course sequence and students with no prior exposure to managerial accounting concepts in a financial accounting course. Table 3 shows the results of the analysis of quiz scores. The results indicate that there was no statistically significant difference in quiz scores between students who had taken the principles of accounting course sequence and students who had taken the financial accounting course. So, although students who had taken the principles course sequence had received two-thirds of a semester of managerial accounting education previously, they did not appear to have retained significant additional knowledge they may have gained in the course as measured by the quiz.

These results, combined with results that attitudes are more positive toward accounting and given that fewer departmental resources would be consumed in teaching one course, support the decision to switch to a financial accounting approach to introductory accounting.

LIMITATIONS

Several limitations of the study exist. The external validity of the study may be limited by studying data gathered from only one university. The circumstances of the curriculum change afforded the relatively unique opportunity to measure student attitudes and performance of two groups of students receiving different treatments with respect to introductory accounting education. Because of the difficulties associated with locating another university going through a similar change contemporaneously and controlling implementation issues, we chose not to add to the external validity of the study by expanding the universities involved.

The study did not examine differences in learning of financial accounting material under the two approaches. The analysis of student learning focused on managerial accounting topics. Support for the financial accounting approach could be positively or negatively affected by evidence suggesting that student learning is affected differentially. Movement toward the user-oriented or hybrid approach toward financial accounting education suggests that learning may be enhanced by the format typically used in the financial accounting classes.

Also, there may be some concern over whether the statistically significant results of the analysis of student attitudes translate to practical significance. Most of the differences are quite small. The 5-point Likert scales tend to limit variability, however, and likely bias against finding significant differences. Perhaps the significant results obtained despite this limitation demonstrate the strength of the association between the financial accounting approach and improved student attitudes toward accounting as a factor in subsequent careers.

CONCLUSIONS

This study may be of interest to accounting educators considering the possibility of curriculum revision. The results indicate that student attitudes are significantly more positive on some of the dimensions examined among students taking a financial accounting course. Student attitudes toward accounting as a discipline were not significantly different between the groups. Student attitudes toward accounting as a factor influencing their careers after graduation were significantly different between the groups, however. This result may be attributable to the user orientation of the course. That is, the user orientation could be effective in demonstrating accounting's importance to users and students may see themselves as users after graduation. Students do not have a significantly more positive attitude toward accounting as a discipline: but because of the user orientation of the course students have a stronger appreciation of the usefulness of accounting after they graduate.

Given that attitudes show some improvement and that learning of key concepts does not appear to be negatively affected, the study suggests that a financial accounting approach may be a more effective and efficient means of achieving the objectives of introductory accounting education. The results imply that educators should consider other relevant factors in considering curriculum revision in an effort to be responsive to calls for reform of accounting education. Other significant factors affecting the one- or two-semester choice could include sufficiency of accounting background for effective business decision making, accreditation requirements, institutional budget and staffing needs, and graduation rates, etc. Incorporating a user orientation is associated with increased esteem for accounting as a tool to assist students in their careers after graduation.

ACKNOWLEDGMENTS

We thank Cindy Thomas for her work in research assistance. We also thank participants in workshops at the American Society of Business and Behavioral Sciences and International Association of Business and Public Administrative Disciplines for comments. We are grateful for the funding assistance provided by the foundations of Charles Wesley Merrit and Phillip K. Livingston.

REFERENCES

Abdelmohammadi, M. J., Brown, C. D., Feldmann, D. A., Gujarathi, M., & Haselkorn, M. (1998). Designing and implementing an AECC complying introductory accounting course: A four-year perspective. *Advances in Accounting Education, 1*, 147–162.

Accounting Education Change Commission (AECC). (1992). Position Statement Number Two. *The First Course in Accounting*. Torrence, CA: AECC

Albrecht, W. S., & Sack, R. J. (2000). *Accounting education: Charting the course through a perilous future*. Sarasota, FL: American Accounting Association.

Allen, A., & Woodland, A. (2006). The 150-Hour requirement and the number of CPA exam candidates, pass rates, and the number passing. *Issues in Accounting Education, 21*(3), 171–193.

American Institute of Certified Public Accountants (AICPA). (2008). *Trends in the supply of accounting graduates and the demand for public accounting recruits*. New York: AICPA.

American Institute of Certified Public Accountants (AICPA) Lewis/Mobilo Research, Wunderman. (2003). *Report of findings: student focus groups and one-on-one interviews*. New York: AICPA.

American Institute of Certified Public Accountants (AICPA) Taylor Research and Consulting Group, Inc. (2000). *Student and academic research study – final quantitative report*. New York: AICPA.

Boone, J. P., & Coe, T. L. (2002). The 150-hour requirement and changes in the supply of accounting undergraduates: Evidence from a quasi-experiment. *Issues in Accounting Education, 17*(3), 253–268.

Chen, C., Jones, K. T., & McIntyre, D. D. (2006). A reexamination of the factors important to the selection of accounting as a major. *Accounting and the Public Interest, 5*, 14–31.

Daroca, F. P., & Nourayi, M. M. (1994). Some performance and attitude effects on students in managerial accounting: Lecture vs. self-study courses. *Issues in Accounting Education, 9*(2), 319–329.

Deberg, C. L., Adams, S. J., & Lea, R. B. (1998). Curricular revision starting at ground zero: The case of introductory accounting. *Advances in Accounting Education, 1,* 163–187.

Geiger, M. A., & Ogilby, S. M. (2000). The first course in accounting: Students' perceptions and their effect on the decision to major in accounting. *Journal of Accounting Education, 19*(1), 1–6.

Hock, C. A., & Bloch, J. M. (2008). Accounting 101: More useful approaches as alternatives to debits and credits. *New Accountant, 174,* 6–9.

Mauldin, S., Crain, J. L., & Mounce, P. H. (2000). The accounting principles instructor's influence on students' decision to major in accounting. *Journal of Education for Business, 75*(3), 142–148.

Monument Information Resource. (2008). *Principles of accounting sales history report.* New Providence, NJ: R. R. Bowker, Inc.

Nelson, I. T., Vendrzyk, V. T., Quirin, J. J., & Allen, R. D. (2002). No, the sky is not falling: Evidence of accounting student characteristics at FSA schools, 1995–2000. *Issues in Accounting Education, 17*(3), 269–287.

Saemann, G. P., & Crooker, K. J. (1999). Student perceptions of the profession and its effect on decisions to major in accounting. *Journal of Accounting Education, 17*(1), 1–22.

Shaftel, J., & Shaftel, T. L. (2005). The influence of effective teaching in accounting on student attitudes, behavior, and performance. *Issues in Accounting Education, 20*(3), 231–246.

Stice, J. D., Swain, M. R., & Worsham, R. G. (1997). The effect of performance on the decision to major in accounting. *Journal of Education for Business, 73*(1), 54–57.

APPENDIX A. ATTITUDINAL SURVEY OF ACCOUNTING

The statements below are designed to survey your attitudes toward the discipline of accounting and courses in accounting. Place an X over the number that best indicates your attitude regarding the statement, where:

1. indicates an attitude that is very closely related to the adjective on the left.
2. indicates an attitude that is closely related to the adjective on the left.
3. indicates an attitude that is neutral regarding the two adjectives.
4. indicates an attitude that is closely related to the adjective on right.
5. indicates an attitude that is very closely related to the adjective on the right.

1. As a discipline, accounting is:

Boring	____ :	____ :	____ :	____ :	____ :	Interesting
	1	2	3	4	5	
Unimportant	____ :	____ :	____ :	____ :	____ :	Important
	1	2	3	4	5	
Irrelevant	____ :	____ :	____ :	____ :	____ :	Relevant
	1	2	3	4	5	
Worthless	____ :	____ :	____ :	____ :	____ :	Valuable
	1	2	3	4	5	
Useless	____ :	____ :	____ :	____ :	____ :	Useful
	1	2	3	4	5	
Meaningless	____ :	____ :	____ :	____ :	____ :	Meaningful
	1	2	3	4	5	

2. In my career after graduation, accounting will be:

Boring	____ :	____ :	____ :	____ :	____ :	Interesting
	1	2	3	4	5	
Unimportant	____ :	____ :	____ :	____ :	____ :	Important
	1	2	3	4	5	
Irrelevant	____ :	____ :	____ :	____ :	____ :	Relevant
	1	2	3	4	5	
Worthless	____ :	____ :	____ :	____ :	____ :	Valuable
	1	2	3	4	5	
Useless	____ :	____ :	____ :	____ :	____ :	Useful
	1	2	3	4	5	
Meaningless	____ :	____ :	____ :	____ :	____ :	Meaningful
	1	2	3	4	5	

APPENDIX B. MULTIPLE CHOICE – CIRCLE THE LETTER FOR THE RESPONSE THAT BEST COMPLETES EACH STATEMENT

1. In determining required production for a manufacturing firm:
   a. desired ending inventory is subtracted from budgeted sales.
   b. beginning inventory is added to budgeted sales.
   c. both of the above.
   d. none of the above.

2. When all units produced are not sold:
   a. inventory carrying costs decrease.
   b. unsold units are included in ending inventory.
   c. both of the above.
   d. none of the above.

3. For most manufactured products, the number of units that will be sold will:
   a. decrease if the selling price is decreased.
   b. increase if sales commissions are decreased .
   c. not be affected by the amount of advertising.
   d. depend on the coordination of a number of elements in the firm.

4. Under variable costing:
   a. fixed factory overhead is included in the cost of goods manufactured.
   b. all variable costs are subtracted from sales to arrive at contribution margin.
   c. contribution margin will always exceed fixed costs.
   d. all variable costs are considered to be product costs.

5. The break-even point in units for a firm:
   a. can be determined by dividing total fixed costs by unit contribution margin.
   b. is the point at which total sales equal total costs.
   c. both of the above.
   d. none of the above.

6. Increasing credit terms from two months to three months will generally:
   a. increase sales
   b. decrease bad debt expense.
   c. both of the above.
   d. none of the above

7. A manufacturing firm will sometimes find it profitable to sell a special order at less than the full manufactured cost:
   a. when not operating at full capacity.
   b. when operating at full capacity.
   c. when variable cost exceeds selling price.
   d. under no circumstances.

8. Determining required production for a manufacturing firm, requires a knowledge of:
   a. plant capacity.
   b. customer credit terms.
   c. both of the above
   d. none of the above.

9. Production efficiency may be increased by:
   a. purchasing new equipment.
   b. increasing the wages of production workers.
   c. both of the above.
   d. none of the above.

10. The decisions to be made in producing a product:
    a. require only a knowledge of expected sales.
    b. do not include applications of managerial accounting.
    c. both of the above.
    d. none of the above.

BUSINESS-STUDENT PARTNERSHIP: LINKING ACCOUNTING INFORMATION SYSTEMS, INTERNAL CONTROL, AND AUDITING

Claire Kamm Latham

ABSTRACT

The American Institute of Certified Public Accounts (AICPA) and the American Assembly of Collegiate Schools of Business (AACSB) encourage experiential learning as a component of accounting and business curriculum. This chapter introduces a business partnership framework for experiential learning in accounting information systems, internal control, and auditing courses. Accounting students establish a partnership with a business client at the beginning of their accounting information systems and internal control study and continue the learning approach through the first auditing course. The framework brings real-world experience to accounting information systems, internal control, and auditing concepts. Accounting students learn to solve unstructured problems in complex realistic business settings, integrating technical and experienced-based knowledge. The project provides a structure for strengthening students' personal competencies including developing

Advances in Accounting Education: Teaching and Curriculum Innovations, Volume 10, 205–255
Copyright © 2009 by Emerald Group Publishing Limited
ISSN: 1085-4622/doi:10.1108/S1085-4622(2009)0000010013

successful team behavior and professional skills. The author has used the
business-partnership model effectively for 15 years.

Describing an integrative two-semester business-student partnership, this
chapter provides a project model that instructors can utilize when applying
concepts learned in accounting information systems, internal control, and
auditing. Accounting students form a relationship with a business entity at
the start of their accounting information systems and internal control study.
The project's approach continues through their first auditing course,
achieving important integration of knowledge.

This chapter provides information about the project's materials, project
overview and objectives, implementation guidance, including the timing of
the project within the courses and deliverables, as well as a discussion of
how the project maps to topic coverage in a conventional accounting
information systems course and an auditing course. I present descriptive
data on the types of entities and subsystems studied as well as student and
business evaluations, attesting to the effectiveness of the partnership. The
remainder of this chapter has six sections. First, I provide motivations for
use of the business-student partnership through reviewing the accounting
profession's call for students developing specific competencies. The second
section details the partnership's university settings, business entities, and
subsystems. The third and fourth sections provide project fundamentals
for use in an Accounting Information Systems and Internal Control class
and an Auditing class respectively. The fifth and the final section provide
implementation considerations for successful project adaptation to a
curriculum and a concluding summary. Appendixes A–C provide the
project handouts for the two-term orientation. Instructors may use these
materials to lower adoption costs.

MOTIVATIONS FOR USE OF
BUSINESS-STUDENT PARTNERSHIP

Development of Personal, Functional, and Broad Business Perspective
Competencies through Experiential Learning

The business-student partnership responds to calls for increased student
interaction with business as an approach to developing personal

competencies. The American Institute of Certified Public Accounts (AICPA) Core Competency framework identifies three major categories of student competencies, personal, functional, and broad business perspective, considered necessary for entry into the accounting profession and for successful accounting careers (AICPA, 1999). Identifying internships, service learning, and class projects where students work with an external entity as part of the curriculum, the AICPA suggests such experiential learning can strengthen all of the competencies, but, in particular, can be instrumental in developing personal competencies (AICPA, 2005). The American Assembly of Collegiate Schools of Business (AACSB) recently highlighted and commended business programs that have increased interaction of students with the business community, including expanding experiential learning opportunities (AACSB International, 2009, pp. 46–50). The AACSB encourages use of active learning, including problem- and project-based methodologies, in collaborative settings (AACSB International, 2008).

Prior research provides support for experiential learning, in its many forms, enhancing personal competencies (Barsky, Catanach, & Lafond, 2008, p. 288; Rama, Ravenscroft, Wolcott, & Zlotkowski, 2000, p. 673; Astin & Sax, 1998, p. 259). Rama et al. (2000, p. 673) suggest these external community connections are important ways to help students develop professional demeanor and interaction, "greater self-awareness and appreciation of and tolerance for others," increasing "students' feelings of connection to community," and improving "teamwork and communication skills." Students engaged in outside community work as part of a class or course reported positive outcomes in terms of interpersonal skills, social self-confidence, leadership ability, and understanding of problems facing the community (Astin & Sax, 1998, p. 259). Barsky et al. (2008, p. 288) offer evidence that experiential learning reflects active learning strengthening students' communication skills and other competencies desired by the profession.

The business-student partnership employs experiential and active learning that supports development of the AICPA personal competencies of professional demeanor, problem solving and decision making, interaction, leadership, communication, project management, and leverage technology (AICPA, 1999). The project also encourages improvement of broad business perspective and functional competencies such as strategic/critical thinking, industry/sector perspective, and risk analysis. Bamber and Bamber (2006, p. 268) note that incorporating real-world business applications into the accounting curriculum speeds up "students' integration of technical with experienced-based knowledge, so the process of expertise development begins while students are still in the classroom." Students "must be active participants in the learning process" and need experience in solving untidy, unstructured problems in more complex realistic business settings (Catanach, Croll, & Grinaker, 2000, p. 587). Realistic business problems in published cases and practice sets in an accounting curriculum serve an important role. The external partnership provides supplemental critical experience that increases the students' exposure to a varied and broad set of business concepts, practices, and problems, some of which are not encountered in published material. Such exposure enhances the students' ability to contribute as a strategic player in a company.

The unstructured business problem at the core of the business-student partnership is the company's approach to internal control. What started out as students documenting a portion of a real-world accounting information system and completing a control matrix has evolved into a more critical internal control examination emphasizing risk analysis and assessment, incorporating client engagement decisions and underscoring the importance of the engagement letter, and developing industry understanding. Fogarty, Graham, and Schubert (2006) note the risk assessment standards place heavy emphasis on understanding internal control and risk assessment as a cornerstone to the audit process. Hence, the need for increased emphasis on accounting students' internal control comprehension, including fundamental risk analysis, also provides incentive for this active learning project.

The next section describes the contexts in which I use the student-business partnership and the entity types and systems students study so that faculty can assess how well the model adapts to their environment.

DESCRIPTIONS OF CONTEXTS, ENTITIES, AND SUBSYSTEMS

Institutional Settings

I have used the partnership model for 15 years, adding the second term component in year 9, in various community settings in Accounting Information Systems and Internal Control and Auditing classes. I implemented an early version of the partnership in Accounting Information Systems classes at an AACSB accredited (business and accounting) state university that serves approximately 24,000 students in an urban location. This institution uses the quarter system. The Accounting Information Systems class is a 300-level course at this institution with average class size of 45 students. In this earlier version, the project constituted 25% of the students' class grade in the class.

I have and currently use the existing partnership projects at Washington State University, an AACSB accredited (business and accounting) university that serves approximately 25,000 students at several urban, suburban, and rural locations across the state. Washington State University uses the semester system. In addition to incorporating the projects in a traditional classroom setting at my resident campus, I use this teaching model when I videoconference the class to another regional campus. I travel to the other campus twice during the semester.

There exists one accounting curriculum for all campuses of this university. The Accounting Information Systems and Internal Control class and the Auditing class are 400-level required courses that students take as part of their senior or 5th year courses. The Accounting Information Systems and Internal Control class is a prerequisite for the Auditing class. These classes are writing-in-the-major courses and, as such, require significant peer and faculty feedback on communication.

Four hundred-level classes are limited to 45 students. The average class size for the partnership courses is 35–40 students. Three to four students comprise a team that yields nine to ten projects per class. My teaching rotation typically includes one project class per semester. The partnership projects always have represented a significant component of the students' grades for the courses; approximately 40% for Accounting Information Systems and Internal Control and 25% for Auditing. The average grade in the preliminary stages of the projects is a mid-C. With considerable feedback and the ability to revise, the average grade on the final component is a low-A so that the overall grade for the project tends to a high-B.

Business Entities and Systems

Table 1 provides descriptive data for a sample of 110 of the partnership projects, representing approximately 70% of all projects students have completed to date. The largest category, 18.18% for manufacturing and construction, includes a wide variety of entities and processes such as order entry for a manufacturer of wooden roof trusses, accounts payable for a LED light manufacturer, and inventory management for an appliance repair shop. Over 50% of the subsystems examined are billing, accounts receivable, and cash receipts, which reflects a common system request of companies students approach.

Table 1. Partnership Business Type and Systems Studied.

Entity Type	Percentage
Manufacturing and construction trades (manufacturing, building contractors, testing, repair)	18.18
Educational institutions (4-year, community colleges, school districts)	11.82
Financial, insurance, and legal entities (credit unions, banks, CPAs, attorneys, insurance, escrow, title)	10.91
Food and beverage trade (wholesale and retail)	10.00
Non-profit entities (low income assistance, churches)	9.09
Medical entities (clinics, hospitals)	8.18
Computer-related businesses (support, hardware, software)	8.18
Transportation services (freight, travel)	7.27
Retail other than food (car dealerships, gas stations, athletic, entertainment)	6.36
Public entities (cities, utility districts)	5.45
Agricultural businesses (farming)	4.55
	100.00

Accounting Information Subsystem	Percentage
Billing/Accounts receivable	26.36
cash receipts	25.45
Order entry/purchasing/accounts payable	20.00
Cash disbursements	13.64
Inventory	6.36
Other	5.45
Payroll	2.73
	100.00

Although the participating business entities are typically small to mid-size, students also examine accounting subsystems of smaller divisions or components of larger companies. For example, students have studied accounts payable for one local department of a financial institution and order entry for a division of an athletic equipment company, both of which are publicly traded entities. Approximately 12% of the sample relates to educational institutions. Some of the projects in this category include studying cash receipts at the university cafeteria, the portals billing system at the university library, credit card processing in an academic department, accounts receivable at the university bookstore, and cash receipts at a local community college. Student groups also assist non-profit entities (9.09%).

Through the business partnership, students gain exposure to a much wider array of software packages than those available for academic use, strengthening the personal competency of leverage technology. Examples from this sample include Nova Time (time tracking for labor costs); Pacifica (industry specific); Pro Shop coordinator; Quickbooks, Quickbooks Pro, and Quickbooks Premier (nonprofit, manufacturing and wholesale, job costing); Peachtree; RAS (remote access software: proprietary version); Sure Close Software (real estate); Timberline; and Yardi (property management). The next section describes the first-term project.

TERM 1: ACCOUNTING INFORMATION SYSTEMS AND INTERNAL CONTROL

Project Materials

Appendix A includes the handouts for the first-term Accounting Information Systems and Internal Control business-student project. I have adapted various project materials provided in Gelinas' *Accounting Information Systems*[1] to include increased emphasis on Committee on Sponsoring Organization (COSO) internal control material and on linking the concepts to auditing. In addition, I have adapted some of the evaluation forms and team contract from my university's business-student partnership manual and management faculty team project material respectively.

Overview and Objectives

In the Term 1 project, student teams document and evaluate, from an internal control perspective, a portion of an actual accounting information system in operation. Students may examine cash receipts, billing, accounts payable, order entry, or other subsystems within the revenue and expenditure cycles. Students also have successfully chosen business processing outside the revenue and expenditure cycles such as personnel hiring. Their investigation includes internal and external stakeholders (impacted users), documents, processes, files, and internal controls.

The project's objectives are to bring to life accounting information systems and foundational internal control concepts and to provide students with the opportunity to examine an actual accounting system in operation. The business-student partnership enhances students' analytical ability, teamwork, and communication skills. A cornerstone of the project is the structured approach by which the students interact with the business entity that serves to provide critical professional skill development.

Project Timing, Topic Coverage, and Deliverables

Table 2 provides an overview of the semester's project timing and maps the project to topic coverage as typically found in a conventional accounting information system course that places heavy emphasis on internal control concepts. I have not reduced topic coverage to include the project in the class. The project provides a continuous learning framework where students apply their knowledge as we cover the topics.

Prior to the First Class Session
I email syllabi for all business courses to students rather than distributing paper copies in the first class session. I electronically send the course syllabi to students at least 1 week prior to the start of classes, with the expectation that students will read the syllabus and come to class prepared for first day's activities. I use an online discussion board where I encourage students to establish teams based on criteria such as site location, availability, and expectations. Entering students typically are aware of the partnership project from the class alumni and from advising activities; hence, most students have formed teams and explored potential business clients by the first class session.

Weeks 1–2: Aligning Expectations and Establishing the Team Contract
The first week of the course, I outline business-student partnership expectations and assist any remaining students in forming teams. Students bring the practice sets, *Systems Understanding Aid* (Arens & Ward, 2008b) and *Computerized Accounting using Microsoft Dynamics GP10.0* (Arens & Ward, 2008a), to class. I initiate both practice sets, with an emphasis on introducing the accounting information systems processing and control concepts that serve as the foundation for the course. Having taught the class with and without the practice sets, I believe the practice sets make several important contributions not redundant with the project. In the first weeks of class, they provide a necessary hands-on refresher of documents and files in the accounting cycle. The practice sets also provide a model accounting information system with good internal control as a basis of comparison to their business clients in the rest of the semester.

Table 2. Term 1 Project: Accounting Information Systems and Internal Control.

Week	Term Project Phase	Due Dates for Term Project Deliverables	Topic Coverage in Class
Students receive syllabus and term project material 1 week prior to classes starting. Students go to the discussion board to establish teams			
1–2	• Student team contract • Initial meeting with business client	• Student team contract due week 2	• Project expectations and business policies regarding group projects • *Systems Understanding Aid* (Arens & Ward, 2008b) and *Computerized Accounting using Microsoft Dynamics GP10.0* (Arens & Ward, 2008a); Manual and computer practice sets emphasizing systems and internal controls
3–4	• Phase I Project Proposal	• Project Proposal due week 3	• Documenting information flows using diagrams and flowcharts • Database Management Systems and relational data bases • Exam #1 covering documenting information flows
5–9	• Phase II Preliminary Project Report – Understanding and documenting Systems	• Preliminary Project Report due week 9 (returned to students week 10)	• Identification of manual and computer controls: *Systems Understanding Aid* and *Computerized Accounting using Microsoft Dynamics GP10.0* turned in • Internal control concepts and the COSO framework • Cases: Internal control failures • Control matrices and questionnaires as evaluative tools

10–14	• Phase III Final Project Report – Documenting and evaluating internal control	• Final Project Report due week 14	• Developing understanding of information flows and controls in cycles:
			  • Order entry
			  • Billing/accounts receivable/cash receipts
			  • Purchasing/accounts payable/cash disbursements
			• Exam #2 covering controls in cycles
			• Student presentations in class

15	• Presentation to business client	• Final Project Report given to business entity • Student team and project evaluations due within 5 days	

During weeks 1 and 2, as part of class, office hours, and through electronic communication, I provide guidance to students concerning potential businesses and subsystems. Outside of class, students complete the team contract, turned in during week 2, and hold an initial meeting with the business client.

Weeks 3–4: Phase I Project Proposal
The Phase I Project Proposal's objective, due week 3, is to establish an agreement with the business. The students use the templates provided in Appendix A to create the following deliverables reflecting the first external entity documentation:

1. Business-student partnership letter of understanding.
2. Confidentiality agreement.
3. Initial student-business partnership meeting report.

I devote class sessions to documenting information flows using data flow diagrams and systems flowcharts. Utilizing tools being learned in class, students more explicitly define the boundaries of their business's system and begin to create a narrative describing the process. Students are completing the *Systems Understanding Aid* (Arens & Ward, 2008b) and *Computerized Accounting using Microsoft Dynamics GP10.0* (Arens & Ward, 2008a) practice set assignments outside of class. An examination in week 4 tests the students' ability to document information flows using data flow diagrams and system flowcharts.

Weeks 5–9: Phase II Preliminary Project Report – Understanding and Documenting Systems
The Preliminary Project Phase II's objective, due week 9, is to produce the following system documentation deliverables:

1. Overview of the business including history, locations, size of entity, and key management.
2. Description of the accounting information system being analyzed, including boundaries of analysis.
3. Operation narrative of the accounting information system being analyzed, as approved by the business.
4. Operation documentation of the accounting system being analyzed, including appropriate flow diagrams and systems flowchart.
5. Additional reports documenting meetings.

Students hand in the two practice sets at the start of class in week 6 and contrast controls through a manual system and a computer system. In class sessions, I cover internal control concepts, the COSO framework, internal control failures, and the use of control matrices and questionnaires as accounting information systems' evaluative tools. I use class time to work on and review their business's system documentation deliverables, concurrent with discussions of their entity's internal control environment. Even though students turn in the system documentation portion at the end of this time, they are preparing information for the Final Project Report as I cover the material in class.

Weeks 10–14: Phase III Final Project Report – Documenting and Evaluating Internal Control
In week 10, I review, grade, and return, with feedback, the Preliminary Project Report. I estimate it takes from 30 minutes, for a strong project, to 1 hour, for a weak project, to grade a preliminary report during the week 9 to week 10 time period (maximum total grading time of 10 hours). Even with the in-class review, these preliminary reports still may contain passive voice, informal language, and flow diagram and flowchart errors. I provide written corrections and suggestions directly on the report. Students are encouraged to revise this material for the Phase III Final Project Report and I recollect the preliminary report to see their changes.

Due week 14, the Phase III Final Project Report's objective is to document and evaluate the business's internal controls. While primary emphasis is on the analysis of the specific accounting information system (e.g., cash receipts processing), students provide an overview of the internal control system using the five components identified in the COSO framework: (a) control environment, (b) risk assessment, (c) control activities, (d) information and communication, and (e) monitoring. The business client receives The Final Project Report, which includes the following:

1. The revised information contained in the Preliminary Project Report.
2. Information detailing the internal control system in which the accounting information system operates, using the COSO framework as a guide.
3. Control matrices that identify present and missing specific control plans and descriptions for the specific analysis of the accounting information subsystem.
4. An assessment based on environment and user needs.

During weeks 10–13, I cover information flows and controls in specific cycles, such as order entry, billing, and purchasing. I use class time to work on and review the internal control deliverables of their business partnerships. Lively discussions about what the text describes versus what students are seeing in their businesses frequently occur at this point in the semester.

In the last class sessions of week 14, student teams present their projects to their classmates as a "test run." Students do not divulge their business client's name during this session to preserve confidentiality. Students must pay particular attention to producing a professional presentation, which is succinct and avoids technical jargon. Class members who are not presenting assume the role of the business partner and provide feedback to each team using a structured evaluation form (see Appendix C). All College of Business students receive team training in a required business core class that is a pre-requisite for upper division major classes. Students embrace the peer feedback process as it is part of the citizenship culture developed through this team training. I witness teams revising their presentation to the business partner due to peer feedback and through seeing approaches that work well for other teams. Following the team presentation class session, I attend the final team presentation at the business partner's work site.

The next section describes the auditing project.

TERM 2: AUDITING

Project Materials, Overview, and Objectives

I provide the handouts for the second-term Auditing business-student project in Appendix B. In this course, student teams assess risks associated with the business client, consider client acceptance issues, and engagement letter responsibilities. They use their understanding to design an audit program, testing controls in the system evaluated in the Accounting Information Systems and Internal Control course. The students also execute at least two of the audit program steps, evaluate the evidence, and discuss the impact of reliance on the controls in the company's subsystem. The students see the connection between the evaluation of internal control they completed in the first project (based on the client's description) and the need to examine what controls actually are present to be able to rely on the initial assessment. The project serves to portray real-life risks, client acceptance activities, the importance of engagement letters, and the impact of reliance on controls and subsequent evidence gathering, making the auditing concepts concrete. I adapt a term-long audit case with a fictitious business, which mirrors the learning objectives of the second-term assignment in circumstances where there is no student or business partnership connection available from the Accounting Information Systems and Internal Control class.

Project Timing, Topic Coverage, and Deliverables

Table 3 provides an overview of the semester's project timing and maps the project to topic coverage found in a conventional first auditing course. Students receive the class syllabi electronically before the first class session.

Weeks 1–5: Aligning Expectations, Establishing Team Contract, and Phase I Project Proposal
I detail business-student partnership expectations and assist in forming student teams for those not continuing with the prior engagement team. Similar to the Accounting Information Systems and Internal Control course, the Phase I Project Proposal's objective (which includes the business client's letter of understanding, the confidentiality agreement, and the first meeting report) is to establish and reinforce the agreement with the client. Students also begin the Phase II Business Entity Risk Assessment as it pertains to topics covered in this portion of the course.

I devote these initial class sessions to framing our auditing study, including exploration of reporting, the professional code of conduct, ethics, legal liability, and engagement issues. Students present famous audit cases and gain first exposure to Audit Command Language (ACL), a data extraction, and analysis software widely used in the audit profession.

Weeks 6–10: Phase II Business Entity Risk Assessment
The objective of the Phase II report, due week 9, is to produce the business entity overview and the risk assessment deliverables:

1. Business Entity Overview using the Accounting Information Systems project information.
2. Engagement considerations.
3. Risk assessment using Audit Risk Model elements as a foundation.

With the business client providing the context, I use class time to discuss client acceptance decisions, evidence concepts, materiality, risks, and fraud potential. Students bring information from their business entities as I cover the material in class. In addition, a community partner from the public accounting industry conducts a Statement on Auditing Standards SAS 99

Table 3. Term 2 Project: Auditing.

Students receive syllabus and term project material 1 week prior to classes starting. Students go to the discussion board to establish teams, if necessary

Week	Term Project Phase	Due Dates for Term Project Deliverables	Topic Coverage in Class
1–5	• Student team contract • Initial meeting with business client • Phase I Project Proposal • Begin Phase II Business Entity Risk Assessment	• Student team contract due week 2 • Phase I Project Proposal due week 3	• Project expectations and business policies regarding group projects • The CPA profession • Reports • Professional ethics • Legal liability • Client acceptance decisions and engagement responsibilities • Audit cases and ACL assignment • Exam #1 covering the profession, reports, ethics, and legal liability
6–10	• Phase II Business Entity Risk Assessment	• Phase II Business Entity Risk Assessment due week 9 (returned to students week 10)	• Evidence • Materiality and risks (Audit Risk Model) • Internal control and control risk • Fraud assessment with SAS 99 work session • ACL assignment • Exam #2 covering evidence, audit risk model, internal control, and fraud
11–12	• Phase III Audit Program (tests of controls and substantive tests of transactions)	• Phase III Audit Program due week 12 (assessed in class)	• Tests of controls in cycles • Attribute sampling
13–15	• Phase IV Fieldwork • Phase V Report of Findings • Discussion of findings	• Phase IV Fieldwork and Phase V Report of Findings due week 15 • Completing the Audit assignment due at Exam #3 • Student teams and project evaluations due within 5 days	• Tests of details of balances in cycles • Monetary unit and variable sampling • Completing the Audit • Class discussion • Exam #3 covering tests of controls, tests of details of balances, sampling, and completing the audit

(AICPA, 2002) audit team "brainstorming" session. I review, grade, and return, with feedback, the Phase II Business Entity Risk Assessment in week 10. Similar to the timing in the first partnership project, I estimate it takes from 45 minutes, for a strong project, to 1 hour, for a weak project, to grade a Phase II report during the week 9 to week 10 time period.

Weeks 11–12: Phase III Design of Audit Program
The Phase III objective is to create an audit program tailored to the business client. In class, I discuss tests of controls and substantive tests of transactions for various cycles as well as attribute sampling. Students create a comprehensive and realistic audit program that includes sampling. I provide audit program guidance for the partnership through (1) developing an example in class based on a case or text problem and (2) sharing, with permission, anonymous programs, and attribute sampling plans from prior semesters. Where possible, the team uses the control matrices provided in the Accounting Information Systems and Internal Control course as a starting point for evaluating key controls, tests of those controls, and potential misstatements for the transaction cycle examined. In class, I review and grade the audit programs and suggest adaptations as necessary for fieldwork. The students select, with approval, only one or two steps from the audit plan to perform so that fieldwork takes approximately 1 hour. For example, in the sales cycle, their tests could include accounting for a sequence of sales invoices in the sales journal and then vouching a sample of those (examining supporting documentation).

Weeks 13–15: Phase IV Fieldwork and Phase V Final Report
In this final stage, students perform the tests outlined in the attribute sampling plan and evaluate the results. They provide an assessment of the audit plan results and decide what they will communicate to the client. In class, I cover tests of details of balances and monetary unit and variable sampling. Though this portion of an audit is not part of the business-student partnership project, the results from the tests of controls become more relevant as students consider its impact on the work they perform in the later auditing stage. I then integrate material from the final stage of audit completion as it relates to the business client.

In the final class sessions, student teams present their findings in a discussion format. As before, students do not divulge their business client's name during this session to preserve confidentiality. The discussion format represents a more realistic portrayal of the auditing team environment before a final meeting with the client concerning the results of testing of internal control. As an instructor-class member team, we discuss our initial understanding and assessment of internal control from our first-term project and compare that understanding to the second term's fieldwork results. This discussion provides additional insight and a fresh perspective for students as they interpret the audit results. During week 14, each team turns in the following:

1. Phase II Business Entity Risk Assessment.
2. Phase III Design of Audit Program.
3. Phase IV Fieldwork (including working papers) and Phase V Final Report.

The student teams present their findings to the business client in week 15. The business-student partnership evaluation form provides evidence that the student team has completed the process.

EFFECTIVENESS OF THE BUSINESS-STUDENT PARTNERSHIP

In addition to receiving informal business entity feedback when I attend the student presentation at the business site, a company representative from each business also evaluates the team's report and presentation on the assessment form (see Appendix A). The business client evaluations of the overall project quality averages 4.6 out of 5 for the sample of projects depicted in Table 1 (see the Business-Student Partnership Project Evaluation of Project by Business Entity, question 4 in Appendix A).

Students also complete an evaluation of the team project on a separate assessment form (see the Business-Student Partnership Project Evaluation of Project by Student in Appendix A) that is in addition to the traditional course assessment. The student assessment form does not contain a project quality scale but garners feedback through several questions. For the question, "In your opinion, do you learn more (a) by working on one or more projects with real-world firms or (b) by working on case studies and textbook material?", 65% of the students chose (a) projects with real-world firms and 35% suggested that a combination of both (a) and (b) is the best learning approach.

Another question asks "How well did the project contribute to the overall learning in this course?" For the sample of projects depicted in Table 1, 93% of students responded positively, using wording such as "very well, very helpful, really helped." Students who did not respond to this question positively cited (1) a negative team issue; (2) being more comfortable with a more structured, case study, or textbook problem; (3) perceiving the project challenged them to analyze before they had adequate understanding; and (4) a desire to have chosen another entity other than the one they studied due to size or scope issues. The second and third comments speak to how the project pushes students, often outside their comfort zone. Comments from a peer review session of this particular project further support this assessment. Students described it as "climbing a mountain," meaning it presented a significant challenge. Based on instructor evaluation comments, students feel anxiety (insecurity) as they go through the project process and find significant accomplishment at the project's conclusion. I address how I counteract negative team issues, anxiety, and business selection concerns in the implementation guidance provided in the next section.

In 2008, one student project received the Accounting Information Systems Educators Association (AISEA) Jack and Maye Stewart Student Project Competition Award. In 2009, a student team presented their project at the annual university Volunteer Showcase as evidence of civic engagement in the community. Table 4 contains quotes taken from both students' and business clients' evaluations, which are representative of the type of feedback received and provide further evidence of the business-student partnership success.

A final evaluative point should not be lost: these clients, many who are entrepreneurs and small business owners, have received concrete suggestions concerning the underpinnings of their accounting information systems and the internal controls that support it (or do not).

IMPLEMENTATION CONSIDERATIONS

The partnership is an active learning framework that provides students opportunities to make meaning from direct experience in a business setting. Arguably, the most compelling outcome is the development of personal competencies such as the respect, pride, and empathy identified in students' quotes. It is a teaching approach that requires a commitment beyond the boundary of the traditional classroom. For example, attending the final business presentations involves commuting to the sites and occupies approximately 20 hours at the end of a semester. Reviewing project components throughout the semester adds to grading responsibilities; yet, the guidance yields a superior student and business experience. Faculty

Table 4.   Business-Student Partnership Feedback.

Student comments
- "The project for this class is invaluable to concept clarification and application. By the time the project was complete I really understood the various plans we were studying as well as the system flow and the means to use the principles to analyze business processes."
- "I gained information and insight into the nuts and bolts operation in the daily work environment and necessary problem solving undertaken by business professionals to achieve their objectives. I learned to respect the co-owners' time constraints. I gained empathy for the many pressures and hard work needed to undertake a business venture."
- "I learned there are a lot of considerations that need to be factored into every decision about internal control, including a cost/benefit analysis and real-world feasibility. It was very satisfying to see our class concepts applied to a real-life situation. I have a deep sense of pride for the work the team did and am (sic) hopeful that it can be used by XX to further their organizational goals."
- "Instead of working as a team to mark debits and credits, suddenly were (sic) applying what we had learned to a much more complex subject (internal control) in a real, dynamic system. It was challenging because there were areas with no concrete right or wrong answers, just individual perspectives on the status of internal control and suggestions to correct vulnerabilities."
- "What I learned most from the project is how to appreciate other's thoughts, communicate with each other, (and) manage our time."
- "Working full time, I like to just do my own work at my own time. HOWEVER ... I did enjoy working on this project because we are actually interacting with a real-world company, instead of just meeting with the group members and turning in a paper when the term ends. I like how this class is set up with the project ... it allowed me to understanding what I am learning. Basically, it was tough for me at times to leave work early to attend meetings, but it was all well worth it at the end."

Business partner comments
- "The team of business students from XXX provided a valuable service to our business as they evaluated a segment of our operation with which we had concerns. They affirmed strengths and made useful recommendations where appropriate and conducted themselves as professional business people."
- "I would recommend that other business people work with a student project group because when you are so close to the system, it is often difficult to see where change may be needed."
- "We gained fresh insight. The final report was surprisingly very good. I highly recommend this student project to other companies."

initially may find it more difficult to address a variety of business systems in different industries, many of which do not have textbook internal control systems, though this challenge lessens as exposure and familiarity develops. My experience has been the benefits accruing to students, and the businesses significantly outweigh the costs associated with additional time. Despite the benefits, potential adopters should consider several commitments integral to the success of the projects: (1) structuring team interaction, (2) engaging business partners, (3) limiting impositions on business time, and (4) ensuring professionalism.

Structuring Team Interaction

The partnership is a team project and as such, team failure, resulting from procrastination, free ridership, dominant leadership, individuals only completing part of the project as opposed to all students working on the entire project or other team problem behaviors, can occur. I use several measures to counteract team problems. All classes that incorporate teamwork use the team contract from the required business core class discussed earlier; students in teams receive a consistent message. For example, if a student fails in a delivering upon a certain responsibility, the team understands it has specific recourse as established in the contract.

Teams establish a weekly meeting time as part of the contract. At the conclusions of meetings, the students assign objectives to achieve by the next meeting time. During each class, I ask "progress and problems" questions as part of a general discussion and in individual meetings with each team. A typical class session will include lecture and discussion on the week's topic, including a mini-case or problem analyses, and then, we spend the remainder of the class time applying the material to the team's business client, with instructor feedback. Early in the semester, students may miss a checkpoint; however, peer influence and class discussion lead them to be active participants in future classes. This structured (contractual) weekly interaction in team meetings and in the class promotes commitment and accountability. Hence, a key success factor for the business-student partnership is the team contract, the specified weekly contact among team members and with the instructor. Even with the contract one or two teams every semester experience personnel challenges. I have learned how to observe and then address problems early on, adhere to the contract, and monitor to ensure the team is successfully overcoming the challenges.

Engaging Business Partners

Potential adopters need to consider the method they will use to access business partners. My students find the business partner with one exception. I receive a company request for a student team for approximately 10% of the projects. Students successfully engage business partners in the urban, suburban, and rural business communities surrounding the campus sites and within the campus community. Several characteristics of the academic environment where the majority of the projects have taken place support this success. First, the business faculty committed to action-oriented learning formed strong connections to the business community approximately a decade ago. The university's Office of Marketing and Communication highlights community partnerships on its website and its literature. At various junctures in the business curriculum, students solve a business problem in the community. For example, in a writing-in-the-major marketing class, the students develop a marketing plan for a real-world entity. Some students use the same company throughout their curriculum.

Second, a recent survey of our undergraduate business students indicates 65% are employed, either part-time or full-time, while attending school. This statistic includes university work study and internships. Students will ask their employer to participate. Third, the university has a small business development office, which companies can contact for assistance with various aspects of their business. At least once a year, I present details on the partnership to the community on behalf of the small business development office. Finally, returning partners request a student team for another cycle in their accounting system.

I witness a stronger commitment to the projects when the student has made an effort to engage the partner. In the first 2 weeks of class, I make students aware of "client engagement" considerations in choosing a partner and project problems that may arise examining a subsystem at a one-person business at one end of the spectrum or a large, complex entity at the other. Although students successfully examine these two contexts and provide good suggestions, entity type can produce too little or too much scope as evidenced by some of the feedback. Students review anonymous project reports and videotaped presentation examples from prior semesters as a way to provide guidance on size and scope. I primarily assist students in defining the boundaries (beginning and end point) of the system they are studying and rarely reject partners. Finally, there have been very few experiences where partners decide not to participate after agreeing to do so.

Limiting Impositions on Business Time

Faculty may be concerned that the student groups take up too much of business partners' time. The project material and class discussions guide the students to make best use of the actual time spent with a company representative designated as a maximum of three or four meetings in each semester, including the final presentation. The students learn an important skill – to be very prepared when you have a limited amount of interaction time – similar to what they may face as an auditor. The feedback received from every participating business does not indicate that time-wasting or imposition is a concern.

The partners commit to the Accounting Information Systems and Internal Control project with no commitment to participate in the Auditing project. After the students report to the partner in the final first-term presentation, they can request company participation in the next semester's project. Approximately 60–70% of business partnerships continue. There are varied company and student reasons for not continuing. For example, the company may have employee turnover or, currently, be facing economic challenges. The student group may have a desire to have chosen another entity other than the one they studied due to size or scope issues. The individuals who do not continue with a business partner may go forward as a team with the fictitious company in the second semester, or, they can dissolve the original group and have the individual members join other teams (see discussion under "Sequencing Courses").

Ensuring Professionalism

Though part of this process is to help students develop professional competencies, faculty may be apprehensive that students expose the university to risk due a lack of professionalism or inappropriate behavior. Our business program has students sign a professionalism agreement as part of participation in external community activities once they are certified as a major. Adopting faculty may wish to consider a similar agreement.

One scenario that has occurred infrequently is students not accurately representing a system and providing suggestions based on an erroneous set of facts. I have been present at concluding partner meetings where the students' representation and recommendations based on those representations are challenged. This uncomfortable circumstance is one that students can face as an auditor, particularly at the junior level. I counteract the problem by reinforcing the need for client narrative review before completing the rest of the project, letting students know of past experiences and stressing their grade is dependent on having the correct system.

To date, I have not received a complaint concerning students breaking confidentiality agreements or behaving inappropriately. Business faculty who use community partner projects have agreements reviewed by appropriate university legal personnel. Similarly, potential adopters should have their own confidentiality agreements approved through their applicable university channels.

Sequencing Courses

I have and currently use the two-term project in university settings where students typically take the first Auditing course in the semester following the primary Accounting Information System and Internal Control course or within a year of taking the systems course. Students develop a new contract and a new confidentiality agreement formed in the second semester if there is a change in team composition including losing a team member through a class withdrawal. On average, one or two students may withdraw from the Auditing class. Though it has varied, approximately 30–35% of teams have formed new contracts. Having at least one member of the original team move forward with the business client has proven successful. Students who join other teams refer to the documentation from that team's Accounting Information Systems and Internal Control class similar to what might be contained in an audit permanent file. These circumstances can mirror audit practice where members of audit teams change, but generally, the senior is the same or someone who was there and was promoted to senior.

Thus, all students develop a relationship with a community partner in the first semester. Not all students continue that same relationship in the second semester, either through becoming a member of another group with another community partner or by applying the term project requirements to a fictitious company. Some students do lose the opportunity of interacting with an outside entity in the second semester though they are exposed to the audit issues surrounding external partners through class interactions. The curriculum integration occurs through continuing the approach of the prior semester of applying class topics to all entities. The class treats the fictitious company as if it is one of the business partners in general class and individual team discussions. For example, one semester the fictitious company may be a winery and the external business entities may be a church, a nonprofit housing organization, an IT outsourcer, and cash receipts at a restaurant. When we discuss client acceptance decisions as a class, students bring in their research covering all of these industry types.

Students gain a wider exposure than they would receive if everyone did the same audit practice case.

SUMMARY

The AICPA challenges educators to provide meaningful professional interaction for students. This educational collaboration provides one such opportunity by engaging students real-world, unstructured problems in the business community. The partnership serves to solidify students' comprehension of internal control and risk concepts. It has helped our accounting students integrate the knowledge and skills they have developed in Accounting Information Systems and Internal Control and in Auditing while providing a valued service to the business community. The business-student partnership requires students to be active participants in the learning process and enriches the classroom experience, rather than take away from the topics covered in the courses. Students come away from this project energized, with a sense of significant accomplishment. The project has raised the visibility of the business school in these local communities and enhanced our reputation. This teaching approach assists in better preparing students for an accounting career by developing key competencies with particular emphasis on the personal competencies requested by the profession.

NOTE

1. I based the original term project on material provided by Ulric J. Gelinas, Jr., Professor of Accountancy at Bentley College, as support for an early edition of his text *Accounting Information Systems*. I use this text that is now its 8th edition (Gelinas & Dull, 2008). The text has a significant amount of term project material available with online guidance. *The Bentley College Accounting Information Systems Term Project Prepared for: A Compendium of Classroom Cases and Tools* (C3) (Gelinas, 2006) by Professor Gelinas includes his term project as it has evolved through his use of the project for over 20 years.

ACKNOWLEDGMENTS

I thank Jane Cote, participants at the 2008 Accounting Information Systems Educators Association Annual Meeting, the 2006 Western American

Accounting Association Annual Meeting, the 2005 American Accounting Association Annual Meeting Teaching Innovation Workshop, and community partners at the 2005 Legislative Aid State Dinner for their invaluable feedback. I thank Jack and Maye Stewart for their recognition of a student project based on the business-student partnership, awarded at the 2008 Accounting Information Systems Educators Association Annual Meeting. I am also grateful for the foundation work and term project development of Ulric J. (Joe) Gelinas, Jr., which provided the initial basis for the first semester of this business-student partnership, and to members of the faculty at Washington State University Vancouver for guidance in the team materials I have included. Finally, I thank my co-editor, Bill N. Schwartz, and two anonymous reviewers for their helpful insight and guidance.

REFERENCES

AICPA – American Institute of Certified Public Accounts. (1999). *AICPA core competency framework for entry into the accounting profession* (Available at http://www.aicpa.org/edu/corecomp.htm. Retrieved on February 6, 2009). New York, NY: AICPA.

AICPA. (2002). *Statement on Auditing Standards (SAS) 99: Consideration of fraud in a financial statement audit*. New York, NY: American Institute of Certified Public Accountants Auditing Standards Board.

AICPA. (2005). *Guidelines for achieving the AICPA core competencies through experiential learning programs* (Available at http://ceae.aicpa.org/Resources/Education+and+Curriculum+Development/Internships+and+Experiential+Learning/Guidelines+for+Achieving+the+AICPA+Core+Competencies+through+Experiential+Learning+Programs.htm.Retrieved on March 5, 2009). New York, NY: American Institute of Certified Public Accountants.

American Assembly of Collegiate Schools of Business (AACSB International). (2008). *Eligibility procedures and accreditation standards for business accreditation*. Tampa, FL: AACSB International.

American Assembly of Collegiate Schools of Business (AACSB International). (2009). New and improved: B-school curriculum. *BizEd Magazine* (January/February), 44–50.

Arens, A. A., & Ward, D. D. (2008a). *Computerized accounting using Microsoft Dynamics GP10.0*. Okemos, MI: Armond Dalton Publishers, Inc.

Arens, A. A., & Ward, D. D. (2008b). *Systems understanding aid*. Okemos, MI: Armond Dalton Publishers, Inc.

Astin, A. W., & Sax, L. J. (1998). How undergraduates are affected by service participation. *Journal of College Student Development, 39*(3), 251–263.

Bamber, E. M., & Bamber, L. S. (2006). Using 10-K reports brings management accounting to life. *Issues in Accounting Education, 21*(3), 267–290.

Barsky, N. P., Catanach, A. H., & Lafond, C. A. (2008). Student turned consultant: Teaching the balanced scorecard using experiential learning. *Advances in Accounting Education, 9*, 287–305.

Catanach, A. H., Jr., Croll, D. B., & Grinaker, R. L. (2000). Teaching intermediate financial accounting using a business activity model. *Issues in Accounting Education, 15*(4), 583–603.

Fogarty, J. A., Graham, L., & Schubert, D. R. (2006). Assessing and responding to risks in a financial statement audit. *Journal of Accountancy Online*, Available at http://www.journalofaccountancy.com/Issues/2006/Jul/AssessingAndRespondingToRisksInAFinancialStatementAudit.htm. Retrieved on July 16, 2008.

Gelinas, U. J., Jr. (2006). *The Bentley College accounting information systems term project prepared for: A compendium of classroom cases and tools (C3)* (Vol. 3). Sarasota, FL: Information Systems Section of the American Accounting Association.

Gelinas, U. J., Jr., & Dull, R. B. (2008). *Accounting information systems.* Florence, KY: South-Western Cengage Learning.

Rama, D. V., Ravenscroft, S. P., Wolcott, S. K., & Zlotkowski, E. (2000). Service-learning outcomes: Guidelines for educators and researchers. *Issues in Accounting Education, 15*(4), 657–692.

APPENDIX A. ACCOUNTING INFORMATION SYSTEMS AND INTERNAL CONTROL TERM 1 BUSINESS-STUDENT PARTNERSHIP PROJECT HANDOUTS

Overview

This team project establishes a partnership with a business entity and has you document and evaluate a portion of that entity's accounting information system. You may examine order entry, billing, cash receipts, purchasing, accounts payable, cash disbursements, or other "subsystems" within the revenue and expenditure cycles. Your examination will include internal and external stakeholders (impacted users), documents, processes, files, and internal controls. The specific objectives of the project are to:

1. Provide you the opportunity to examine an accounting information system in operation.
2. Provide you the opportunity to apply tools used in our profession, such as diagrams, flowcharts, internal control matrices, and questionnaires, as we learn them in class.
3. Enhance your understanding of foundational accounting information systems and internal control concepts.
4. Enhance your analytical ability, teamwork, and oral and written communication and professional skills.

Your team is responsible for finding the business entity within the first 2 weeks of the semester. We will have time in the first class session to discuss potential partners and I encourage you to contact me with any questions regarding entity types and the boundaries of subsystems you are considering. From past experience, team members usually need to meet with representative(s) of the business entity four to five times. Except for the final presentation, not all team members need to be present at these meetings. If you plan to record (tape) the meeting, you will need to gain permission from the business entity representative.

Project Phases and Deliverables

The project has deliverables (specific items to be turned in at the start of class on the due date). All deliverables should include the requested forms, be word processed and *in all other ways represent the work of a professional*.

Team Contract (due at start of class on XX). The team contract form, based on your Management XXX team contract, is included herein. All team members should participate in developing the contract. A five-point deduction will be made from the team project if it is not completed and turned in by the designated time.

Phase I Project Proposal (due at start of class XX). The objective of the Phase I Project Proposal is to establish an agreement with the business entity. You will need to have had one meeting with the business entity in order to complete the proposal stage. I provide you with templates you can adapt to your accounting information system for the three deliverables noted below:

1. A signed business entity letter of understanding adapted to the system you have identified.
2. A signed confidentiality agreement.
3. An initial report of your first meeting with the business entity.

In the weeks that follow turning in the Project Proposal, we will be covering system documentation in class. It is critical that you bring business entity material with you to each class session (e.g., overview of the business entity, accounting information system, narrative, diagrams, flowchart) so you benefit from peer and faculty review. I expect to meet with teams on a weekly basis to assess progress.

Phase II Preliminary Project Report – Understanding and Documenting the System (due at start of class XX). The objective of the Preliminary Project Phase II is to produce the system documentation deliverables in seven sections:

1. Title page (alpha order on team members unless work load differed)
2. Table of contents (page i)
3. Overview of the business entity including but not limited to answering the following questions (Overview starts on page 1 of the report) – hint: good research done here helps you in your next class, Auditing):
   - What type of entity (for-profit, manufacturing, government, etc.)? What is its purpose?
   - Where is its primary location? Is it one of several locations?
   - When was it founded? In what state?
   - What is its size (number of employees, revenue generated, in comparison to other similar entities, etc.)? You may wish to include an organizational chart.
   - Is there a change on the horizon for the company, for example, are they expanding, introducing a new product?
4. Description of the accounting information system being analyzed including but not limited to answering the following questions:
   - What accounting information system is your team examining (be sure to state it in the report)? What are the boundaries, that is, at what point are you starting and where does your examination end? What are the external and internal entities of this system? You may wish to include a portion of an organizational chart here again.
   - What are the objectives of the system you are examining? For example, if you chose cash receipts, you may wish to say the primary objective is to process cash receipts promptly and accurately. You should be prepared to list several objectives here. These objectives will appear in your control matrix in the final report.
   - How many transactions does the company post through this subsystem on a monthly basis? Is there a delay in posting transactions (are transactions gathered for a period of time and then posted).
   - What is the hardware and software used in the system you are examining? Please sure to specify databases, modules used.
5. Narrative of operation of the accounting information system being analyzed, *which has been approved by the business entity*. This narrative should be similar to the narratives we did in class, describing data flows, processes, forms, reports, and files. It should be approximately one page

unless it is a more complex system. Please use active voice. The narrative should be input into a table of entities and activities as demonstrated in class.

6. Documentation of operation of the accounting system being analyzed, including
   - appropriate flow diagrams (context, physical and logical)
   - systems flowchart

   Note: Please check – your diagrams should be in balance and you should have the same files with similar data flows in and out of the files in the different documentation types.

7. Additional reports documenting any meetings with business entity

I return the Phase II Report within a week. At this point in the term, we are covering information flows and controls in specific cycles, such as order entry, billing, and purchasing. We will be using class time to work on and review the internal control deliverables of your entities as described below so please bring your business entity material with you to class.

Phase III Final Project Report – Documenting and Evaluating Internal Control. The objective of the Phase III Final Project Report is to document and evaluate the internal control of the business entity. While primary emphasis is on the specific accounting information system you are analyzing (e.g., cash receipts processing), you also provide an overview of the internal control environment using the five areas identified in the COSO framework. The deliverable is the final project report that is given to the business entity that includes the following:

1. The revised information contained in the preliminary report (items 1–9 detailed above).
2. Overview of the internal control environment in which the accounting information system operates using the COSO framework as a guide. For example, you might discuss management's attitude and policies regarding control, how they approach risk assessment, the organization's office and computer facilities and the physical security over those facilities, and segregation of duties (or lack thereof). These examples are not meant to be exhaustive. You may wish to develop a set of questions to ask the business entity representative(s).
3. Control matrices identifying present and missing specific control plans and descriptions for the specific accounting information subsystem being analyzed. Annotate your systems flowchart with the controls noted on the matrices.

4. An assessment based on environment and user needs. Please refrain from wording such as "weakness" and "lack of controls" and present findings positively. You should include with your assessment a description of any changes that are pending as well as your suggestions for enhancing the system.

Project Presentation. In our final class session, you will present a "test run" of your business entity presentation. Your classmates will provide suggestions for improvement. No company names should be given during the class presentation. The presentation should be in PowerPoint™ (or other presentation software), last a maximum of 10–15 minutes, *not include* detailed data flow diagrams, systems flowcharts, or matrices, but include the following:

- Brief background on the business entity
- Overview of the accounting information system you analyzed (start and stop points, internal and external entities)
- Overview of internal control environment
- Controls present and missing
- System strengths
- Suggestions for enhancements.

The team should arrange to present their findings with the business entity during the time period of XX. I will be at these final presentations, thus it is important to schedule the time for this presentation early in the semester. I recommend you bring the business entity evaluation form and a stamped envelope with my name and address on it to the presentation so that I receive the evaluation form in a timely manner. In addition, I recommend you provide a thank you note signed by all team members. Again, a professional presentation is considered an integral part of this project.

Evaluation Forms. Students should turn in completed student and business entity evaluation forms by *XX*.

BUSINESS-STUDENT PARTNERSHIP
TERM 1 GRADING SHEET

Student Name(s)_____

Preliminary Project

Category	Possible Points	Score
1. Company overview	5	
2. System narrative and table (s)	10	
3. Context diagram	5	
4. Physical DFD	5	
5. Logical DFD	5	
6. Systems Flowchart	25	
7. Overall Appearance/Product Professionalism	10	
TOTAL	65	

Final Project

Category	Possible Points	Score
1. Revised Preliminary information	5	
2. Internal Control Description	10	
3. Control Matrix and entry explanations	15	
4. Assessment and recommendations	15	

Continued

Category	Possible Points	Score
5. Overall Appearance/ Product Professionalism (including presentation)	20	
6. Individual Student Assessment	20	
TOTAL	85	

Please attach this form to your preliminary and final projects before turning in.

Honor Statement:

I have neither given nor received unauthorized assistance on this assignment

Student(s) Signature(s)   Date

BUSINESS-STUDENT PARTNERSHIP BUSINESS ENTITY LETTER OF UNDERSTANDING (TERM 1)

Note: Template is shown using accounts receivable and should be adapted to your system
Date

ABC Company
1234 Accounting Way
Systems, NJ 07777

Dear Ms. Debit:

This letter confirms our intent to pursue the Business-Student Partnership project during our X semester (dates) as discussed with you, describes our understanding of what we hope to accomplish, and provides detail on the interaction and information we need to complete these tasks.

The focus of our project with be ABC Company's Accounts Receivable (A/R) accounting information system. We intend to document and evaluate the A/R accounting information system from an internal control perspective. Our documentation will include:

1. An overview of your company including history, locations, size of entity, and key management

2. A narrative detailing the operation of the A/R system. The narrative will describe the system's entities, data flows, processes, forms and files.
3. A set of data flow diagrams and a systems flowchart combining the physical and logical aspects of the A/R system.
4. A description of the internal control environment in which the accounting information system operates.
5. A control matrix which assists in evaluating the potential effectiveness of controls by matching control goals to relevant control plans.
6. An overall analysis of the A/R system based on its environment and user needs.

To accomplish the above, we will need an overview of the A/R system and a walkthrough of tasks performed, a review of our initial narrative and diagrams, and a discussion regarding internal controls. We expect to generate useful recommendations as a result of the Business-Student partnership. Our goal is to provide a final written report and an oral briefing for you by XX.

Thank you for giving us this opportunity to apply our knowledge and skills in an actual business environment. We are pleased to answer any questions and have included the contact information for our professor with this letter if you wish to learn about our accounting curriculum and the use of this project at our university.

Sincerely,
Students   Enclosure: Faculty business card

BUSINESS-STUDENT PARTNERSHIP PROJECT
MEETING REPORT (USED IN TERM PROJECT 1 AND 2)

Business-Student Partner_____

Meeting #/Date	Location	Person Met/ Title	Team Members Present	Tasks Accomplished	Actions for Next Meeting (set date for next meeting)

BUSINESS-STUDENT PARTNERSHIP PROJECT
CONFIDENTIALITY AGREEMENT
(USED IN TERM PROJECT 1 AND 2)

Business-Student Partner _____

Date _____

IN CONSIDERATION of being permitted to participate in the Business-Student Partnership Project, I agree:

1. I will treat in strict confidence all information received by me from any business firm to be provided under this project. The only exception to this commitment will be another member of the Project Team and the faculty member supervising the project.

2. I will not recommend to any business firm purchase of goods or services from sources in which I or other members of the Project Team may be interested, nor will I accept fees, commissions, gratuities or other benefits from any firm I or another member of the Project Team may recommend to the business firm.

   Student Signature _____

   Student Signature _____

   Student Signature _____

   Student Signature _____

   One copy for business entity
   One copy for faculty member

BUSINESS-STUDENT PARTNERSHIP PROJECT
EVALUATION OF PROJECT BY STUDENT
(USED IN TERM PROJECT 1 AND 2)

Business-Student Partner _____

Student Name_____

1. What were your specific expectations when you started working on the project?

2. What did you gain from interacting with the business entity during the semester?

3. How well did the project contribute to the overall learning in this course?

4. In your opinion, do you learn more (a) by working on one or more projects with real-world firms or (b) by working on case studies and textbook material? Explain.

BUSINESS-STUDENT PARTNERSHIP PROJECT EVALUATION OF PROJECT BY BUSINESS ENTITY (USED IN TERM PROJECT 1 AND 2)

Name of Company_____

Your Name and Phone No._____

1. What were your specific expectations when you decided to have students work on the project?

2. What did you gain from interacting with the students during the semester?

3. How useful was the final report (or reports) for your firm?

4. Please evaluate the quality of the work of the student group on a 1- to 5-point scale. Please circle the appropriate number.

1	2	3	4	5
Poor	Below average	Average	Above average	Excellent

5. Would you recommend to other businesspeople you know that they work with a student project group? Why or why not?

—

Thank you again for your involvement. If you wish to provide any other feedback, we provide space below.

APPENDIX B. AUDITING TERM 2
BUSINESS-STUDENT PARTNERSHIP
PROJECT HANDOUTS

Overview

This team project continues the partnership with the business entities engaged with in Accounting Information Systems and Internal Control (Accounting XXX). You may continue with the same entity or "audit" different business entities than those that you documented and evaluated in the Accounting XXX class. I encourage you to continue with the same team but understand and support the myriad of reasons where it is not possible. If you are not continuing with the same team (any team member absent), you need to complete a new team contract (template provided herein). We will have time in the first class session to discuss team compositions and business partners and I encourage you to contact me with any questions regarding the partnerships you are considering. You will also need to establish another understanding with the business entity. From past experience, team members usually need to meet with representative(s) of the business entity three times. *All team members need to be present for fieldwork and the final report of findings.*

You have previously documented your understanding of an accounting information system. This is the first step in an audit plan that contains some reliance on internal control. The primary objectives of this assignment are to design an audit program to test the controls in a system and to execute (actually test) at least two of the program steps.

The specific objectives of the project are to provide you the opportunity to:

1. Examine the complexities of client acceptance decisions.
2. Assess the different risks associated with the audit of a business entity, with specific focus on an accounting information system in operation.
3. Develop and apply tools used in our profession, such as an audit program and statistical sampling plan, as we learn them in class.
4. Develop an understanding of the impact of internal control testing on the remainder of the audit, including substantive testing and evidence gathered when completing the audit.
5. Enhance your analytical ability, in particular as it relates to risk assessment and fieldwork, teamwork, and oral and written communication and professional skills.

Project Phases and Deliverables

The project has deliverables (specific items to be turned in at the start of class on the due date). All deliverables should include the requested forms, be word processed and *in all other ways represent the work of a professional.*

Team Contract (due at start of class on XX). If you are not continuing with the same team, the team contract form, based on your Management XXX team contract and included herein, should be completed. All team members should participate in developing the contract. A five-point deduction will be made from the team project if it is not completed and turned in by the designated time.

Phase I Project Proposal (due at start of class XX). As we did in the Accounting Information Systems and Internal Control class, the objective of the Phase I Project Proposal is to establish an agreement with the business entity. You will need to have had one meeting with the business entity in order to complete the proposal stage. I provide you with templates you can adapt to your accounting information system for the three deliverables noted below.

1. A signed business entity letter of understanding
2. A signed confidentiality agreement
3. An initial report of your first meeting with the business entity

Starting in week X, we will be covering evidence and auditing planning including the audit risk model and materiality in class. You should bring your business entity material with you to each class session (e.g., engagement considerations, business entity risk assessment) so you benefit from peer and faculty review. I expect to meet with teams on a weekly basis to assess progress.

Phase II Business Entity Risk Assessment (due at start of class XX). The objective of the Phase II is to produce the business entity overview and the risk assessment deliverables.

1. Title page (alpha order on team members unless work load differed)
2. Table of contents (page i)
3. Business entity overview (use the Accounting Information Systems project overview if possible)
   • What type of entity (for-profit, manufacturing, government, etc.)? What is its purpose?
   • Where is its primary location? Is it one of several locations?

- When was it founded? In what state?
- What is its size (number of employees, revenue generated, in comparison to other similar entities, etc.)? You may wish to include an organizational chart.
- Is there a change on the horizon for the company, for example, are they expanding, introducing a new product?

4. Engagement Considerations: we have discussed client acceptance decisions. Provide information on the following (as applicable):
   - What service would your business entity most request (audit, review, compilation, other) and why?
   - What specific client business and industry factors should be considered in assessing the engagement (e.g., information technology, regulatory requirements, global activities, industry factors such as product obsolescence, competition, major sources of revenue and key customers and suppliers, unique accounting requirements, related party issues)
   - What staff would be needed for this type of engagement?
   - Would the engagement require outside specialists?

5. Risk Assessment (Audit Risk Model elements as foundation)
   - What factors affect *acceptable audit risk* related to the business entity (e.g., the degree to which external users rely on reporting, the likelihood that the client will have financial difficulties, the evaluation of management integrity)
   - What factors affect *inherent risk* related to the business entity (e.g., nature of the business; related parties; non-routine transactions, population, and judgment required related to cycle you are examining, factors related to misappropriation of assets and fraud in cycle you are examining)
   - What factors affect *control risk* related to the business entity (e.g., assessment of the five components of the COSO framework, identification of any significant deficiencies: all of these items were completed in Accounting XXX)

Phase III Design of Audit Program (due at start of class XX). The objective of Phase III is to create an audit program. Using the format presented in class, create a table of audit control objectives (e.g., occurrence, completeness) and tests of those controls as follows:

- For each of the *audit control objectives* in the cycle you are examining, identify the *internal control procedure or key existing control,* the appropriate *test of control,* and the *potential misstatement* for the transaction cycle previously flowcharted and analyzed. The control matrix from Accounting XXX should be helpful in preparing this portion of the assignment. The start of a suggested template is provided.

Audit Objective	Control	Test of Control	Potential Misstatement
Recorded sales are for shipments made to valid customers (occurrence)	Sales are supported by authorized shipping documents	Examine sales invoice for supporting bill of lading	Invalid sale
Continue...			

- Using the format presented in class and in your text, prepare an *Performance Audit Plan for Tests of Controls and Substantive Tests of Transactions* for the transaction cycle. At this juncture, do not include your sampling plan (i.e., sample size). The start of a suggested template is provided.

Tests of Controls and Substantive Tests of Transactions in Performance Format

1. Obtain the sales journal for the year and perform the following:
    a. Foot the journal for XX months and reconcile to the general ledger (use audit software).
    b. Review for unusual items
    c. Account for a sequence of sales invoice numbers.
Continue...

- For at least two of the steps in your Performance Audit Plan for Tests of Controls and Substantive Tests of Transactions, delineate an *attribute sampling plan*. A suggested template, based on your text and class material, is provided.

Business entity: ABC Company
Audit area: Tests of Controls and Substantive Tests of Transactions in Billing
Year-end: 12/31/XX
Population: Sales invoices for period 1/1XX to 12/31/XX. First invoice = X; Last invoice = Y;
Sampling unit: Sales invoice number, recorded in sales journal sequentially, selected through random number generation

Attribute	Attribute Sampling Plan					Actual Results		
	Expected population exception rate	Tolerable exception rate	Acceptable rate of assessing control risk too low	Initial sample size	Sample Size	Number of Exceptions	Sample Exception Rate	Computed Upper Exception Rate
Sales are supported by authorized shipping documents	0	4	5	74				
Continue…								

- These templates comprise the audit program, are reviewed in class and graded, and adapted as necessary for fieldwork (Note: once your sampling plan is approved, add the information to your Performance Audit Plan where appropriate).

Phase IV Fieldwork and Phase V Final Report along with revised Phase II and III (due at start of class XX). In this final stage, you execute the plan (perform the tests outlined in your attribute sampling plan) and evaluate the results. You will fill out the "Actual Results" of the sampling plan and provide the following assessment at the bottom the attribute sampling plan:

Effect on Audit Plan:
Are the controls tested through identified attributes operating effectively given the size of the allowance for sampling error? Do any exceptions fall in one category or are they pervasive? Is the population acceptable? Should we revise assessed control risk? What is the impact on evidence, that is, substantive tests of details of balances?

Communication to Management:
The exceptions should be discussed with appropriate personnel (i.e., dependent on entity, audit committee or management). Specific recommendations made as appropriate.

Project Conclusion. At the start of last class session, you will be turning in the following:

1. Phase II Business Entity Risk Assessment.
2. Phase III Design of Audit Program.
3. Phase IV Fieldwork (including working papers) and Phase V Final Report.

In this session, student teams present their findings to the class in a discussion format. As before, no business partner names are divulged in class. The discussion format represents a more realistic portrayal of the auditing team environment. As a team, we compare our initial understanding and assessment of internal control from our term one project to fieldwork results with individuals (class members and the instructor) providing additional insight and a fresh perspective on interpreting results.

The team should arrange to present their findings with the business entity during the time period of XX. The student teams then present the findings to the business entity in the subsequent week. The business student partnership evaluation form provides evidence of the student team completing the process. I will not be at these final presentations. I recommend you bring the business entity evaluation form and a stamped envelope with my name and address on it to the presentation so that I receive the evaluation form in a timely manner. I recommend you provide a thank you note signed by all team members.

Evaluation Forms. Students should turn in completed student and business entity evaluation forms by *XX*.

BUSINESS-STUDENT PARTNERSHIP
TERM 2 GRADING SHEET

Student Name(s)_____

Category	Possible Points	Score
Phase II	25	
1. Business Overview (5)		
2. Engagement Considerations (10)		
3. Business Entity Risk Assessment (10)		
Phase III	30	
1. Audit control objectives, tests of controls, potential misstatements (10)		
2. Performance program (10)		
3. Sampling Plan (10)		
Phase IV: Fieldwork	10	
Phase V: Final Report	15	
Overall Appearance/Product Professionalism	10	
Individual Student Assessment	10	
TOTAL	100	

Please attach this form to the phases of your projects before turning in.

Honor Statement:

I have neither given nor received unauthorized assistance on this assignment

Student(s) Signature(s)   Date

BUSINESS-STUDENT PARTNERSHIP
BUSINESS ENTITY LETTER OF
UNDERSTANDING (TERM 2)

Note: Template is shown using accounts receivable and should be adapted to your system
Date

ABC Company
1234 Accounting Way
Systems, NJ 07777

Dear Ms. Debit:

This letter confirms our intent to pursue the Business-Student Partnership project during our X semester (dates) as discussed with you, describes our understanding of what we hope to accomplish, and provides detail on the interaction and information we need to complete these tasks.

The focus of our project with be ABC Company's Accounts Receivable (A/R) accounting information system. We intend to document and evaluate the A/R accounting information system from an internal control perspective. Our documentation will include:

1. A business entity risk assessment.
2. An audit program
3. Fieldwork results and discussion of findings

To accomplish the above, we will need an overview of the A/R system and a walkthrough of tasks performed, a review of our initial narrative and diagrams, and a discussion regarding internal controls. We expect to generate useful recommendations as a result of the Business-Student partnership. Our goal is to provide a final written report and an oral briefing for you by XX.

Thank you for giving us this opportunity to apply our knowledge and skills in an actual business environment. We are pleased to answer any questions and have included the contact information for our professor with this letter if you wish to learn about our accounting curriculum and the use of this project at our university.

Sincerely,
Students

Enclosure: Faculty business card

APPENDIX C. BUSINESS-STUDENT PARTNERSHIP TEAMWORK CONTRACT (USED IN TERM PROJECT 1 AND 2)

Acctg XXX Teamwork Contract

(Adapted from Mgt XXX Team Contract developed by Management faculty)

Team Number _____ (will be assigned by instructor)

This contract will be given to me by XX at the start of class. For this contract to be a successful document that guides the conduct of the group members it is vital that each group member participate honestly. This is not a wish list indicating how the group hopes to work; it is a contract that specifies how the group will work together. When you sign your name at the end of the contract you have made a commitment that you will be expected to honor. It is critical that all group members be present during the discussion and preparation of this contract. Note: the contract cannot override anything that is in the class syllabus.

For each section, first discuss the relevant points and issues and then compose the group's statement (word processing is required). Upon completion, sign your names and make copies for each member and the professor.

Section 1: Norm Statement

A. What will your group's policy be concerning participation level? Most student groups assume and expect equal participation from each member. Will that be your policy? If so, specifically outline what your group means by equal participation. Alternatively, will there be exceptions, situations in which a member could carry more or less of the load for a period of time or permanently? If so, specifically outline the circumstances under which the effort load will be shifted and the procedures for approving changes in effort.

B. What will your group's policy be concerning leadership? Most student groups resist the appointment of a leader or leaders. Will that be your plan or is there a type of leadership your group would consider to improve your product? When outlining the policy, make sure to indicate how the group will work toward meeting goals (i.e., if shared leadership is the policy how will that operate). If a leadership structure is adopted indicate who will be taking responsibility, what their leadership role will be and how that person(s) will be expected to exert his/her authority.

C. What will your group's policy concerning communication between group members?
   1. If contact is necessary between class periods, what method of communication is preferred: face-face, email, phone?
   2. What is the procedure for scheduling a meeting (i.e., how much notice before the meeting time, normal location, etc.)
   3. If problems surface what is your policy for discussing issues concerning member behavior? Should everyone be present for certain types of conversations?
D. "Groupthink" can be fatal in some situations because alternatives are ignored that could have been critical to success. This especially applies to groups where one or two members present their positions so confidently and authoritatively that other group members suppress their perspectives. What policy will your group have to avoid groupthink and encourage group members to express opinions, even if they are different from the majority in the group?

Section 2: Vision Statement

A vision statement describes how the group is expected to work together. Will your group focus on efficiency, excellence, having fun, respecting differences, and so on? Develop a statement, which captures the *team atmosphere* each group member will work toward achieving.

Section 3: Performance Standard

A performance standard quite simply is how good to you want your product to be. Some groups strive for excellence and perfection while others work toward survival or adequate performance. Be very honest here in defining the level of performance you will be working toward. You may specify your performance standard generally or you may want to quantify your performance standards, such as 100% on 80% of assigned tasks.

Section 4: Group Goals and Approach to the Tasks

A. How will your group work together to complete the tasks?
B. What level of preparation is expected before coming to each class?
C. As a group, what goals do you have for your team interactions?
D. Other goals and strategies for successful teamwork?

Section 5: Behavioral Expectations and Consequences

A. What is your group's policy concerning the following issues?:
   1. Group member comes to class unprepared for the task.
   2. Group member cannot meet a deadline for work assigned to him/her.
   3. Group member cannot attend a scheduled group meeting.
   4. Other expectations.
B. What will your group do if a member is not meeting behavioral expectations? Outline a series of steps to be followed that are designed to work with the person to get them aligned with group's expectations (e.g., step 1: a designated team member contacts the group member, if that interaction fails to produce the intended behavior then; step 2: a special team meeting is called). It may be necessary to create an individual contract between the team member and the group to outline the steps expected to re-align the person with the group's expectations.

What is the tentative meeting time each week that all members are available?

The responses supplied above represent the commitments we as a team have made to each other as members of a working group. Each one of us listed below will abide by this agreement.

Group Number_____   Date _____

Group Member Names (print name)   Signatures

_____   _____

_____   _____

_____   _____

BUSINESS-STUDENT PARTNERSHIP CONFIDENTIAL INTRA-TEAM PROJECT EVALUATION FORM (USED IN TERM PROJECT 1 AND 2)

The purpose of this form is for you to evaluate each member of your team, including yourself. The scores from the evaluations (excluding your self-evaluation) will be used to measure your performance within the group. Please **prepare one form for each team member.**

Total number of people in group _____

Your Name _____   Team Member's Name _____

		Strongly Disagree		Neutral			Strongly Agree
1	Team member provided ideas and directions for the project.	1	2	3	4	5	6	7
2	She/He helped to execute the work necessary for the project.	1	2	3	4	5	6	7
3	What percentage of the total project effort did this person contribute?	10 20 30	40 50 60 Other ____	70 80 90 100 %			
4	She/He completed assigned tasks on time.	1	2	3	4	5	6	7
5	Team member attended group meetings.	1	2	3	4	5	6	7
6	When meetings were missed he/she gave advance notice and provided as much input as possible.	1	2	3	4	5	6	7
7	After absent from a meeting, he/she followed up to learn what was accomplished and what needed to be done.	1	2	3	4	5	6	7

Continued

		Strongly Disagree			Neutral			Strongly Agree
8	Assigned role was accomplished satisfactorily.	1	2	3	4	5	6	7
9	Quality of his/her share of work was at the level expected.	1	2	3	4	5	6	7
10	He/She was open minded and flexible when considering others' input.	1	2	3	4	5	6	7
11	He/She demonstrated enthusiasm for the project.	1	2	3	4	5	6	7
12	His/Her interaction within the group was honest and aimed at moving the project forward.	1	2	3	4	5	6	7
13	I would willingly work with this person again.	1	2	3	4	5	6	7

14. Describe one event that captures the essence of this person's work on the team.

15. What was this person's key strength? Give an example.

16. What was this person's key weakness? Give an example.

BUSINESS STUDENT PARTNERSHIP
EVALUATION OF TEAM PRESENTATIONS IN CLASS
(USED IN TERM 1 PROJECT ONLY)

(Adapted from form developed by Management faculty)
Group #:
Team members:

The following scale will be used to make ratings:
1 = Strongly Disagree 2 = Disagree 3 = Neutral 4 = Agree 5 = Strongly Agree
NA = Not Applicable

Introduction/Appearance of Team:

Team members were introduced to the audience	1 2 3 4 5 NA
Team member's roles in presentation were outlined	1 2 3 4 5 NA
Presenters looked like business professionals	1 2 3 4 5 NA
Presenters acted like business professionals	1 2 3 4 5 NA

Class Project Presentation:

Flow of presentation was smooth and easy to follow	1 2 3 4 5 NA
Presented material in a creative fashion	1 2 3 4 5 NA
Held audience's attention throughout	1 2 3 4 5 NA
Generated appropriate class conversation	1 2 3 4 5 NA
Responded articulately to questions	1 2 3 4 5 NA
Used appropriate nonverbal communication (eye contact)	1 2 3 4 5 NA
Used appropriate vocabulary throughout	1 2 3 4 5 NA

Content of Presentation:

Discussed relevant issues regarding the topic	1 2 3 4 5 NA
Examined the topic in sufficient breadth	1 2 3 4 5 NA
Examined the topic in sufficient depth	1 2 3 4 5 NA
Presented clearly specified issues and facts	1 2 3 4 5 NA
Conclusion/recommendations were workable and practical	1 2 3 4 5 NA

Overall Comments:
• The team presentation as a whole was:
___ **Unsatisfactory** ___ **Marginal** ___ **Satisfactory** ___ **Above Satisfactory**
___ **Outstanding**

The best feature of this team presentation was:
Additional Comments/Recommended Improvements for client presentation: